Table of Contents

Chapter 1: Understanding Unreal's Core Concepts

1.1. The Architecture of Unreal Engine

Unreal Engine is a powerful and versatile game development platform used to create a wide range of interactive experiences, from video games to architectural visualizations and virtual reality simulations. To fully harness its potential, it's essential to understand the underlying architecture of Unreal Engine.

Engine Components

Unreal Engine consists of several core components, each playing a crucial role in the development process:

1. **Editor**: The Unreal Editor is the graphical interface where developers and designers create and manipulate assets, scenes, and gameplay elements. It provides a WYSIWYG (What You See Is What You Get) environment for designing levels and scripting gameplay.

2. **Engine Code**: Unreal Engine's source code, written in C++, provides the foundation for the engine's functionality. It includes libraries, systems for rendering, physics, audio, and more. Developers can extend and modify the engine's behavior through code.

3. **Content Browser**: This tool allows you to manage and organize assets such as 3D models, textures, materials, and animations. It's where you import, create, and edit assets for your projects.

4. **Blueprints**: Blueprints are a visual scripting system in Unreal Engine that enables designers and non-programmers to create gameplay logic and interactions. They are represented as node graphs, making it accessible to a wide range of users.

5. **Rendering**: Unreal Engine boasts a robust rendering system that supports high-quality graphics. It employs techniques like Physically Based Rendering (PBR), Global Illumination, and dynamic lighting to achieve stunning visuals.

6. **Physics**: Unreal Engine has a built-in physics engine that allows objects to interact realistically. It supports features like collision detection, rigid body dynamics, and soft-body physics.

7. **Audio**: The engine offers a comprehensive audio system for implementing 3D sound, ambient effects, and interactive music. It supports spatial audio to enhance immersion.

Entity-Component System

Unreal Engine follows an Entity-Component System (ECS) architecture, where game objects (entities) are composed of components that define their behavior and appearance. Key ECS components include:

- **Actor**: The fundamental building block in Unreal Engine. Actors can represent characters, objects, lights, and more. They can contain components like meshes, colliders, and scripts.

- **Components**: These are modular building blocks that define an actor's functionality. Examples include Static Mesh Component (for rendering), Collision Component (for collision detection), and Blueprint Script Component (for custom logic).

- **World**: The game world is a container for all actors and objects within a level. Unreal Engine supports seamless level streaming, allowing large and complex worlds to be divided into manageable sections.

Asset Pipeline

Unreal Engine's asset pipeline facilitates the management of game assets. Developers import assets like 3D models, textures, and audio files into the engine via the Content Browser. The engine's import settings allow for fine-tuning asset properties and optimization.

Scripting Languages

Unreal Engine supports two scripting languages:

- **Blueprints**: Visual scripting language that empowers designers and non-programmers to create gameplay logic using a node-based interface. Blueprints are versatile and accessible, making them a popular choice for prototyping and production.

- **C++**: Unreal Engine's native programming language, which provides full access to the engine's source code. Developers use C++ for performance-critical tasks and creating custom functionality.

Understanding Unreal Engine's architecture is essential for effective development. Whether you're a designer using Blueprints or a programmer working with C++, this knowledge forms the foundation of creating interactive and immersive experiences. In the following sections of this chapter, we'll delve deeper into advanced Blueprint scripting techniques, 3D modeling essentials, lighting and texturing for realism, and Unreal Engine's physics and AI systems, providing you with a comprehensive understanding of the engine's core concepts.

1.2. Advanced Blueprint Scripting Techniques

In Unreal Engine, Blueprints provide a powerful and accessible way to create gameplay logic and interactions without writing code. In this section, we'll explore advanced Blueprint scripting techniques that can help you take your game development skills to the next level.

Custom Events and Event Dispatchers

Custom events and event dispatchers allow you to define your own events within Blueprints. These events can be triggered when specific conditions are met or when you want to create a custom interaction. To create a custom event:

1. **Create Custom Event Node**: In the Blueprint graph, right-click and select "Add Custom Event." Give it a meaningful name.

2. **Define Event Logic**: Connect the custom event node to the nodes that define the event's logic. You can add conditions, actions, and functions just like in regular Blueprint graphs.

3. **Triggering the Event**: You can call your custom event from other parts of the Blueprint graph or even from other Blueprints.

Event dispatchers work similarly but allow you to create events that can be called from outside the Blueprint, making them useful for communication between different objects or Blueprints.

Blueprint Interfaces

Blueprint Interfaces are a way to define a set of functions that multiple Blueprints can implement. This is useful when you want different objects to respond to certain events or have shared functionality. Here's how to use Blueprint Interfaces:

1. **Create the Interface**: In the Content Browser, right-click and select "Blueprint Class." Choose "Interface" as the parent class. Define the functions that the interface will contain.

2. **Implement the Interface**: In a Blueprint that should use the interface, you can implement it by right-clicking on the graph and selecting "Add Interface." Then, you can add the functions defined in the interface to your Blueprint.

3. **Implement Function Logic**: Customize the logic for each function implemented in your Blueprint.

4. **Use the Interface**: Now, any Blueprint that implements this interface will have access to these functions.

Macros and Custom Nodes

Blueprint Macros and Custom Nodes allow you to create reusable pieces of logic within your Blueprints. Macros are like functions, but they are defined directly within the Blueprint graph and can include nodes and connections.

To create a Macro:

1. **Create a New Macro Node**: Right-click on the graph and select "Create Macro."

2. **Define Input and Output Pins**: Just like with functions, you can define input and output pins for your Macro. These pins determine how data flows in and out of the Macro.

3. **Add Logic**: Inside the Macro, you can add nodes and connections to create your custom logic.

Custom Nodes, on the other hand, are created by extending Unreal Engine with C++ code. These nodes can be added to the Blueprint graph and provide custom functionality that isn't achievable with standard Blueprint nodes.

Blueprint Optimization

As your Blueprints become more complex, it's crucial to optimize them for performance. Here are some optimization techniques:

- **Function and Macro Usage**: Use functions and macros to encapsulate and reuse logic to avoid redundancy in your Blueprints.

- **Variable Management**: Minimize the use of expensive operations on variables by caching results when possible.

- **Use Tick Sparingly**: The "Tick" event can be resource-intensive. Use it only when necessary, and consider using timers or events when appropriate.

- **Debugging and Profiling**: Utilize Unreal Engine's built-in debugging and profiling tools to identify performance bottlenecks in your Blueprints.

Advanced Blueprint scripting techniques open up a world of possibilities for creating complex gameplay mechanics and interactions without delving into C++ code. When used effectively, Blueprints can streamline your development process and help you create engaging and interactive experiences.

1.3. 3D Modeling Essentials in Unreal

Understanding 3D modeling is fundamental for creating immersive environments and assets in Unreal Engine. In this section, we'll explore the essential concepts and techniques you need to know to work effectively with 3D models within the engine.

Importing 3D Models

Unreal Engine supports various 3D model formats, including FBX, OBJ, and more. To import a 3D model:

1. **Prepare Your Model**: Ensure that your 3D model is properly UV-mapped, textured, and rigged (if it's a character). It's also essential to consider the model's scale, as Unreal Engine uses a real-world scale by default.

2. **Import Model**: In the Unreal Editor, go to the Content Browser, right-click, and select "Import." Choose your 3D model file, and Unreal will analyze and import it.

3. **Import Options**: Unreal Engine provides various import options, including materials and animations. Adjust these settings according to your model's requirements.

4. **Review and Save**: Review the imported model in the Content Browser. You can create a new folder to organize your assets and save the imported model.

Working with Static Meshes

Static Meshes are 3D models that don't have any dynamic behavior, making them suitable for objects like props, buildings, or terrain. To work with Static Meshes in Unreal Engine:

1. **Create a Static Mesh Actor**: In the Content Browser, right-click and select "Static Mesh." Choose the mesh you want to use as your Static Mesh Actor.

2. **Placing the Mesh**: Drag and drop the Static Mesh Actor into your level. You can then use the Transform tools to position, rotate, and scale the mesh as needed.

3. **Materials**: Apply materials to your Static Mesh to define its appearance. Materials control the mesh's visual properties, such as color, texture, and reflectivity.

Skeletal Meshes and Animation

For characters and objects with dynamic animations, Skeletal Meshes are used. These meshes are rigged to a skeleton and can be animated. To work with Skeletal Meshes:

1. **Import Skeletal Mesh**: Follow a similar process to importing a Static Mesh, but ensure your Skeletal Mesh has an associated skeleton and animations.

2. **Creating Animations**: You can create animations within Unreal Engine using the Animation Editor. You can define animations for various actions like walking, running, and attacking.

3. **Blueprints and Character Controllers**: Use Blueprints to create character controllers that allow you to control the Skeletal Mesh's animations based on player input or in response to in-game events.

Level Design and Terrain

In Unreal Engine, you can design expansive levels and terrains to create realistic game environments. The Landscape tool allows you to sculpt and paint terrain, and it's particularly useful for outdoor scenes. To work with landscapes:

1. **Creating a Landscape**: Go to the Landscape Mode in the Unreal Editor and create a new Landscape. You can define its size and resolution.

2. **Sculpting Terrain**: Use the sculpting tools to modify the terrain's shape. You can create hills, valleys, and other natural features.

3. **Texturing**: Apply textures and materials to the landscape to give it a realistic appearance. You can use the Landscape Material system to control texture blending.

4. **Foliage and Props**: Populate your terrain with foliage, trees, and props to enhance the environment's realism. Unreal Engine provides tools for efficiently placing and managing these assets.

Optimization and LODs

Optimizing 3D models and environments is crucial for maintaining good performance. Unreal Engine offers tools to help with Level of Detail (LOD) management, which involves displaying lower-poly versions of assets as the camera moves away. This reduces the computational load. LODs are automatically generated during the import process, but you can customize them for better performance.

Understanding these 3D modeling essentials in Unreal Engine is key to creating visually stunning and interactive game environments. Whether you're importing 3D assets, working with Static or Skeletal Meshes, designing terrain, or optimizing for performance, these skills are fundamental to your game development journey.

1.4. Lighting and Texturing for Realism

Lighting and texturing play a significant role in achieving realism and visual quality in Unreal Engine. This section delves into the essential aspects of lighting and texturing to help you create immersive and visually stunning environments for your games or simulations.

Lighting in Unreal Engine

Unreal Engine's lighting system is robust and capable of simulating realistic lighting scenarios. Here are some key concepts and techniques:

1. **Light Sources**: Unreal supports various light types, including Directional Lights (sunlight), Point Lights (omnidirectional), Spot Lights (focused beams), and more. Each light type has its purpose and characteristics.

2. **Global Illumination (GI)**: GI simulates indirect lighting, allowing light to bounce off surfaces and affect nearby objects. Unreal Engine provides tools for baking GI into your levels, which greatly enhances realism.

3. **Light Mobility**: Lights can have different mobility settings. "Static" lights are baked into the environment, while "Stationary" lights can move but still contribute to GI. "Dynamic" lights can move and affect dynamic objects in real-time.

4. **Light Probes**: Light probes help capture and blend the lighting information between different areas of your level. They are especially useful for maintaining consistent lighting in large, open worlds.

5. **Lightmass**: Unreal Engine's Lightmass is a powerful tool for baking realistic lighting. It can generate high-quality lightmaps that greatly enhance the visual quality of your scenes.

6. **Real-Time Lights**: Unreal also supports real-time lights that can be used for dynamic lighting effects like flickering torches or vehicle headlights.

7. **Materials and Reflections**: Materials play a crucial role in how objects interact with light. PBR materials accurately simulate how surfaces reflect light, making materials essential for achieving realism.

Texturing and Materials

Textures and materials define the visual appearance of objects in your scenes. Unreal Engine employs a Physically Based Rendering (PBR) approach for materials, resulting in realistic and consistent visuals. Here's what you need to know about texturing and materials:

1. **Albedo Maps**: These define the base color of a material. They include information about the object's surface color, making them fundamental to achieving realism.

2. **Normal Maps**: Normal maps simulate surface detail and add the illusion of depth to objects. They affect how light interacts with surfaces, enhancing the perception of 3D geometry.

3. **Roughness Maps**: Roughness maps control the surface roughness of materials. They determine how shiny or matte a material appears. In PBR, roughness is a crucial parameter for realism.

4. **Metallic Maps**: Metallic maps specify which parts of a material are metal and which are non-metallic. This affects how light reflects off the surface.

5. **Emissive Maps**: Emissive maps allow you to make parts of an object emit light, useful for creating glowing materials, signs, or futuristic elements.

6. **Material Instances**: Unreal Engine supports material instances, which allow you to create variations of a material without duplicating assets. This is invaluable for efficient content creation.

7. **Material Functions**: Material functions enable you to create reusable material components that can be applied across different materials, improving workflow and consistency.

Texturing and UV Mapping

Proper UV mapping is essential for correctly applying textures to 3D models. Unreal Engine offers tools to help with UV mapping and texturing:

1. **Unwrap UVs**: You can use Unreal's UV unwrapping tools to create and edit UV maps for your models. These maps determine how textures are applied to the model's surface.

2. **UV Channel**: Unreal Engine supports multiple UV channels, which can be used for different purposes, such as lightmaps or secondary textures.

3. **Texture Streaming**: To optimize performance, Unreal Engine employs texture streaming, which loads textures dynamically based on the camera's location. This ensures that high-resolution textures are used where they are most needed.

4. **Material Blending**: You can blend multiple materials and textures on a single object to create complex and realistic surfaces. This is particularly useful for terrain or architectural elements.

5. **Texture Compression**: Unreal Engine provides various texture compression options to balance visual quality and performance. Understanding which compression settings to use is essential for optimization.

Lighting and texturing are critical aspects of game development in Unreal Engine. By mastering these techniques, you can create visually captivating and realistic environments that immerse players or users in your interactive experiences. Whether you're simulating natural lighting scenarios or crafting detailed materials, these skills will elevate the quality of your projects.

1.5. Unreal Engine's Physics and AI Systems

Unreal Engine provides powerful physics and AI systems that are essential for creating interactive and dynamic experiences. In this section, we'll explore these systems and their fundamental concepts.

Physics in Unreal Engine

Unreal Engine's physics system allows you to simulate realistic physical interactions between objects in your game world. Key aspects of the physics system include:

1. **Collision Detection**: Unreal Engine handles collision detection, allowing objects to interact with each other physically. You can define collision shapes for objects and determine how they respond to collisions.

2. **Rigid Bodies**: You can assign rigid body properties to objects to simulate their mass, inertia, and physical behavior. This enables realistic movement and interactions.

3. **Constraints**: Constraints are used to restrict the movement of objects. For example, you can create hinges, sliders, and other constraints to build complex mechanical systems.

4. **Physics Materials**: Physics materials define how objects interact when they collide. You can specify friction, restitution (bounciness), and other properties to control the physics simulation.

5. **Cloth Simulation**: Unreal Engine includes a cloth simulation system that allows you to create realistic cloth and fabric animations for characters and objects.

6. **Vehicles and Wheeled Vehicles**: Unreal Engine provides built-in support for simulating vehicles and wheeled vehicles, making it ideal for creating driving and racing games.

Setting Up Physics

To utilize the physics system effectively, you need to configure objects and actors properly:

1. **Enabling Physics**: You can enable physics simulation for an actor by checking the "Simulate Physics" option in its properties. This allows the actor to respond to physical forces.

2. **Collision Shapes**: Define accurate collision shapes for objects to ensure precise collision detection. You can use simple shapes like spheres, boxes, or complex shapes for more realistic collisions.

3. **Mass and Density**: Set the mass and density of objects to determine how they interact with forces like gravity. Heavier objects respond differently from lighter ones.

4. **Friction and Restitution**: Adjust friction and restitution values for physics materials to control how objects slide and bounce when they collide.

5. **Blueprints and Scripting**: You can use Blueprints or C++ scripting to create custom interactions and behaviors in response to physics simulations.

AI in Unreal Engine

Unreal Engine's AI system empowers you to create intelligent and responsive non-player characters (NPCs) and enemies. Key features of the AI system include:

1. **Navigation Mesh (NavMesh)**: The NavMesh system allows AI characters to navigate the game world intelligently. It generates a mesh representing walkable surfaces and helps AI characters plan their paths.

2. **Behavior Trees**: Unreal Engine employs behavior trees for defining AI behaviors. Behavior trees consist of nodes that represent AI actions and decisions, allowing you to create complex AI logic.

3. **Blackboards**: Blackboards are data containers that store information for AI decision-making. They can be used in conjunction with behavior trees to make dynamic decisions based on game conditions.

4. **Sensing and Perception**: AI characters can sense and perceive their surroundings, detecting other characters, objects, and events. This information influences their decision-making.

5. **AI Controllers**: AI characters are controlled by AI controllers, which execute the logic defined in behavior trees and respond to stimuli from the game world.

6. **Waypoints and Pathfinding**: Unreal Engine provides tools for defining waypoints and implementing pathfinding algorithms, enabling AI characters to navigate complex environments.

Creating AI Behavior

To create AI behavior in Unreal Engine, you can follow these steps:

1. **Define Behavior Trees**: Create behavior trees that represent the decision-making process of your AI characters. This involves defining tasks, conditions, and sequences of actions.

2. **Set Up Blackboards**: Configure blackboards to store relevant data for AI decision-making. Blackboards can hold variables like target locations, enemy locations, and more.

3. **AI Perception**: Configure AI perception components to allow AI characters to sense and react to their environment. This can include sight, sound, and other sensory inputs.

4. **Navigation and Pathfinding**: Implement pathfinding logic to enable AI characters to find their way around the game world. Waypoints and NavMeshes play a crucial role in this process.

5. **Testing and Iteration**: Test your AI behaviors in the game and iterate to fine-tune their responses and actions. You can adjust parameters, modify behavior tree nodes, and refine blackboard data as needed.

Unreal Engine's physics and AI systems are foundational for creating interactive and dynamic gameplay experiences. Whether you're simulating physical interactions, building intelligent AI characters, or designing complex behaviors, these systems provide the tools and capabilities to bring your games and simulations to life.

Chapter 2: Enhancing User Experience

2.1. Designing Intuitive User Interfaces

Designing intuitive user interfaces (UI) is crucial for creating engaging and user-friendly experiences in your Unreal Engine projects. In this section, we'll explore the principles and techniques for designing effective UI in Unreal Engine.

Importance of UI Design

User interfaces serve as the bridge between players or users and the game world. A well-designed UI can significantly enhance the overall user experience. Here are some reasons why UI design is essential:

1. **User Engagement**: An intuitive and visually appealing UI keeps players engaged and immersed in the game.

2. **Information Presentation**: UI elements convey important game information, such as health, inventory, objectives, and more.

3. **Navigation**: UI menus and navigation systems help users explore the game world, access settings, and switch between different game modes.

4. **Feedback**: UI provides feedback on user actions, making interactions more meaningful and responsive.

Unreal Motion Graphics (UMG)

Unreal Engine uses the Unreal Motion Graphics (UMG) system for creating user interfaces. UMG is a powerful visual UI designer that allows you to design and implement UI elements using a drag-and-drop interface. Here's an overview of using UMG for UI design:

1. **UMG Widgets**: Widgets are the building blocks of your UI. They can represent buttons, text, images, sliders, and more. You can create and customize widgets in the UMG Designer.

2. **Canvas Panel**: The Canvas Panel is a container that holds widgets and controls their position and layout. It's a fundamental element for structuring your UI.

3. **Anchors and Alignment**: You can anchor widgets to specific corners or edges of the screen, ensuring they adapt to different screen resolutions and aspect ratios.

4. **Event Handling**: UMG widgets can respond to user interactions through event handling. You can define what happens when a button is clicked or when the mouse hovers over an element.

5. **Animations**: UMG supports animations, allowing you to create transitions, fades, and dynamic UI effects to enhance the user experience.

Design Principles

When designing UI in Unreal Engine, it's essential to adhere to design principles that ensure usability and aesthetics. Here are some key principles to consider:

1. **Clarity and Readability**: Ensure that text and graphics are clear and easy to read. Use appropriate fonts, sizes, and color contrasts.

2. **Consistency**: Maintain a consistent visual style and layout throughout your UI. Consistency helps users understand how to navigate and interact with the interface.

3. **User-Centered Design**: Design your UI with the user's perspective in mind. Consider their needs, preferences, and expectations when creating interface elements.

4. **Minimalism**: Avoid clutter and unnecessary elements. Keep the UI clean and focused on essential information and interactions.

5. **Visual Hierarchy**: Use visual cues like size, color, and positioning to emphasize important elements and create a clear hierarchy of information.

6. **Responsive Design**: Design your UI to be responsive to different screen sizes and resolutions. Test your UI on various devices to ensure it scales appropriately.

Blueprint Integration

You can integrate UMG widgets and UI logic with Blueprints to create interactive UI elements. For example:

1. **Button Click Events**: You can use Blueprints to define what happens when a button is clicked. This can trigger in-game actions, open menus, or perform other functions.

2. **Dynamic UI Updates**: Blueprints can update UI elements dynamically based on in-game events or changing conditions. For instance, you can display the player's health or inventory status.

3. **UI Animation Control**: You can control UI animations and transitions using Blueprints, allowing for more interactive and visually appealing UI experiences.

Testing and Iteration

UI design is an iterative process. It's essential to test your UI with real users or playtesters to gather feedback and make improvements. Additionally, consider usability testing to ensure that your UI is intuitive and user-friendly.

Designing intuitive user interfaces in Unreal Engine is a vital aspect of creating compelling and immersive games or applications. By understanding UMG, adhering to design principles, and integrating UI with Blueprints, you can craft interfaces that enhance user engagement and provide a seamless experience.

2.2. Implementing Responsive Controls

Implementing responsive controls in Unreal Engine is essential for creating games and applications that feel intuitive and engaging to users. In this section, we'll explore techniques for designing and implementing controls that respond smoothly to user input.

Input Handling in Unreal Engine

Unreal Engine provides a robust input system that allows you to capture and process various types of user input, including keyboard, mouse, touch, and gamepad input. Here's an overview of input handling in Unreal:

1. **Input Axes and Actions**: Unreal Engine defines input axes and actions. Axes represent analog input, such as mouse movement or joystick positions, while actions represent discrete input events, like button presses.

2. **Input Mapping**: Input mapping allows you to associate physical input devices with in-game actions. This mapping can be configured in the project settings to define how input should be interpreted.

3. **Input Components**: Actors in Unreal Engine can have input components that capture and process input events. These components can be used to define how an actor responds to user input.

4. **Blueprints and C++**: You can handle input in Blueprints or C++ code. Blueprints provide a visual scripting interface for defining input logic, while C++ allows for more extensive customization.

Implementing Responsive Mouse Controls

Implementing responsive mouse controls is crucial for games and applications that rely on precise aiming, camera movement, or object selection. Here are some tips for responsive mouse controls in Unreal Engine:

1. **Sensitivity Settings**: Allow users to adjust mouse sensitivity in the game settings. This gives players control over how quickly their view or cursor moves in response to mouse input.

2. **Smooth Camera Movement**: Implement smooth camera movement by interpolating between current and target positions or orientations. This eliminates jerky or abrupt camera motions.

3. **Mouse Smoothing**: Apply mouse smoothing to reduce jittery movements and ensure that mouse input feels natural and comfortable.

4. **Inverted Controls**: Provide an option for users to invert mouse controls if they prefer to move the mouse in the opposite direction for specific actions, such as camera panning.

5. **Cursor Interaction**: When implementing cursor-based interactions, such as selecting objects or UI interaction, ensure that the cursor responds accurately to mouse movements and clicks.

Implementing Responsive Touch Controls

For mobile and touchscreen devices, responsive touch controls are essential for creating enjoyable experiences. Here's how to implement them effectively in Unreal Engine:

1. **Touch Gestures**: Recognize common touch gestures like tapping, swiping, pinching, and dragging. Map these gestures to relevant in-game actions.

2. **Multi-Touch Support**: Ensure that your application or game can handle multiple simultaneous touch inputs. This is essential for multi-touch gestures and interactions.

3. **Virtual Joysticks and Buttons**: Implement virtual on-screen joysticks, buttons, and controls that respond to touch input. These controls should be intuitive and easy to use.

4. **UI Scaling**: Adjust the size and layout of UI elements for different screen sizes and resolutions to ensure that touch controls remain accessible and responsive.

5. **Feedback and Visuals**: Provide visual feedback, such as highlighting buttons upon touch, and tactile feedback, like haptic vibrations, to confirm user interactions.

Implementing Gamepad Controls

Gamepad controls are common for console and PC gaming. Implementing responsive gamepad controls requires consideration of input mapping, dead zones, and button remapping:

1. **Input Mapping**: Define input mappings for various gamepad types, such as Xbox, PlayStation, or custom controllers. Ensure that button layouts are intuitive.

2. **Dead Zones**: Implement dead zones to filter out small, unintended joystick movements, preventing unwanted character or camera drift.

3. **Button Remapping**: Allow users to customize button mappings to accommodate different preferences and controller configurations.

4. **Controller Vibration**: Utilize controller vibration to provide haptic feedback for in-game events, enhancing the gaming experience.

5. **Responsive Menus**: Ensure that menus and UI elements can be navigated and interacted with using gamepad controls.

Implementing responsive controls across different input devices is essential for creating inclusive and accessible experiences. By considering the specific needs of mouse, touch, and gamepad input, you can provide users with a smooth and enjoyable interaction with your Unreal Engine project.

2.3. Audio Integration for Immersive Gameplay

Audio integration is a crucial aspect of game development in Unreal Engine, contributing significantly to the immersive and engaging experience of players. In this section, we'll explore the principles and techniques for effectively integrating audio into your Unreal Engine projects.

The Role of Audio in Games

Audio serves various critical roles in games:

1. **Immersive Environment**: Audio helps create a believable game world by providing ambient sounds like wind, rain, or background chatter.

2. **Feedback and Interaction**: Sound effects provide feedback on in-game actions, such as footsteps, weapon shots, or object interactions.

3. **Emotional Impact**: Music and soundscapes evoke emotions, enhancing the overall storytelling and player engagement.

4. **Gameplay Clues**: Audio cues can be used to guide players, hint at hidden secrets, or provide clues for solving puzzles.

Audio Assets and Formats

Unreal Engine supports various audio formats, including WAV, MP3, and FLAC, and provides tools to import and manage audio assets. When working with audio assets, consider the following:

1. **Quality vs. Size**: Balance audio quality with file size. High-quality audio may be essential for music and key sound effects, but background or ambient sounds can use compressed formats to save space.

2. **Stereo vs. Spatial Audio**: Choose between stereo audio for general sounds and spatial audio for immersive experiences. Spatial audio simulates 3D sound positioning, enhancing realism.

3. **Looping**: For continuous audio, like background music or environmental sounds, enable looping to ensure a seamless experience.

4. **Variation**: Create variations of sound effects to prevent repetition and add diversity to the audio experience. For example, footsteps can have different variations to avoid monotony.

Audio Components

In Unreal Engine, audio is controlled using Audio Components, which can be added to Actors or objects in your scene. Audio Components allow you to manage playback, spatialization, and attenuation of audio.

1. **Audio Sources**: Audio Components represent sound sources in the game world. You can attach them to objects like characters or items to emit sound.

2. **Spatialization**: Unreal Engine's audio system spatializes audio based on the listener's position, creating a 3D audio experience. This means sounds appear to come from their sources in the game world.

3. **Attenuation**: Attenuation settings control how audio volume diminishes with distance from the source. You can adjust attenuation settings to match the realism of your game world.

Sound Cues and Blueprints

Sound Cues are assets that define how audio behaves in your game. You can create complex audio behaviors by combining multiple sound cues. Unreal Engine also allows you to manipulate audio using Blueprints:

1. **Sound Cue Editor**: Use the Sound Cue Editor to design intricate audio behaviors. You can create loops, delays, and modify audio properties over time.

2. **Dynamic Audio**: In Blueprints, you can trigger sound cues dynamically in response to in-game events. For example, you can play footstep sounds when a character moves or trigger a dramatic music change during a boss fight.

Interactive Music and Soundscapes

Interactive music systems in Unreal Engine enable music to adapt to gameplay situations. For instance, the intensity of the music may increase during combat or change based on the player's location. To implement interactive audio:

1. **Music Tracks**: Compose and arrange music tracks for different moods and situations in your game.

2. **Music Blueprints**: Use Blueprints to control the playback of music tracks based on game events or player actions. You can seamlessly transition between tracks for a dynamic musical experience.

3. **Soundscapes**: Create dynamic soundscapes that adapt to the game environment. For instance, the sound of a forest should change as the player moves from a clear meadow to a dense woodland.

Optimizing audio performance is essential to maintain a smooth gaming experience. Unreal Engine provides tools for optimizing audio:

1. **Concurrency Management**: Set limits on the number of simultaneous audio instances to prevent audio overload.

2. **Distance-Based Prioritization**: Prioritize audio sources based on their distance from the player to reduce CPU load.

3. **Occlusion and Sound Occlusion**: Implement occlusion settings to ensure that audio is realistically muffled when objects or walls block the sound source.

4. **Streaming and Caching**: For large audio assets, use streaming and caching techniques to minimize memory usage.

Testing and Iteration

Testing audio in your game is crucial to ensure that it enhances the player's experience. Regularly playtest your game, gather feedback, and iterate on audio assets and behaviors to fine-tune the immersive qualities.

Incorporating audio effectively into your Unreal Engine projects can elevate the overall user experience and immersion. By understanding the role of audio, managing audio assets, utilizing audio components, and implementing interactive audio systems, you can create games that not only look great but also sound fantastic.

2.4. Optimizing Performance for Different Platforms

Optimizing performance for different platforms is a critical step in game development with Unreal Engine. Whether you're targeting PC, consoles, or mobile devices, ensuring that your game runs smoothly and efficiently is essential for a positive user experience. In this section, we'll explore the key considerations and techniques for optimizing performance across various platforms.

Platform Considerations

Each platform has its hardware specifications and capabilities, so it's important to consider the following when optimizing for different platforms:

1. **Hardware Limitations**: Understand the limitations of the target platform, including CPU, GPU, memory, and storage constraints.

2. **Resolution and Graphics Settings**: Adjust the resolution and graphics settings to match the capabilities of the platform while maintaining visual quality.

3. **Input Methods**: Consider how users interact with the game on different platforms, whether it's with a keyboard and mouse, a gamepad, or touch controls.

4. **Performance Profiling**: Use performance profiling tools provided by Unreal Engine to identify bottlenecks and areas that require optimization specific to each platform.

Unreal Engine Scalability Settings

Unreal Engine provides scalability settings that allow you to adjust the level of detail and quality of graphics and effects dynamically. These settings are particularly useful for optimizing performance on different platforms:

1. **Scalability Groups**: Unreal Engine categorizes graphics settings into scalability groups, such as "Epic," "High," "Medium," "Low," and "Minimum." These groups control the overall quality of graphics.

2. **Automatic Quality Adjustments**: You can enable automatic quality adjustments based on the platform's performance capabilities. Unreal Engine will dynamically adjust graphics settings to maintain a target frame rate.

3. **Per-Platform Scalability**: Customize scalability settings for each platform to ensure the best performance while adhering to hardware limitations.

Level of Detail (LOD)

Level of Detail (LOD) is a technique used to optimize performance by reducing the detail of objects based on their distance from the camera. Unreal Engine provides tools to manage LOD effectively:

1. **Static Mesh LODs**: Set up different versions of 3D models with varying levels of detail. Unreal Engine will automatically switch between LODs as objects move closer or farther from the camera.

2. **Texture LODs**: Create texture mipmaps to reduce texture quality at a distance. This reduces memory and GPU bandwidth usage.

3. **Material Complexity**: Simplify materials for distant objects, using fewer shaders and effects to save GPU processing power.

Texture Compression

Texture compression is crucial for optimizing memory usage and loading times on different platforms. Unreal Engine supports various texture compression formats, including:

1. **ASTC (Adaptive Scalable Texture Compression)**: Suitable for mobile devices, ASTC provides excellent quality with variable compression levels.

2. **BC (Block Compression)**: Used for consoles and PC, BC formats offer good quality and compression ratios.

3. **Texture Streaming**: Enable texture streaming to load textures dynamically based on the camera's location, reducing memory usage.

Optimizing game logic and code is essential for achieving smooth performance on all platforms. Consider the following:

1. **Avoid Costly Operations**: Minimize expensive operations like complex mathematical calculations and iterations in game logic.

2. **Asynchronous Loading**: Use asynchronous loading to load assets and resources in the background to prevent hitches and frame drops.

3. **Culling and Occlusion**: Implement frustum culling and occlusion culling techniques to avoid rendering objects that are not visible to the camera.

4. **Memory Management**: Be mindful of memory usage and optimize data structures and resource allocation to avoid excessive memory consumption.

5. **Garbage Collection**: Minimize garbage collection by reusing objects and avoiding excessive dynamic memory allocations.

6. **Profiling and Optimization Tools**: Regularly profile your game to identify performance bottlenecks and use optimization tools provided by Unreal Engine.

Testing on Target Platforms

Finally, thorough testing on each target platform is crucial. Test performance, stability, and gameplay experience on real hardware to ensure that your game runs smoothly and meets the performance requirements of the platform.

Optimizing performance for different platforms is an ongoing process in game development. By considering platform-specific limitations, using Unreal Engine's scalability settings, managing LODs and texture compression, optimizing code and logic, and conducting thorough testing, you can deliver a high-quality gaming experience across a variety of platforms, reaching a broader audience of players.

2.5. Debugging and Troubleshooting Common Issues

Debugging and troubleshooting are essential skills for any Unreal Engine developer. In this section, we'll explore techniques and tools to help you identify and resolve common issues that may arise during the development process.

Logging is a fundamental debugging technique that allows you to output messages to the console or log files. Unreal Engine provides a robust logging system through its UE_LOG macro. Here's how you can use it:

```
UE_LOG(LogTemp, Warning, TEXT("This is a warning message."));
```

- LogTemp is the log category, which you can customize for different parts of your code.
- Warning is the verbosity level, indicating the severity of the message.
- TEXT("This is a warning message.") is the message text.

Logging is valuable for tracking the flow of your code, identifying issues, and verifying that specific functions are being called correctly.

Breakpoints and Debugging Tools

Unreal Engine integrates with popular integrated development environments (IDEs) like Visual Studio and Visual Studio Code, offering powerful debugging tools:

1. **Breakpoints**: Set breakpoints in your code to pause execution at specific points. You can inspect variable values, step through code, and analyze program flow.

2. **Watch and Autos Windows**: These windows allow you to monitor variable values in real-time while debugging.

3. **Call Stack**: The call stack shows the sequence of function calls leading to the current point in your code, helping you trace the path of execution.

4. **Conditional Breakpoints**: You can set breakpoints with conditions, allowing you to pause execution only when specific conditions are met.

Assertion Checks

Assertion checks are used to validate assumptions about your code. Unreal Engine provides the check and ensure macros for this purpose:

- check(expression) verifies that expression is true; otherwise, it triggers an error and halts execution.
- ensure(expression) performs a similar check but continues execution even if the condition is false.

These checks are valuable for catching unexpected issues early in development.

Profiling and Performance Analysis

Profiling tools help you analyze the performance of your game and identify bottlenecks:

1. **Unreal Insights**: Unreal Insights is a profiling tool that provides detailed performance data, including CPU and GPU usage, memory allocation, and frame timings.

2. **Stat Commands**: Unreal Engine offers built-in stat commands that allow you to gather real-time performance data from the console, such as `stat unit`, `stat fps`, and `stat memory`.

3. **GPU Profiling**: Tools like NVIDIA Nsight and AMD GPU PerfStudio can help you profile GPU performance and identify rendering bottlenecks.

Error Handling and Exception Handling

Implementing proper error handling in your code is essential to gracefully handle unexpected situations. Use try-catch blocks in C++ to capture and handle exceptions:

```cpp
try {
    // Code that may throw an exception
}
catch (const std::exception& e) {
    // Handle the exception
}
```

In Blueprints, you can use "Execute Console Command" nodes to capture and handle errors using console commands.

Replicating and Network Debugging

For multiplayer games, debugging network-related issues is crucial. Unreal Engine offers tools to help diagnose and resolve networking problems:

1. **Replication Graph**: Use the replication graph to visualize how data replicates between clients and the server, helping you identify replication issues.

2. **Replication Viewer**: The Replication Viewer tool provides detailed information about network replication, allowing you to inspect replicated actors and variables.

3. **NetDiagnostics**: Unreal Engine's NetDiagnostics tool assists in analyzing network traffic, helping you identify and resolve network-related problems.

Crash Reports and Bug Tracking

When your game crashes, Unreal Engine can generate crash reports that provide information about the crash's cause. These reports are essential for diagnosing and fixing issues. Additionally, using bug tracking software like Jira or Trello can help you manage and prioritize bug fixes efficiently.

Community and Documentation

The Unreal Engine community and official documentation are valuable resources for troubleshooting. Forums, discussion boards, and community support can provide insights and solutions to common problems. Additionally, the official Unreal Engine documentation offers extensive information on various aspects of development and debugging.

Debugging and troubleshooting are integral parts of the game development process. By utilizing logging, debugging tools, assertion checks, profiling, error handling, network debugging, crash reports, bug tracking, and community resources, you can effectively identify and resolve common issues that arise during Unreal Engine development, ensuring the stability and quality of your project.

Chapter 3: Advanced Level Design

3.1. Creating Complex Environments

Creating complex environments is a fundamental aspect of level design in Unreal Engine. Whether you're crafting vast open worlds, intricate indoor scenes, or detailed landscapes, understanding the principles and techniques for creating complex environments is essential. In this section, we'll explore the key considerations and methods for crafting immersive and visually stunning game environments.

Planning and Conceptualization

Before diving into level design, it's crucial to plan and conceptualize your environment. Consider the following aspects:

1. **Theme and Setting**: Define the theme, setting, and mood of your environment. Is it a post-apocalyptic wasteland, a lush fantasy forest, or a futuristic sci-fi cityscape?

2. **Gameplay Requirements**: Determine how gameplay elements will interact with the environment. Are there puzzles, combat encounters, or exploration challenges that need to be accommodated?

3. **Story Integration**: Ensure that the environment aligns with the game's narrative and contributes to storytelling. Environments can convey lore and context.

4. **Player Flow**: Design the flow of the environment to guide players naturally through the level. Use level geometry and visual cues to direct player movement.

World Building and Level Design

Once you have a clear plan, you can start building your environment:

1. **Blockout**: Begin with a rough blockout of the level. Use simple geometric shapes to define the layout of spaces, paths, and major landmarks. This helps you establish proportions and scale.

2. **Asset Placement**: Populate the environment with assets such as static meshes, props, and interactive objects. Consider asset variation to avoid repetition.

3. **Terrain and Landscape**: If your environment includes natural landscapes, use Unreal Engine's landscape tools to sculpt terrain, add foliage, and paint textures. Pay attention to erosion, blending, and detail.

4. **Lighting**: Lighting plays a significant role in creating ambiance. Experiment with different lighting sources, day-night cycles, and dynamic weather effects.

5. **Materials and Textures**: Apply materials and textures to surfaces to enhance realism. Utilize material layers for terrain and complex material functions for dynamic effects.

Detail and Polish

The devil is in the details, and adding fine details to your environment can make a substantial difference:

1. **Decals**: Use decals to add dirt, grime, or damage to surfaces. Decals can break up uniformity and add realism.

2. **Particle Effects**: Implement particle effects for environmental details such as falling leaves, blowing dust, or flowing water. Particle systems add life and movement.

3. **Audio Ambiance**: Include ambient sounds and environmental audio to enhance immersion. Audio cues like birdsong, wind, or distant footsteps can breathe life into the environment.

4. **Interactive Elements**: If applicable, create interactive elements like doors, levers, or hidden passages that players can interact with.

5. **Optimization**: Optimize the environment for performance. Use Level of Detail (LOD) models, culling techniques, and occlusion culling to maintain frame rates.

Gameplay Integration

To create engaging gameplay experiences, integrate gameplay elements seamlessly into your environment:

1. **Puzzles and Challenges**: Design puzzles and challenges that make use of the environment's features and props. Ensure that solutions are logical within the context of the environment.

2. **Enemy Encounters**: Place enemies strategically within the environment to create tension and combat scenarios. Consider the layout for cover and tactical advantages.

3. **Exploration Rewards**: Hide collectibles, secrets, or lore within the environment to encourage exploration. Use visual clues to guide players to these rewards.

4. **Environmental Hazards**: Incorporate environmental hazards such as traps, collapsing structures, or changing weather patterns to add variety and challenge.

Testing and Iteration

Testing and iteration are crucial for refining your environment:

1. **Playtesting**: Have playtesters navigate the environment and provide feedback on gameplay, flow, and visual appeal.

2. **Performance Testing**: Test the environment on target hardware to ensure optimal performance. Address any frame rate drops or technical issues.

3. **Feedback Incorporation**: Act on feedback and make iterative improvements to the environment's design, visuals, and gameplay elements.

Creating complex environments is a rewarding and creative process in Unreal Engine level design. By carefully planning, world-building, adding detail, integrating gameplay, and iterating based on testing and feedback, you can craft environments that captivate players and enhance the overall gaming experience.

3.2. Effective Use of Landscaping Tools

Effective use of landscaping tools is vital for creating diverse and visually appealing outdoor environments in Unreal Engine. Whether you're crafting sprawling natural landscapes, terrains with complex vegetation, or unique biomes, understanding the landscaping tools and techniques is essential. In this section, we'll delve into the key aspects of utilizing Unreal Engine's landscaping tools effectively.

Landscape Creation and Sculpting

Creating a landscape in Unreal Engine involves defining the terrain's shape, size, and basic features. Here's how to start:

1. **Landscape Actor**: Begin by adding a Landscape Actor to your level. This serves as the canvas for your terrain.

2. **Landscape Size**: Define the size of your landscape, considering the scale of your environment. You can choose different grid sizes and resolutions to suit your needs.

3. **Sculpting**: Use the Landscape Sculpting tools to modify the terrain's shape. You can raise, lower, smooth, and flatten the landscape to create hills, valleys, and other features.

4. **Erosion and Noise**: Apply erosion and noise filters to add realism and variation to the terrain. This simulates natural processes and breaks up uniformity.

Layered Materials and Textures

Layered materials and textures allow you to paint different textures onto the landscape for a realistic appearance. Here's how to effectively use them:

1. **Material Layers**: Create material layers in the Landscape Material, defining the textures for grass, dirt, rock, and more. These layers can be blended seamlessly.

2. **Texture Painting**: Use the Landscape Layer Blend node in the Material Editor to paint textures onto the landscape. You can adjust brush settings for different effects.

3. **Weightmaps**: Weightmaps control the distribution of textures on the landscape. They allow you to specify where each material layer should appear with precision.

4. **Foliage Painting**: Incorporate foliage, such as trees, bushes, and grass, onto the landscape. Unreal Engine provides tools for painting and controlling the density of foliage.

Landscape Sculpting Techniques

Effective landscape sculpting involves mastering various techniques to achieve the desired results:

1. **Smooth Transitions**: Ensure smooth transitions between different terrain features, such as cliffs meeting grassy slopes or riverbanks merging with sandy shores.

2. **Ridges and Valleys**: Create ridges and valleys using the sculpting tools to define natural topography.

3. **Caves and Overhangs**: Experiment with negative sculpting to create caves, tunnels, or overhangs within the landscape.

4. **Detail Sculpting**: Pay attention to detail sculpting for fine features like cracks, pebbles, and erosion patterns.

Foliage and Vegetation

Adding foliage and vegetation to your landscape enhances its realism and visual appeal. Consider the following:

1. **Foliage Types**: Use a variety of foliage types, each with its own set of assets and density settings. This creates diversity in the environment.

2. **Density Painting**: Adjust the density of foliage based on environmental conditions and biomes. For example, dense forests may have more foliage than open meadows.

3. **Wind and Animation**: Implement wind animations for foliage to simulate natural movement and make the environment feel alive.

4. **LOD and Performance**: Set up Level of Detail (LOD) for foliage to maintain performance. Unreal Engine's LOD system reduces the complexity of distant foliage for better frame rates.

Environmental Effects

To enhance the overall realism and atmosphere of your landscape, consider environmental effects:

1. **Dynamic Lighting**: Utilize dynamic lighting and day-night cycles to cast realistic shadows and create varying moods throughout the day.

2. **Particle Systems**: Implement particle systems for environmental effects like falling leaves, rain, snow, or fog.

3. **Water Bodies**: Integrate water bodies, such as rivers, lakes, or oceans, into your landscape using Unreal Engine's water tools.

4. **Post-Processing**: Apply post-processing effects to enhance visuals. Effects like depth of field, color grading, and bloom can dramatically impact the environment's appearance.

Testing and Optimization

Lastly, testing and optimization are crucial when working with landscapes:

1. **Performance Testing**: Regularly test the performance of your landscape on target hardware. Adjust landscape resolution and LOD settings as needed to maintain frame rates.

2. **Collision**: Ensure that collision settings for the landscape are appropriate to prevent players and objects from clipping through terrain.

3. **Culling and Occlusion**: Implement culling techniques and occlusion culling to optimize rendering performance, especially for large landscapes.

Effective use of landscaping tools in Unreal Engine requires a combination of artistic creativity and technical proficiency. By mastering landscape creation and sculpting, layered materials and textures, foliage and vegetation, environmental effects, and optimizing for performance, you can craft breathtaking outdoor environments that captivate players and enhance the immersion of your game.

3.3. Dynamic Weather and Environmental Effects

Dynamic weather and environmental effects play a significant role in creating immersive and realistic game worlds in Unreal Engine. These effects can greatly enhance the player's experience by adding variety, mood, and interactivity to the environment. In this section, we'll explore how to implement dynamic weather and environmental effects in your Unreal Engine projects.

Dynamic Weather Systems

Dynamic weather systems allow you to simulate changing weather conditions, such as rain, snow, fog, and wind, in your game world. Here are the key components and techniques to implement dynamic weather:

1. **Weather States**: Define different weather states, such as clear, rainy, snowy, or foggy. Each state corresponds to specific weather conditions.

2. **Transition Logic**: Create transition logic to smoothly change between weather states over time. This can be based on in-game triggers, time of day, or scripted events.

3. **Particle Systems**: Use particle systems to generate raindrops, snowflakes, or fog particles. Unreal Engine's Cascade particle editor allows you to customize the appearance and behavior of these particles.

4. **Lighting and Skydome**: Adjust the lighting conditions and skydome to match the selected weather state. For example, overcast weather may result in diffuse lighting and a gray sky.

5. **Audio Effects**: Implement audio effects to accompany weather changes. Rainfall sounds, thunder during storms, or wind gusts add to the immersive experience.

Material and Shader Techniques

Materials and shaders are essential for achieving realistic environmental effects. Here's how to use them effectively:

1. **Wet Surfaces**: Modify material properties to make surfaces appear wet during rainy weather. You can adjust reflectivity and specular highlights to achieve the desired effect.

2. **Snow Accumulation**: Implement a snow accumulation system that gradually covers surfaces with snow during snowy weather. This can be achieved by altering the material and texture properties.

3. **Fog and Atmospheric Scattering**: Use fog and atmospheric scattering techniques to create realistic foggy conditions. These effects enhance depth and atmosphere in your scenes.

4. **Dynamic Sky and Lighting**: Utilize dynamic sky and lighting systems to simulate changes in natural lighting conditions as the weather changes. This includes variations in sunlight, sky colors, and shadows.

Weather Interactivity

Adding interactivity to weather systems can engage players and affect gameplay:

1. **Player Influence**: Allow players to influence weather changes through in-game actions or decisions. For example, a player might trigger rain by solving a specific puzzle.

2. **Gameplay Effects**: Integrate weather conditions into gameplay mechanics. For instance, rainy weather could make surfaces slippery, affecting character movement.

3. **Environmental Puzzles**: Design puzzles that require players to adapt to changing weather conditions. Solving these puzzles may involve using weather-related tools or finding shelter from a storm.

4. **Visual Feedback**: Provide visual feedback to players when weather changes occur. This can include on-screen effects like raindrops on the screen or snow accumulation on the character.

Performance Optimization

Optimizing performance when implementing dynamic weather and environmental effects is crucial for maintaining smooth gameplay:

1. **Particle System Optimization**: Optimize particle systems to avoid performance bottlenecks. Limit the number of particles and use LOD settings for particle effects.

2. **Dynamic Lighting**: Be mindful of the performance impact of dynamic lighting changes. Use light culling and LOD settings to optimize lighting effects.

3. **Texture Streaming**: Ensure that textures for environmental effects are efficiently streamed to minimize memory usage.

4. **Bounding Volumes**: Implement bounding volumes to limit the scope of weather effects. For example, confine rain effects to specific areas rather than applying them globally.

Testing and Iteration

Thorough testing and iteration are essential to fine-tune dynamic weather and environmental effects:

1. **Playtesting**: Have playtesters experience and provide feedback on weather transitions, visual quality, and gameplay interactions related to weather.

2. **Performance Testing**: Test the impact of weather effects on different hardware configurations to ensure smooth performance across various platforms.

3. **Feedback Incorporation**: Act on feedback and make iterative improvements to weather systems, materials, shaders, and gameplay mechanics affected by weather.

Implementing dynamic weather and environmental effects in Unreal Engine can elevate your game's immersion and visual quality. By creating realistic weather states, using materials and shaders effectively, adding interactivity, optimizing performance, and conducting thorough testing and iteration, you can craft game worlds that respond dynamically to changing weather conditions, enhancing the player's overall experience.

3.4. Level Streaming and Seamless World Building

Level streaming and seamless world building are essential techniques in Unreal Engine for creating vast and interconnected game environments. These techniques allow you to efficiently manage large game worlds, load and unload sections of the world as needed, and maintain a seamless player experience. In this section, we'll delve into the key concepts and methods for implementing level streaming and achieving seamless world building.

Understanding Level Streaming

Level streaming is the process of loading and unloading different parts of a game world dynamically to optimize performance and memory usage. Unreal Engine provides tools and features to facilitate level streaming:

1. **Level Streaming Volumes**: Level streaming volumes are trigger areas that define when and where level streaming should occur. When a player enters or exits a volume, associated levels are loaded or unloaded.

2. **Persistent Levels**: Unreal Engine allows you to have a persistent level that contains common assets and actors that remain loaded throughout gameplay. This can include the player character, UI elements, and essential gameplay systems.

3. **Sublevels**: Sublevels are individual levels that can be streamed in and out of the persistent level. You can organize your game world into multiple sublevels, each representing a specific area or section.

4. **Streaming Levels**: Streaming levels are sublevels that can be dynamically streamed in or out based on player proximity or other criteria. This allows you to create a seamless and expansive game world.

Seamless World Building Techniques

Achieving seamless world building involves several techniques to ensure a continuous and immersive player experience:

1. **Level Transition Areas**: Create smooth transition areas between streaming levels to avoid jarring transitions. Use natural landmarks, tunnels, or visually obscured areas.

2. **Streaming Distance**: Adjust the streaming distance and activation ranges for sublevels to control when and how they load. This prevents distant areas from loading prematurely.

3. **Loading Screens**: Implement loading screens or transitions to mask level loading and provide a more polished experience. Loading screens can include tips, lore, or interactive elements.

4. **Streaming Optimization**: Optimize the content of sublevels to minimize memory usage and loading times. Use Level of Detail (LOD) models and texture streaming to improve performance.

Streaming for Gameplay

Incorporate level streaming into gameplay to enhance the player experience and gameplay mechanics:

1. **Open World Exploration**: Design your game to encourage open-world exploration. Allow players to discover new areas seamlessly as they explore.

2. **Quest and Mission Structure**: Integrate level streaming with quests and missions. Load specific areas when players accept quests or reach mission objectives.

3. **Dynamic Events**: Trigger dynamic events or encounters as players move between streaming levels. This keeps gameplay engaging and unpredictable.

4. **Multiplayer Compatibility**: Ensure that level streaming works seamlessly in multiplayer environments. Synchronize level streaming across all connected players to maintain consistency.

Testing and Optimization

Testing and optimization are critical to ensuring that level streaming and seamless world building function smoothly:

1. **Performance Testing**: Test level streaming performance on target hardware to identify potential issues like frame rate drops or streaming delays.

2. **Memory Management**: Monitor memory usage and manage assets efficiently to prevent excessive memory consumption. Unload levels that are no longer needed.

3. **Collision and Navigation**: Verify that collision and navigation data remain accurate when levels are streamed in or out. Adjust navigation meshes and collision volumes as needed.

4. **Quality Assurance**: Conduct thorough quality assurance testing to identify any issues related to level streaming, such as loading errors or level transition problems.

5. **Feedback and Iteration**: Gather feedback from playtesters and address any issues or suggestions related to level streaming. Make iterative improvements to ensure a seamless player experience.

Implementing level streaming and seamless world building in Unreal Engine can significantly enhance the scope and depth of your game worlds. By understanding level streaming concepts, using level streaming volumes, optimizing streaming levels, and integrating level streaming into gameplay, you can create expansive and immersive game environments that captivate players and provide a seamless gaming experience.

3.5. Incorporating Multiplayer Elements

Incorporating multiplayer elements into your Unreal Engine game is essential for creating dynamic and interactive experiences that allow players to connect and play together. Whether you're developing a cooperative adventure, competitive multiplayer, or a massive online world, Unreal Engine provides robust tools and features to facilitate multiplayer gameplay. In this section, we'll explore key concepts and methods for incorporating multiplayer elements into your game.

Multiplayer Architecture

Unreal Engine's multiplayer architecture is based on a client-server model, where one player acts as the server and others as clients. Understanding this architecture is crucial:

1. **Server**: The server is responsible for maintaining the game's authoritative state. It manages game logic, physics, and player interactions.

2. **Clients**: Clients connect to the server to receive updates and send input commands. Clients primarily focus on rendering and local input handling.

3. **Replication**: Replication is the process of synchronizing data between the server and clients. Replicating relevant game state ensures that all players have a consistent view of the game world.

Replication and Remote Function Calls (RPCs)

Replication is the mechanism that allows information to flow between the server and clients. Unreal Engine uses Remote Function Calls (RPCs) to execute functions on remote objects:

1. **Server RPCs**: Functions marked as "Run on Server" are executed only on the server. They are used to update game state and perform authoritative actions.

2. **Client RPCs**: Functions marked as "Run on Owning Client" are executed on the owning client of the object. These are often used for client-specific actions.

3. **Multicast RPCs**: Multicast functions are executed on both the server and all relevant clients. They are useful for events that should be visible to all players.

Replication Conditions

To optimize network bandwidth and improve performance, Unreal Engine provides replication conditions:

1. **Role-Based Replication**: Use the `Role` property to determine whether an object is a server, client, or autonomous proxy. Execute functions conditionally based on the role to minimize unnecessary replication.

2. **Net Dormancy**: Unreal Engine automatically "dormants" objects that are far from the player's view or don't need frequent updates. Dormant objects consume fewer network resources.

Player Controller and Character

The Player Controller and Character classes play pivotal roles in multiplayer gameplay:

1. **Player Controller**: The Player Controller represents a player's input and actions. It handles player input and sends commands to the controlled character.

2. **Character**: The Character class represents a playable character in the game. It handles movement, animations, and interactions. Characters are often replicated to ensure consistency across clients.

Networked Variables and State

To maintain consistent game state across all players, Unreal Engine provides networked variables and state synchronization:

1. **Replicated Variables**: You can mark variables as replicated, ensuring that changes to these variables are synchronized between the server and clients.

2. **RepNotify**: RepNotify functions are triggered when a replicated variable changes. They allow you to respond to state changes and update UI or gameplay accordingly.

Cheat Protection and Security

In multiplayer games, it's essential to protect against cheating and ensure a fair gaming experience:

1. **Server Authority**: Most critical game logic should run on the server to prevent client-side manipulation and cheating.

2. **Anti-Cheat Measures**: Implement anti-cheat measures to detect and prevent cheating behavior, such as aimbots or speed hacks.

3. **Network Security**: Use secure networking protocols and encryption to protect against data tampering and unauthorized access.

Playtesting and Debugging

Thorough playtesting and debugging are essential for multiplayer game development:

1. **Dedicated Servers**: Test your game with dedicated servers to simulate real-world network conditions and identify potential synchronization issues.

2. **Replication Debugging**: Use Unreal Engine's built-in replication debugging tools to inspect and diagnose replication-related problems.

3. **Lag Compensation**: Implement lag compensation techniques to ensure that player actions remain responsive even in high-latency situations.

Incorporating multiplayer elements into your Unreal Engine game opens up opportunities for engaging and competitive gameplay experiences. By understanding multiplayer architecture, replication, RPCs, replication conditions, player controllers, character classes, networked variables, and security measures, you can create multiplayer games that provide a seamless and enjoyable experience for players around the world. Thorough playtesting and debugging are essential to ensure that your multiplayer game functions as intended and remains free of cheating or synchronization issues.

Chapter 4: Scripting and Gameplay Mechanics

4.1. Advanced Blueprint Scripting for Gameplay

Advanced Blueprint scripting in Unreal Engine is a powerful way to implement gameplay mechanics without delving into complex C++ code. Blueprints provide a visual scripting interface that allows designers and developers to create and manipulate game logic, events, and interactions. In this section, we'll explore advanced techniques for using Blueprints to script gameplay mechanics.

Blueprint Classes and Components

Unreal Engine organizes game objects as Blueprint classes, and these classes can contain various components and scripts. Here's how to work with Blueprint classes and components for advanced gameplay scripting:

1. **Creating Blueprint Classes**: Start by creating Blueprint classes for your game objects, such as characters, weapons, or interactive items.

2. **Adding Components**: Attach components to Blueprint classes to define their functionality. Components can include static meshes, collision volumes, particle systems, and more.

3. **Scripting Event Graphs**: Use the Event Graph within a Blueprint class to script behaviors and interactions. The Event Graph is where you define the logic that responds to events, such as player input or collisions.

Advanced Event Handling

Advanced Blueprint scripting involves handling events and triggers efficiently:

1. **Custom Events**: Create custom events within Blueprints to trigger specific actions or behaviors. Custom events are versatile and can be called from different parts of the Blueprint.

2. **Event Dispatchers**: Event dispatchers allow Blueprints to communicate with each other. You can define custom event dispatchers in one Blueprint and bind functions in other Blueprints to respond to those events.

3. **Input Mapping**: Customize input mapping in Blueprints to handle player input for actions like shooting, jumping, or interacting with objects.

State Machines

Implementing state machines in Blueprints is crucial for managing complex gameplay logic:

1. **Enum-Based State Machines**: Use enumerations (enums) to define different states for game objects or characters. Enum values can represent various states such as idle, walking, running, and attacking.

2. **Switch on Enum**: Employ the "Switch on Enum" node in Blueprints to handle different state transitions. This node allows you to route logic based on the current state of an object.

3. **State Entry and Exit**: Set up logic for state entry and exit within the Blueprint. This is where you define what happens when an object transitions between states.

Data Tables and Gameplay Data

Managing gameplay data efficiently is essential for creating dynamic and data-driven games:

1. **Data Tables**: Unreal Engine provides data tables that allow you to store game-related data in a structured format. You can use data tables for managing item properties, enemy statistics, and more.

2. **Reading Data Tables**: Use Blueprint nodes to read data from data tables during gameplay. This allows you to access information about items, enemies, and other game elements.

Animation and Blend Spaces

Animating characters and objects in Blueprints requires an understanding of animation and blend spaces:

1. **Animation Blueprint**: Create Animation Blueprints to define character animations based on gameplay logic. These Blueprints control animation transitions and blending.

2. **Blend Spaces**: Implement blend spaces to smoothly interpolate between different animations based on input or states. Blend spaces are particularly useful for character movement.

Debugging and Profiling

Debugging and profiling Blueprints are essential for identifying and resolving issues:

1. **Print and Debug Nodes**: Utilize print and debug nodes to display variable values, debug messages, and execution flow during Blueprint execution.

2. **Profiling Tools**: Unreal Engine provides profiling tools to analyze Blueprint performance. Use these tools to identify bottlenecks and optimize your Blueprints.

Blueprint Interfaces

Blueprint interfaces enable communication between unrelated Blueprint classes:

1. **Creating Interfaces**: Define Blueprint interfaces that contain a set of functions that can be implemented by various Blueprint classes.

2. **Implementing Interfaces**: Implement interfaces in specific Blueprint classes to ensure that they respond to interface-defined functions.

Advanced Blueprint scripting in Unreal Engine empowers developers and designers to create complex gameplay mechanics and systems visually. By using Blueprint classes, custom events, state machines, data tables, animation, debugging tools, and Blueprint interfaces, you can build intricate and dynamic gameplay experiences without writing extensive code. Thorough debugging and profiling ensure that your Blueprints perform efficiently and deliver a polished gaming experience.

4.2. Implementing AI Behaviors and Pathfinding

Implementing artificial intelligence (AI) behaviors and pathfinding in Unreal Engine is crucial for creating lifelike and responsive NPCs (non-playable characters) that interact with the player and their environment. In this section, we'll explore the key concepts and techniques for implementing AI behaviors and pathfinding in your game using Unreal Engine's built-in tools.

AI Controllers and Characters

AI controllers and characters are fundamental components for implementing AI behaviors:

1. **AI Controller**: Each AI character is associated with an AI controller. The controller is responsible for making decisions and executing AI behaviors.

2. **AI Character**: AI characters are derived from the Character class and represent the physical representation of NPCs in the game world.

Blackboards and Behavior Trees

Unreal Engine provides a visual scripting system called Behavior Trees to define AI behaviors:

1. **Behavior Trees**: Behavior Trees are visual graphs that describe AI decision-making processes. They consist of nodes that represent tasks, conditions, and control flow.

2. **Blackboards**: Blackboards are used to store and share information between AI tasks. They allow AI characters to access and modify variables that influence their behavior.

Tasks and Actions

Tasks and actions define specific AI behaviors and actions:

1. **AI Tasks**: AI tasks are nodes in the Behavior Tree that represent actions like moving, attacking, or interacting with objects. You can customize AI tasks to suit your game's needs.

2. **Custom Actions**: Create custom actions to implement unique AI behaviors. These actions can include complex decision-making logic or interactions with game-specific mechanics.

AI characters need to perceive their surroundings to make decisions:

1. **Sensing Components**: Unreal Engine provides sensing components like sight, hearing, and damage sensing. These components allow AI characters to detect nearby players or events.

2. **Perception System**: The Perception System helps AI characters gather information about the game world. It provides a framework for handling sensory data and reacting to it.

NavMesh and pathfinding are essential for AI movement and navigation:

1. **NavMesh**: The NavMesh is a representation of the game world that AI characters use for pathfinding. It defines walkable areas, obstacles, and navigation bounds.

2. **Pathfinding Algorithms**: Unreal Engine employs pathfinding algorithms like A* (A star) to calculate the shortest path between two points on the NavMesh.

3. **AI Move To**: Use the "AI Move To" node in Blueprints to command AI characters to navigate to specific locations. You can customize navigation settings and behavior.

Debugging AI behaviors and Behavior Trees is crucial for identifying and resolving issues:

1. **Behavior Tree Debugger**: Unreal Engine offers a Behavior Tree Debugger to visualize the execution flow of Behavior Trees. It helps diagnose logic errors and inefficiencies.

2. **AI Debugging Tools**: Utilize AI debugging tools to inspect AI character perceptions, decision-making, and navigation paths in real-time.

Finite State Machines are useful for organizing complex AI behaviors:

1. **FSM Nodes**: Implement Finite State Machines in Behavior Trees using FSM nodes. Each state represents a specific AI behavior or decision-making process.

2. **Transitions**: Define transitions between states based on conditions. FSMs allow AI characters to switch between states as the game situation changes.

For advanced AI behaviors and complex interactions, you may need to implement custom AI logic in Blueprints or C++:

1. **Custom Blueprint Logic**: Use Blueprints to create custom AI logic that goes beyond the capabilities of Behavior Trees and tasks. This can include intricate decision-making processes or complex character interactions.

2. **C++ AI Classes**: For highly specialized AI behaviors, consider developing custom AI classes in C++ that extend Unreal Engine's AI framework.

Implementing AI behaviors and pathfinding in Unreal Engine allows you to create engaging and challenging NPCs that enhance your game's immersion. By utilizing AI controllers, Behavior Trees, Blackboards, tasks, perception systems, NavMesh, debugging tools, Finite State Machines, and custom AI logic, you can design AI characters that respond intelligently to player actions and navigate the game world effectively. Thorough testing and iteration are essential to fine-tune AI behaviors and ensure that they align with your game's design and objectives.

4.3. Creating Custom Game Mechanics

Creating custom game mechanics in Unreal Engine allows game developers to design unique and engaging gameplay experiences tailored to their specific vision. In this section, we'll explore the process of designing and implementing custom game mechanics using Unreal Engine's Blueprint scripting and C++ programming capabilities.

Conceptualizing Custom Game Mechanics

Before diving into implementation, it's crucial to conceptualize your custom game mechanics thoroughly. Consider the following steps:

1. **Idea Generation**: Brainstorm and conceptualize your game mechanics. What unique gameplay elements do you want to introduce, and how will they enhance the player experience?

2. **Design Documentation**: Document your game mechanics with clear diagrams, flowcharts, or written descriptions. Define the rules, interactions, and intended player outcomes.

3. **Prototype**: Create a prototype or mockup of your custom game mechanics using simple placeholders. This allows you to test the concept before investing in full implementation.

Blueprint Scripting for Game Mechanics

Unreal Engine's Blueprint visual scripting system provides a flexible and accessible way to implement custom game mechanics:

1. **Event Graph**: Use the Event Graph within Blueprint classes to script game mechanics. This is where you define how your mechanics react to player input, events, or conditions.

2. **Custom Variables**: Create custom variables within Blueprints to store information related to your game mechanics. These variables can represent player scores, power-ups, or any other relevant data.

3. **Custom Functions**: Define custom functions in Blueprints to encapsulate specific game logic related to your mechanics. This promotes code reuse and organization.

4. **Timelines**: Timelines in Blueprints enable you to create time-based animations and behaviors for your game mechanics, such as character animations or environmental changes.

Integrating C++ for Performance and Complexity

While Blueprint scripting is a powerful tool, complex game mechanics may benefit from integration with C++ code:

1. **Blueprint Native Events**: Implement Blueprint Native Events in C++ to expose hooks for custom game mechanics. This allows you to combine the flexibility of Blueprints with the performance of C++.

2. **Performance Optimization**: For resource-intensive mechanics, consider implementing critical sections in C++ for performance optimization. C++ offers fine-grained control over memory and processing.

3. **AI and Navigation**: Custom AI behaviors and navigation logic may require C++ programming for efficient implementation. This is especially relevant for complex AI-driven game mechanics.

Iteration and Playtesting

Iterative development and playtesting are essential for refining custom game mechanics:

1. **Playtesting**: Regularly playtest your game mechanics to gather feedback and identify areas for improvement. Pay attention to player satisfaction, balance, and usability.

2. **Balancing**: Adjust and fine-tune your game mechanics to achieve balance and fairness. This includes tweaking variables, difficulty levels, and player rewards.

3. **Usability Testing**: Ensure that your game mechanics are intuitive and accessible to players. Conduct usability testing to identify any usability issues or barriers.

Custom game mechanics often require corresponding user interface elements:

1. **HUD Elements**: Create custom HUD (Heads-Up Display) elements to display relevant information to the player. This can include scores, timers, or status indicators.

2. **UI Widgets**: Design UI widgets using Unreal Engine's UMG (User Interface Markup Language) system to create menus, buttons, and other interactive elements tied to your mechanics.

Documentation and Tutorials

Proper documentation is essential for sharing your custom game mechanics with other team members or the community:

1. **Internal Documentation**: Document your code, Blueprints, and mechanics thoroughly to make it easier for team members to understand and maintain.

2. **Tutorials and Guides**: Consider creating tutorials or guides for your custom game mechanics to help other developers or modders use and extend them.

Creating custom game mechanics in Unreal Engine allows for innovation and creativity in game design. By conceptualizing, prototyping, and implementing your mechanics through Blueprint scripting and, when necessary, C++ programming, you can craft unique and engaging gameplay experiences. Don't forget to iterate, playtest, and fine-tune your mechanics to ensure they align with your game's vision and provide an enjoyable player experience.

4.4. Integrating Physics-Based Interactions

Integrating physics-based interactions into your game can add a layer of realism and immersion, making the virtual world feel more dynamic and interactive. Unreal Engine offers robust tools for handling physics simulations and interactions, and in this section, we'll explore how to implement physics-based mechanics effectively.

Unreal Engine's Physics Engine

Unreal Engine features a powerful built-in physics engine that can handle various aspects of physics, including:

1. **Collision Detection**: Unreal Engine's physics engine can accurately detect collisions between objects, whether they are static or dynamic.

2. **Rigid Body Dynamics**: You can simulate rigid body dynamics for objects such as boxes, characters, and vehicles. This allows for realistic movement and interaction.

3. **Constraints**: Constraints and joints enable you to connect objects together with specific behaviors. For example, you can create hinge joints for doors or rope constraints for swinging objects.

4. **Physics Materials**: Physics materials allow you to define friction, restitution, and other physical properties for materials, making surfaces behave realistically.

Physics-Based Interactions with Blueprint

Unreal Engine's Blueprint visual scripting system allows you to implement physics-based interactions without extensive coding:

1. **Physics Assets**: Use the Physics Asset Tool to create complex skeletal mesh physics simulations. This is useful for characters and creatures with realistic movements.

2. **Physics Simulation**: Enable physics simulation for specific objects or actors within the Blueprint. You can toggle physics on and off based on game events.

3. **Forces and Impulses**: Apply forces and impulses to objects within Blueprints to simulate external influences. For example, you can push a physics-enabled crate with a character.

4. **Raycasting**: Implement raycasting in Blueprints to detect objects hit by a line or ray. This is helpful for interactions like shooting or pointing.

5. **Custom Physics Logic**: Create custom physics logic within Blueprints to define unique interactions and behaviors. For example, you can script a pinball game's flippers and bumpers.

Constraints and Joints

To create more complex physics-based interactions, you can use constraints and joints:

1. **Hinge Joints**: Hinge joints allow objects to pivot around an axis, simulating doors, gates, or rotating platforms.

2. **Ball and Socket Joints**: Ball and socket joints enable multi-axis rotations and are useful for complex machinery or robotic arms.

3. **Physics Constraints**: Use the Physics Constraint Component to set up custom constraints between objects. This is helpful for scenarios like attaching a rope to a hook.

Ragdoll Physics

Implementing ragdoll physics can make character deaths or impacts more realistic:

1. **Ragdoll Physics Asset**: Create a ragdoll physics asset for characters to define how their body parts react to physics simulations.

2. **Blend Poses**: Blend between animated and ragdoll poses to smoothly transition between character animations and ragdoll physics when needed.

Particle Systems and Effects

Physics-based interactions often involve particle systems and effects:

1. **Particle Systems**: Use Unreal Engine's Niagara or Cascade particle systems to create realistic smoke, fire, water splashes, and other dynamic effects.

2. **Physical Materials**: Assign physical materials to particle effects to control how they interact with the environment, such as bouncing off surfaces or adhering to them.

Optimization and Performance

To ensure smooth gameplay, optimize physics-based interactions:

1. **Collision Complexity**: Adjust collision complexity settings for objects to balance accuracy and performance. Use simple collision shapes when detailed collisions are unnecessary.

2. **Physics Substepping**: Configure physics substepping to handle fast-moving or complex interactions more accurately.

3. **Culling and LOD**: Implement culling and Level of Detail (LOD) techniques to reduce the physics simulation load on distant objects.

4. **Collision Channels**: Use collision channels to control which objects interact with each other. This can help optimize complex scenes.

Integrating physics-based interactions into your Unreal Engine game can enhance gameplay, realism, and player engagement. By leveraging Unreal Engine's built-in physics engine, Blueprint scripting, constraints, ragdoll physics, particle systems, and optimization techniques, you can create dynamic and interactive environments that respond realistically to player actions. Thorough playtesting and iteration are crucial to ensure that physics-based interactions align with your game's design and provide an immersive experience.

4.5. Developing Adaptive Enemy AI

Creating adaptive enemy AI is essential for providing challenging and engaging gameplay experiences in your Unreal Engine game. Adaptive AI allows enemies to react intelligently to the player's actions, making encounters more dynamic and exciting. In this section, we'll explore techniques for developing adaptive enemy AI in Unreal Engine.

Effective adaptive AI begins with perception and sensing mechanisms that allow enemies to gather information about the player:

1. **Sight and Hearing**: Utilize Unreal Engine's built-in sensory systems to enable enemies to see and hear the player. Configure detection ranges, angles, and line of sight for realistic behavior.

2. **Perception Stimuli**: Use perception stimuli to simulate various sensory cues that enemies can react to. These can include noise, visual stimuli, or even custom events generated by the player.

3. **Custom Senses**: Implement custom senses if your game requires unique perception mechanics, such as tracking the player's scent or detecting vibrations.

Behavior Trees and Decision-Making

Unreal Engine's Behavior Trees provide a powerful framework for defining adaptive enemy behavior:

1. **Behavior Tree Nodes**: Create custom behavior tree nodes that encapsulate specific AI behaviors. This allows you to design complex decision-making logic.

2. **Blackboards**: Use Blackboards to store and share information between behavior tree nodes. Blackboards allow AI to remember and react to changes in the game world.

3. **Dynamic Decision Trees**: Implement decision trees within behavior trees to make decisions based on factors such as the player's proximity, health, or inventory.

Learning and Adaptation

To make enemy AI truly adaptive, consider incorporating learning and adaptation mechanisms:

1. **Machine Learning**: Explore machine learning techniques to train AI agents that adapt and learn from player interactions. This can lead to AI that improves its strategies over time.

2. **Dynamic Difficulty Adjustment**: Implement dynamic difficulty adjustment mechanisms that scale enemy AI behaviors based on the player's performance, ensuring a balanced challenge.

State Machines

State machines are valuable for organizing adaptive AI behaviors:

1. **AI States**: Define different AI states, such as "patrol," "alert," "attack," and "retreat." Transition between these states based on sensory input and player interactions.

2. **State Transitions**: Create state transition rules that determine when and how AI switches between states. For example, an enemy might transition to an alert state when it hears a gunshot.

To create challenging adaptive AI, predict the player's actions:

1. **Player Behavior Modeling**: Analyze the player's behavior and predict likely actions. For instance, if the player tends to take cover, AI can adapt by flanking or using grenades.

2. **Anticipation**: Implement anticipatory behaviors in AI to react proactively to expected player actions. This can include pre-emptive strikes or taking cover in advance.

Continuous feedback and iteration are crucial for fine-tuning adaptive enemy AI:

1. **Playtesting**: Playtest your game extensively to gather data on player interactions with the AI. This helps identify areas where AI behaviors can be improved.

2. **Balancing**: Adjust AI difficulty and behavior based on playtest feedback to strike the right balance between challenge and fairness.

3. **Bug Testing**: Rigorously test AI behaviors to identify and fix any bugs or unintended interactions. Ensure that AI doesn't become too predictable or erratic.

Consider a modular AI design that allows you to mix and match behaviors for different enemies:

1. **Behavior Components**: Create behavior components that can be attached to various enemy types, making it easier to reuse and adapt AI logic.

2. **Parameterization**: Use parameterization to customize AI behaviors and attributes for different enemies. This allows you to create diverse and challenging enemy encounters.

Developing adaptive enemy AI in Unreal Engine is a dynamic and creative process. By implementing perception and sensing, designing behavior trees, incorporating learning and adaptation, using state machines, predicting player actions, and continuously iterating based on feedback, you can create intelligent and responsive enemy AI that enhances your game's immersion and challenge. Balancing AI difficulty and variety is key to delivering a satisfying gameplay experience.

Chapter 5: Animation and Character Design

5.1. Character Modeling Techniques

Character modeling is a fundamental aspect of game development, responsible for bringing virtual characters to life in your Unreal Engine game. In this section, we'll explore various character modeling techniques that allow you to create detailed and visually appealing characters that fit seamlessly into your game world.

Character Design

Character modeling begins with character design. Consider the following steps:

1. **Concept Art**: Start with concept art to visualize the character's appearance, personality, and role in the game. Concept art serves as a reference throughout the modeling process.

2. **Silhouette**: Focus on creating a recognizable silhouette for your character. A distinct silhouette helps players identify characters easily, even from a distance.

3. **Reference Images**: Gather reference images for inspiration and to ensure accuracy in modeling. Reference images can include photographs, illustrations, or existing 3D models.

Character Mesh

The character's mesh is the foundation of its 3D representation. Here's how to approach character mesh modeling:

1. **Topology**: Pay attention to the topology of the character mesh. Clean and efficient topology ensures smooth deformations during animation.

2. **Edge Flow**: Create proper edge flow to define muscle and joint structures. Well-placed edge loops aid in deformation and rigging.

3. **Symmetry**: Model one half of the character in symmetry, then mirror it to create the other half. This ensures consistency and saves time.

High-Poly vs. Low-Poly

Character modeling often involves creating both high-poly and low-poly versions of the character:

1. **High-Poly**: The high-poly model contains a high level of detail and is used for rendering close-up shots or generating normal maps for the low-poly model.

2. **Low-Poly**: The low-poly model is optimized for real-time rendering. It's used for in-game character representation to ensure optimal performance.

Sculpting and Detailing

To add intricate details to your character, consider using sculpting software like ZBrush or Mudbox:

1. **Normal Maps**: Create normal maps from high-poly models to transfer surface details to low-poly models. Normal maps enhance the appearance of low-poly characters.

2. **Baking Textures**: Bake various textures, such as normal maps, ambient occlusion, and curvature maps, to add depth and realism to character models.

UV Mapping and Texturing

UV mapping and texturing are critical for giving characters their unique appearance:

1. **UV Unwrapping**: Properly unwrap the character's UVs to ensure that textures are applied accurately and without distortion.

2. **Texturing**: Use software like Substance Painter or Photoshop to paint textures. Pay attention to skin, clothing, and accessory details.

Rigging and Animation

Character modeling goes hand in hand with rigging and animation:

1. **Skeleton Rigging**: Create a skeletal rig for your character to define how it moves. Rigging includes bones, joints, and controls for animators.

2. **Weight Painting**: Weight painting assigns how vertices are influenced by bones. Accurate weight painting ensures smooth and realistic character movements.

Blend Shapes and Morph Targets

Blend shapes, also known as morph targets, are essential for facial expressions and character customization:

1. **Facial Blend Shapes**: Create a set of blend shapes to control facial expressions like smiles, frowns, and blinks. This adds emotional depth to characters.

2. **Customization**: Implement blend shapes to allow players to customize their character's appearance, such as adjusting facial features or body proportions.

LODs (Level of Detail)

Optimize character models with LODs to improve performance:

1. **LOD Levels**: Create multiple LOD levels with decreasing detail. Use LODs to ensure characters look good at different distances.

2. **Automatic LOD Generation**: Unreal Engine provides tools for automatically generating LODs based on your high-poly model.

Test character models in different game scenarios and iterate based on feedback:

1. **Animation Testing**: Animate your character to test rigging and animations. Ensure that animations work well with the model.

2. **Performance Testing**: Test character performance in-game to identify any issues with polygon counts or textures that impact frame rate.

3. **User Testing**: Gather feedback from playtesters to gauge player satisfaction with character design and animation.

Creating captivating characters through effective modeling techniques is crucial for immersing players in your game world. By following the steps outlined in this section and paying attention to character design, mesh topology, sculpting, UV mapping, rigging, blend shapes, LODs, and continuous testing and iteration, you can bring your characters to life and enhance the overall gaming experience.

5.2. Rigging and Skinning for Realism

Rigging and skinning are essential processes in character modeling, responsible for creating realistic and dynamic character animations in your Unreal Engine game. Rigging involves setting up a skeleton and controls, while skinning ensures that the character's mesh deforms naturally when animated. In this section, we'll explore rigging and skinning techniques to achieve realism in character movement.

Skeleton Rigging

Rigging begins with creating a skeleton that serves as the character's internal framework:

1. **Bones and Joints**: Define bones and joints for the character's body. Pay close attention to the placement of bones in areas like the spine, limbs, and facial features.

2. **Hierarchy**: Organize bones into a hierarchical structure. This hierarchy determines how bones influence each other during animation.

3. **Controls**: Implement control objects, such as IK (Inverse Kinematics) handles and FK (Forward Kinematics) controllers, to simplify animation tasks.

Inverse Kinematics (IK) and Forward Kinematics (FK)

Understanding the difference between IK and FK is crucial for rigging:

1. **IK Rigging**: Use IK for limbs and body parts that require precise positioning, such as arms and legs. IK allows you to place a character's hand on an object or keep their feet planted on the ground while walking.

2. **FK Rigging**: FK is suitable for parts that move naturally with rotational motion, like the spine or neck. FK controls are used for fluid and intuitive movement.

Rigging for Facial Animation

Facial rigging is vital for conveying emotions and expressions:

1. **Blend Shapes**: Create a set of blend shapes or morph targets for facial expressions. These control the deformation of the character's face to achieve various emotions.

2. **Rigged Facial Features**: Rig individual facial features like eyelids, eyebrows, and mouth corners to allow precise control over expressions.

3. **Bone-Based Rigging**: Implement bone-based facial rigs to provide animators with flexibility in shaping the character's face.

Weight Painting

Weight painting is the process of assigning how vertices on the character's mesh are influenced by bones:

1. **Smooth Deformation**: Carefully paint weights to ensure that the character's mesh deforms smoothly and naturally when bones are manipulated.

2. **Testing Deformations**: Test character poses and animations to identify areas where weight painting may need adjustments. Iterate until deformations look realistic.

Skinning and Binding

Skinning binds the character's mesh to the skeleton:

1. **Skinning Methods**: Choose between different skinning methods, such as linear skinning, dual quaternion skinning, or blend skinning, depending on the desired level of realism and performance.

2. **Painting Skin Weights**: Use skin weight painting tools to refine how each bone influences the surrounding vertices. This fine-tunes the character's deformations.

Rigging Plugins and Tools

Unreal Engine provides plugins and tools to streamline the rigging process:

1. **Unreal Engine Rigging Tools**: Take advantage of Unreal Engine's built-in rigging tools to simplify rig creation and management.

2. **Third-Party Plugins**: Explore third-party plugins and scripts for advanced rigging techniques and automation.

Rigging for Specialized Characters

Consider the unique needs of specialized characters:

1. **Quadrupeds**: Rig quadruped characters like animals or creatures with four legs. Adapt rigging techniques to account for differences in anatomy.

2. **Non-Humanoid Characters**: Rig characters with non-humanoid anatomy, such as monsters or fantasy creatures, by designing custom bone structures and controls.

Rigging Optimization

Optimize rigs for better performance:

1. **LODs**: Create LODs for character rigs, reducing the complexity of the rig as the character moves farther from the camera.

2. **Culling**: Implement culling techniques to disable parts of the rig that are not visible, conserving resources.

3. **Rig Complexity**: Balance rig complexity with performance considerations, ensuring that character animations run smoothly.

Testing and Iteration

Rigging and skinning require extensive testing and iteration:

1. **Animation Tests**: Animate the character to evaluate how well the rig performs during various movements and actions. Identify and fix issues like joint popping or mesh distortion.

2. **Collaboration**: Collaborate with animators to gather feedback and make adjustments to the rig based on their needs and preferences.

3. **Performance Testing**: Test the character rig's impact on game performance and make necessary optimizations.

Rigging and skinning are integral parts of character modeling that significantly influence the quality of character animations in your Unreal Engine game. By following the rigging and skinning techniques outlined in this section, you can create character rigs that allow for realistic movement, facial expressions, and specialized character designs. Rig optimization and continuous testing and iteration are key to delivering polished and lifelike character animations.

5.3. Advanced Animation Tools in Unreal

Unreal Engine offers a robust set of advanced animation tools that empower developers and animators to create complex and realistic character animations for their games. In this section, we'll explore these tools and techniques for achieving sophisticated character animations.

Animation Blueprints

Animation Blueprints allow you to create complex character animations through a node-based visual scripting system. Here's how to make the most of them:

1. **State Machines**: Use State Machines within Animation Blueprints to define various animation states such as idle, walking, running, and attacking. Transitions between states can be controlled based on conditions like player input or character status.

2. **Blend Spaces**: Implement Blend Spaces to smoothly interpolate between different animations based on multiple parameters. This is especially useful for character movement and aiming animations.

3. **Montage Animations**: Montage Animations enable you to create sequences of animations that can be triggered and played dynamically during gameplay. They are often used for special attacks or scripted sequences.

4. **Animation Notifies**: Add Animation Notifies to trigger events during specific frames of an animation. This can be used for things like footstep sounds or particle effects synchronized with animations.

Animation Retargeting

Unreal Engine's animation retargeting system allows you to reuse animations across characters with different skeletal structures. Here's how to utilize it effectively:

1. **Skeleton Hierarchy Mapping**: Define a mapping between bones of different skeletons. Unreal Engine can then adapt animations from one skeleton to another based on this mapping.

2. **Retargeting Options**: Configure retargeting options to control how animations are adapted, including bone translation, rotation, and scaling.

3. **Virtual Bones**: Use Virtual Bones to handle differences in bone hierarchies between source and target skeletons, making retargeting more flexible.

Animation Blending

Achieve smooth and realistic character animations through various blending techniques:

1. **Blend Poses by Bone**: Blend individual bone transformations to create precise and fine-grained animations, such as facial expressions or detailed hand movements.

2. **Layered Animations**: Combine multiple animations using layered animation blending, allowing characters to perform complex actions while maintaining responsiveness.

3. **Aim Offset Blending**: Implement Aim Offset Blending to smoothly transition between different aim directions while aiming weapons, providing a fluid and responsive feel to gunplay.

Root Motion

Root Motion is a technique that moves a character's root bone (usually the pelvis) to drive character movement and animations:

1. **Character Locomotion**: Use Root Motion to control character locomotion based on animations. This technique is particularly valuable for cinematic sequences and character interactions.

2. **Root Motion Extraction**: Extract root motion data from animations and apply it to character movement in real-time, enabling more dynamic and responsive gameplay animations.

Animation Curves

Fine-tune animations with animation curves that control various aspects of motion:

1. **Time-Based Curves**: Adjust animation speed and timing by manipulating time-based curves, allowing for slow-motion effects or dramatic action sequences.

2. **Morph Curves**: Use morph curves to control morph targets (blend shapes) for facial expressions, enabling precise and nuanced character emotions.

Animation Sequencer

Unreal Engine's Animation Sequencer is a powerful tool for creating cinematic sequences and cutscenes:

1. **Camera Animation**: Animate cameras and camera properties to create dynamic camera movements and cinematic shots.

2. **Character Animation**: Animate characters, objects, and events within the Sequencer timeline to craft engaging storytelling sequences.

3. **Audio Integration**: Sync animations with audio tracks for accurate lip-syncing and sound effects timing.

Physics-Based Animation

Integrate physics-based animation for realistic interactions and dynamic character movements:

1. **Ragdoll Physics**: Implement ragdoll physics for characters upon death or impact, enhancing realism in character deaths and falls.

2. **Cloth Simulation**: Simulate cloth and fabric physics for character clothing, adding realism and immersion to character animations.

Unreal Engine allows you to retime animations to adjust their speed or timing:

1. **Time Warping**: Apply time warping to animations to create dramatic slow-motion or fast-forward effects during gameplay or cutscenes.

2. **Timeline Scrubbing**: Utilize timeline scrubbing to preview and adjust animation timing directly within the Unreal Engine editor.

Advanced animation tools in Unreal Engine empower developers and animators to create immersive and dynamic character animations. By mastering Animation Blueprints, animation retargeting, blending techniques, root motion, animation curves, Animation Sequencer, physics-based animation, and animation retiming, you can craft compelling character animations that enhance the storytelling and gameplay experiences in your game. These tools open up possibilities for creating lifelike characters and engaging cinematic sequences, adding depth and realism to your project.

5.4. Facial Animation and Lip Syncing

Facial animation and lip syncing are critical aspects of character design, bringing a character's expressions and speech to life in your Unreal Engine game. In this section, we'll delve into techniques and tools for creating convincing facial animations and synchronizing character lip movements with dialogue.

Effective facial animation begins with a well-rigged face that can convey a wide range of emotions:

1. **Blend Shapes**: Implement blend shapes (morph targets) to control specific facial features like eyebrows, eyelids, lips, and cheeks. Each blend shape represents a different expression.

2. **Joint-Based Rigging**: Create joint-based facial rigs for more intricate control over facial movements. Joint-based rigs allow for nuanced expressions and realistic deformations.

3. **Control Rigging**: Utilize control rigging to provide animators with easy-to-use controllers for shaping facial expressions. These controllers simplify the animation process.

Motion Capture for Realism

Motion capture is a powerful tool for capturing realistic facial animations:

1. **Facial Motion Capture**: Record actors' facial performances using motion capture technology. This data can be applied directly to character rigs, preserving natural facial movements.

2. **Cleanup and Editing**: After capturing, perform cleanup and editing to refine the facial animation data, ensuring it aligns perfectly with your character model.

Phoneme and Viseme-Based Lip Syncing

Lip syncing involves matching a character's lip movements to spoken dialogue. Two common approaches are phoneme-based and viseme-based lip syncing:

1. **Phoneme-Based Lip Syncing**: Sync character lip movements with individual phonemes (speech sounds) in the spoken language. Unreal Engine provides phoneme recognition tools for this purpose.

2. **Viseme-Based Lip Syncing**: Utilize visemes, which are mouth shapes that correspond to specific speech sounds. Viseme-based lip syncing simplifies the process and is more accessible for many languages.

Lip Sync Plugins and Tools

Unreal Engine offers plugins and tools to facilitate lip syncing:

1. **LipSync Plugin**: Take advantage of Unreal Engine's LipSync Plugin, which integrates with external lip syncing software, automating the process and saving time.

2. **Text-to-Speech (TTS)**: Implement TTS solutions to convert text-based dialogue into audio and phoneme data, simplifying the creation of lip sync animations.

Manual Lip Syncing

Manual lip syncing may be required for precise control or when working with languages not supported by automated tools:

1. **Reference Videos**: Animate lip sync by closely studying reference videos of people speaking the dialogue. This method is effective for achieving natural and accurate results.

2. **Timeline Scrubbing**: Use Unreal Engine's timeline scrubbing features to synchronize lip movements frame by frame with the spoken dialogue.

Emotion and Expression

Facial animations should reflect the character's emotions and the context of the dialogue:

1. **Emotion Matching**: Ensure that facial expressions match the emotional tone of the dialogue. Expressions should be consistent with the character's feelings.

2. **Contextual Expressions**: Adjust facial expressions based on the context of the conversation. Characters should emote differently during casual chats and intense confrontations.

Animation Blending

Blend facial animations seamlessly to avoid abrupt transitions:

1. **Transition Blending**: Implement blend animations between different facial expressions and lip syncs to achieve smooth transitions during dialogue changes.

2. **Real-Time Blending**: For interactive conversations, use real-time blending to smoothly switch between character animations and responses.

Testing and Iteration

Thorough testing and iteration are crucial for refining facial animations and lip syncing:

1. **Animation Playtesting**: Playtest character animations in different scenarios and gather feedback to identify areas for improvement.

2. **Dialogue Review**: Review lip syncing animations in context with the dialogue to ensure that mouth movements match the spoken words accurately.

3. **Expression Tweaking**: Continuously tweak and refine facial expressions to enhance character believability and emotional depth.

Effective facial animation and lip syncing enhance the immersion and storytelling in your game. By rigging faces for expressions, leveraging motion capture, implementing phoneme or viseme-based lip syncing, using Unreal Engine's lip sync plugins and tools, manually synchronizing lip movements, considering emotion and expression, mastering animation blending, and conducting thorough testing and iteration, you can create characters with compelling and realistic facial animations that captivate players and bring your game world to life.

5.5. Integrating Motion Capture Data

Integrating motion capture data into your Unreal Engine project can elevate the quality and realism of character animations. Motion capture, often abbreviated as mocap, involves recording real-world movements and applying them to 3D character models. In this section, we'll explore the process of integrating motion capture data effectively.

The motion capture workflow typically consists of the following steps:

1. **Recording**: Perform motion capture sessions using specialized equipment and markers placed on actors' bodies. This records their movements in a controlled environment.

2. **Data Cleanup**: After recording, clean up the captured data by removing noise and unwanted artifacts. This ensures that the motion data is precise and ready for integration.

3. **Retargeting**: Map the motion capture data onto the skeleton of your 3D character model. This process is called retargeting and involves aligning the markers to the character's bones.

4. **Adaptation**: Adjust the retargeted motion to fit your character's proportions and rig. This step ensures that the animation looks natural on your character.

5. **Integration**: Import the cleaned and adapted motion capture data into Unreal Engine for use in your game.

Unreal Engine's Mocap Tools

Unreal Engine provides tools and features to streamline the integration of motion capture data:

1. **Animation Blueprints**: Use Animation Blueprints to create animation state machines that incorporate motion capture animations seamlessly. This allows for dynamic transitions between different mocap animations.

2. **Animation Montages**: Organize motion capture animations into Animation Montages, which can be triggered at specific moments during gameplay or cutscenes.

3. **Blend Spaces**: Implement Blend Spaces for smooth transitions between mocap animations, especially in situations where the character's movements vary.

4. **Root Motion**: Utilize root motion data captured during mocap to drive character movement, making animations more realistic.

Mocap Cleanup and Optimization

Cleaning up motion capture data and optimizing it for real-time use is essential:

1. **Noise Reduction**: Remove noise and unwanted artifacts from the motion capture data using filtering and smoothing techniques.

2. **Looping**: Create seamless loopable animations for actions like walking, running, or idle stances to ensure a continuous and natural look in the game.

3. **Animation Compression**: Compress mocap animations to reduce memory usage and improve runtime performance while maintaining visual quality.

Real-Time Retargeting

Unreal Engine's real-time retargeting tools allow you to adapt mocap data in real-time to different characters:

1. **Live Link**: Use Unreal Engine's Live Link feature to connect to motion capture systems and see real-time retargeting results in the editor.

2. **IK Solvers**: Implement Inverse Kinematics (IK) solvers to adapt mocap animations to characters with different proportions, such as robots or non-humanoid creatures.

Facial Motion Capture

Facial mocap data can be integrated to enhance character expressions:

1. **Facial Rigging**: Ensure that your character's facial rig is compatible with facial mocap data. Create a mapping between facial markers and rig controls.

2. **Expression Blending**: Blend facial expressions captured through mocap with other animations to create dynamic and emotionally rich character performances.

Interaction and Realism

To make the most of motion capture data, consider interactions and realism:

1. **Physics Interactions**: Implement physics-driven interactions to make characters react realistically to the environment and other objects.

2. **Layered Animations**: Combine motion capture animations with other animations, such as hand-crafted combat moves or scripted interactions, to achieve complex and dynamic character behavior.

Testing and Fine-Tuning

Thoroughly test and fine-tune mocap-integrated animations:

1. **Playtesting**: Playtest animations in different game scenarios to ensure that they respond well to player input and environmental conditions.

2. **Animation Blending**: Pay attention to animation blending to ensure smooth transitions between motion capture data and other animations.

3. **Visual Feedback**: Gather feedback from testers and animators to make necessary adjustments for realism and immersion.

Integrating motion capture data into Unreal Engine offers a powerful way to achieve lifelike character animations. By following the motion capture workflow, leveraging Unreal Engine's mocap tools, cleaning up and optimizing data, exploring real-time retargeting, integrating facial mocap, considering interactions and realism, and conducting thorough testing and fine-tuning, you can create characters that move and behave realistically, enhancing the overall gaming experience.

Chapter 6: Visual Effects and Particle Systems

6.1. Creating Realistic Fire, Smoke, and Explosions

In this section, we will delve into the intricate process of creating realistic fire, smoke, and explosions using Unreal Engine's powerful visual effects and particle systems. These elements are essential for adding immersion and dynamism to your game environments, whether you're working on a high-octane action game or a cinematic experience.

Fire Effects

Creating convincing fire effects in Unreal Engine requires a combination of particle systems and materials. You can start by defining the behavior of the fire, including its shape, intensity, and movement. Here's an example of a basic fire particle system:

```
Particle System: Fire

- Particle Emitter
  - Initial Size: Random between 50 and 100
  - Initial Color: Warm orange and yellow tones
  - Lifetime: Random between 1 and 3 seconds
  - Initial Velocity: Upward and slightly erratic
  - Gravity: Some upward force to simulate the rising effect

- Material
  - Use a dynamic material that changes color and opacity over time
  - Add distortion and turbulence for a realistic look
```

You can further enhance fire effects by adding sparks, embers, and smoke particles to create a more immersive experience.

Smoke and Explosions

Simulating smoke and explosions involves complex particle systems. You can create a smoke plume with the following settings:

```
Particle System: Smoke Plume

- Particle Emitter
```

- Initial Size: Random between 100 and 200
- Initial Color: Shades of gray and black
- Lifetime: Random between 2 and 5 seconds
- Initial Velocity: Upward and outward with some randomness
- Gravity: Affecting particles to make them rise and disperse

- Material
  - Use a translucent material with noise and turbulence
  - Adjust opacity and alpha blending for a more realistic appearance

Explosions often consist of multiple particle systems, including an initial burst, shockwave, and lingering smoke. These systems can be triggered in sequence to create a convincing explosion effect.

Remember to consider performance optimization when working with complex particle systems. Unreal Engine provides tools for culling and LOD (Level of Detail) to ensure your effects run smoothly on various hardware.

Creating realistic fire, smoke, and explosions in Unreal Engine can greatly enhance the visual quality and immersion of your game. Experiment with different parameters and textures to achieve the desired look and feel for your project.

6.2. Water and Fluid Simulations

In this section, we will explore the fascinating world of water and fluid simulations within Unreal Engine. Water is a fundamental element in many game environments, whether it's a serene lake, a flowing river, or a turbulent ocean. Unreal Engine provides robust tools to create realistic water and fluid effects that can greatly enhance the visual appeal and interactivity of your game worlds.

Basic Water Surfaces

Creating a basic water surface in Unreal Engine can be achieved using the built-in Water Plane Actor. Here's a simple example of setting up a calm water surface:

1. Create a Water Plane Actor in your level.
2. Adjust the dimensions and location to fit your scene.
3. Customize the Material applied to the Water Plane for desired colors and t ransparency.
4. Configure the Water Plane's properties such as wave height, speed, and ref raction.

This basic approach can be used for ponds, lakes, and other calm water bodies. For more realistic water simulations, consider using the Water Body Actor, which allows for dynamic interaction with the environment, including splashes and ripples.

Advanced Water Effects

Unreal Engine also supports advanced water effects such as dynamic oceans with waves and foam. These effects are often achieved using complex shader and simulation techniques. Here's an overview of the steps to create an ocean-like effect:

```
1. Use the Water Body Actor to define the ocean's volume and properties.
2. Implement a shader that simulates wave displacement, taking into account f
actors like wind direction and intensity.
3. Add foam and whitecaps using particle systems triggered by wave intensity
and collisions.
4. Fine-tune the materials to achieve realistic water color, transparency, an
d reflection.
```

These advanced water effects can transform your game's coastal or maritime scenes into immersive and dynamic experiences. Be prepared for some performance considerations when working with complex water simulations, as they can be resource-intensive.

Fluid Simulations

Fluid simulations, such as flowing rivers or pouring liquids, can be challenging but rewarding to implement in Unreal Engine. You may consider using third-party plugins or tools that specialize in fluid dynamics to achieve realistic results. These tools often provide integration with Unreal Engine through custom nodes or APIs.

In conclusion, water and fluid simulations in Unreal Engine offer a wide range of possibilities for enhancing your game's visual appeal and interactivity. Whether you need serene water surfaces or dynamic ocean waves, Unreal Engine provides the tools and flexibility to bring your virtual water worlds to life. Experimentation and iteration are key to achieving the desired level of realism and immersion in your game's aquatic environments.

6.3. Implementing Post-Processing Effects

In this section, we will explore the concept of post-processing effects in Unreal Engine. Post-processing effects are a crucial part of game development that can greatly impact the visual quality and mood of your game. These effects are applied after the rendering process to enhance or modify the final image that the player sees. Unreal Engine provides a wide range of post-processing options that allow you to achieve various artistic styles and visual enhancements.

Basic Post-Processing Stack

Unreal Engine organizes post-processing effects into a stack, where each effect is applied in a specific order. The basic post-processing stack typically includes:

4. **Tonemapping**: Adjusts the overall color and brightness of the image, making it visually appealing.

5. **Bloom**: Creates a soft glow around bright objects or light sources, enhancing the sense of light and atmosphere.

6. **Color Grading**: Allows you to adjust the color balance, contrast, and saturation to achieve a specific look or mood.

7. **Depth of Field**: Simulates the camera's focus, blurring objects in the foreground or background for cinematic effects.

8. **Motion Blur**: Adds blur to fast-moving objects or camera movements, contributing to a more realistic and cinematic feel.

9. **Anti-Aliasing**: Reduces jagged edges and aliasing artifacts for smoother visuals.

Custom Post-Processing Effects

Unreal Engine also enables you to create custom post-processing effects using Material Editor and Material Instances. This gives you full control over the visual style of your game. Here's a simplified example of creating a custom vignette effect:

1. Create a Material with a Post-Process Material Domain.
2. Add a Texture Parameter representing the vignette texture.
3. Use a Pixel Depth Offset to apply the vignette effect based on screen depth.
4. Apply the Material to a Post-Process Volume in your level.
5. Adjust parameters like the intensity and size of the vignette.

This example demonstrates how you can create a custom post-processing effect using Unreal Engine's Material Editor. You can apply similar techniques to create a wide range of unique visual effects.

Performance Considerations

While post-processing effects can greatly enhance your game's visuals, they can also impact performance, especially on lower-end hardware. It's essential to consider the performance implications of each effect and optimize accordingly. Unreal Engine provides tools like the GPU Profiler to help identify performance bottlenecks related to post-processing.

In conclusion, post-processing effects in Unreal Engine are a powerful tool for shaping the visual style and mood of your game. Whether you want to create a gritty, post-apocalyptic atmosphere or a dreamy, ethereal world, understanding how to implement and customize post-processing effects is a valuable skill for game developers. Experimentation and iteration are key to finding the right balance of effects to achieve your desired artistic vision while maintaining optimal performance.

6.4. Optimizing Particle Systems for Performance

Optimizing particle systems is a critical aspect of game development in Unreal Engine. While particle systems can add dynamic and visually appealing effects to your game, they can also be resource-intensive. In this section, we'll explore strategies and techniques to optimize particle systems for better performance without sacrificing visual quality.

LOD (Level of Detail) for Particles

Unreal Engine allows you to set different levels of detail for particle systems based on the player's distance from the effect. For example, you can use a high-detail particle system when the player is up close and switch to a simplified version when they are farther away. This helps reduce the computational load and improves performance. To implement LOD for particles:

```
1. Create multiple versions of your particle system with varying levels of de
tail.
2. Set up LOD settings in the particle system's details panel.
3. Adjust the distance thresholds at which each LOD level is used.
4. Unreal Engine will automatically switch between LODs based on player proxi
mity.
```

Particle Culling

Culling is the process of determining which particles are within the player's view frustum and should be rendered. Unreal Engine includes efficient culling mechanisms to avoid rendering particles that are outside the player's field of view. To make the most of particle culling:

```
1. Enable "Use View Frustum Culling" in your particle system's settings.
2. Ensure that the bounds of your particle system are correctly set to encaps
ulate the particles' positions.
3. Unreal Engine will automatically exclude particles outside the view frustu
m from rendering.
```

Spawn Rate and Lifetime Optimization

The spawn rate and lifetime of particles can significantly impact performance. Be mindful of these factors when designing your particle systems:

- **Spawn Rate**: Reduce the spawn rate of particles, especially for effects that are not in the player's immediate focus. Lower spawn rates mean fewer particles to simulate and render.

- **Lifetime**: Shorten the lifetime of particles that don't need to persist for a long time. For example, smoke or sparks can have shorter lifetimes than persistent effects like rain.

Texture and Material Optimization

The textures and materials used by particles can consume GPU resources. To optimize them:

- Use smaller texture resolutions when possible.
- Employ texture compression techniques to reduce memory usage.
- Avoid complex and expensive materials unless necessary for the effect.

Particle Collisions

Enabling collisions for particles can add realism but also increase CPU usage. Use collision sparingly and only for effects where it's essential, like sparks bouncing off surfaces or raindrops hitting the ground.

GPU Particles

Unreal Engine 4.26 introduced GPU particle simulations, which can significantly boost performance for certain particle effects. GPU particles offload the simulation work from the CPU to the GPU, allowing for larger and more complex particle systems. To use GPU particles:

```
1. Set the "Required Simulation Type" to GPU in your particle system's settin
gs.
2. Adjust GPU-specific parameters like Max GPU Particles and Max Lifetime.
3. Test and fine-tune to achieve the desired balance between visual quality a
nd performance.
```

In conclusion, optimizing particle systems is essential for maintaining a smooth and enjoyable player experience in Unreal Engine. By implementing LOD, culling, adjusting spawn rates and lifetimes, optimizing textures and materials, and considering GPU particles, you can strike the right balance between visual fidelity and performance in your game's particle effects. Remember that performance optimization is an iterative process, and testing on a variety of hardware configurations is crucial to ensure your game runs smoothly for all players.

6.5. Using Niagara for Complex VFX

Niagara is Unreal Engine's powerful visual effects system that offers advanced tools for creating complex and dynamic visual effects (VFX). In this section, we'll delve into using Niagara to achieve stunning and intricate VFX for your games.

Introduction to Niagara

Niagara is designed to provide greater flexibility and performance compared to the older Cascade particle system. It uses a node-based system, making it more accessible for artists and designers to create complex VFX without extensive coding. Here's a high-level overview of using Niagara:

10. **Create a Niagara System**: Begin by creating a Niagara System Asset, which serves as the container for your VFX.

11. **Emitter Modules**: Inside your Niagara System, you'll use Emitter Modules to control how particles are spawned, updated, and rendered. Modules include Spawn, Update, and Renderer modules.

12. **Node Graph**: Niagara uses a node-based graph system to create logic and control particle behavior. You can create custom nodes and parameterize your VFX.

Realistic Particle Movement

One of Niagara's strengths is its ability to simulate realistic particle movement. You can achieve this by controlling forces and velocities. For example, to create swirling smoke:

```
1. Use the Curl Noise module to add turbulence and swirling motion to your pa
rticles.
2. Adjust the turbulence intensity and scale to achieve the desired effect.
3. Combine this with other forces like gravity and wind to create complex, re
alistic movement.
```

This level of control over particle motion allows you to simulate a wide range of natural phenomena, from wind-blown leaves to turbulent water currents.

Parameterization and Dynamic VFX

Niagara allows you to parameterize your VFX, making it easy to create variations and dynamic effects. For example, you can create a fire VFX with customizable parameters like flame intensity, color, and size. These parameters can be exposed to designers and artists, allowing them to tweak the effect in real-time without needing code changes.

```
1. Create parameters in your Niagara System, such as FlameIntensity, FlameCol
or, and FlameSize.
2. Expose these parameters in the Niagara Details panel.
3. Designers can adjust these parameters in real-time within the Unreal Engin
e editor, facilitating rapid iteration.
```

Advanced Rendering Techniques

Niagara offers advanced rendering techniques to make your VFX stand out. For example, you can use GPU sprites for highly performant and visually appealing effects like sparks or magical projectiles. You can also enable soft particles to create smooth transitions between particles and opaque surfaces.

```
1. In the Niagara Renderer module, select the GPU Sprites rendering method fo
r high-performance sprite rendering.
2. Enable Soft Particles to achieve smooth particle blending with surfaces.
```

Audio and Visual Integration

Niagara can be integrated with Unreal Engine's audio system to synchronize VFX with sound effects. For example, you can create a Niagara VFX that emits particles in sync with a music beat or an explosion sound.

1. Use Blueprint or scripting to trigger Niagara events in response to audio cues.
2. Connect Niagara events to your VFX parameters, such as particle emission rate or size, to sync with the audio.

In conclusion, Niagara is a powerful tool for creating complex and dynamic visual effects in Unreal Engine. Whether you're designing realistic natural phenomena, magical spells, or explosive destruction, Niagara's node-based system, parameterization, and advanced rendering techniques provide the flexibility and performance needed to bring your VFX to life. Experimentation and iteration are key to mastering Niagara and achieving the desired visual impact in your games.

Chapter 7: Networking and Multiplayer Setup

7.1. Understanding Unreal's Networking Model

Unreal Engine's networking capabilities are a crucial aspect of developing multiplayer and online games. Understanding how Unreal handles networking is essential for creating seamless multiplayer experiences. In this section, we'll delve into Unreal's networking model and its key components.

Replication

Unreal Engine uses a system called replication to synchronize game state across multiple clients in a multiplayer game. Replication ensures that players on different machines see the same game world and interact with each other correctly.

- **Server Authority**: In Unreal's networking model, the server is the authoritative source of the game state. It decides what happens in the game and sends updates to clients.

- **Client Prediction**: To provide a responsive feel to players, Unreal uses client-side prediction. Clients predict the results of their actions locally and then receive corrections from the server.

Replication Modes

Unreal Engine offers three primary replication modes:

13. **Not Replicated**: Objects set to this mode are not synchronized across the network. Typically used for objects that don't affect gameplay.

14. **Replicated**: Objects set to this mode are replicated from the server to clients. Players on different machines will see and interact with these objects.

15. **Replicated Movement**: Objects in this mode have their transforms replicated, allowing synchronized movement across the network.

Remote Function Calls

Unreal uses Remote Function Calls (RPCs) to execute functions on remote objects. These are essential for triggering actions on other players' clients or on the server itself.

Here's an example of defining an RPC in Unreal:

```
UFUNCTION(Server, Reliable, WithValidation)
void ServerFunctionExample(int32 Value);

void ServerFunctionExample_Implementation(int32 Value)
{
    // Implementation of the server function.
```

```
}

bool ServerFunctionExample_Validate(int32 Value)
{
    // Validation logic for the server function.
    return true;
}
```

- `Server`: Specifies that this function is executed on the server.

- `Reliable`: Ensures that the function call is guaranteed to reach its destination.

- `WithValidation`: Includes a validation function that Unreal calls before executing the RPC.

Network Conditions

Unreal Engine provides tools to deal with varying network conditions, including packet loss and latency. These tools include:

- **Replication Condition**: You can set conditions for replication to control when and how often an object is replicated.

- **Ping-Based Replication**: Unreal can adjust the replication rate based on a player's ping to maintain a smooth experience.

Replication Graph

Unreal Engine 4.26 introduced the Replication Graph, a system for optimizing replication in large-scale multiplayer games. It allows developers to customize how objects are replicated based on their relevance and importance to the player.

In summary, Unreal Engine's networking model revolves around replication, which synchronizes game state across clients and the server. Understanding replication modes, RPCs, network conditions, and advanced features like the Replication Graph is crucial for creating robust and enjoyable multiplayer experiences in Unreal Engine.

7.2. Implementing Multiplayer Gameplay

Implementing multiplayer gameplay in Unreal Engine is a complex and exciting task. It allows players to connect and interact with each other in a shared game world. In this section, we will explore the fundamental concepts and steps required to implement multiplayer functionality in your Unreal Engine game.

Game Modes and Game State

In Unreal Engine, multiplayer games often use different game modes and game states to manage the flow of gameplay. Game modes define the rules and settings for a particular game type, while game states track the overall state of the game and manage things like scorekeeping and round transitions.

To create a multiplayer game, you typically start by extending the existing game mode and game state classes to handle multiplayer-specific functionality. This may include managing player spawns, scoring, and network replication.

Player Replication

In multiplayer games, each player's actions need to be replicated to all other players in the game. Unreal Engine's replication system handles this process automatically for replicated variables, functions, and properties.

To replicate variables, you can use the Replicated keyword in your class declaration. For example:

```
UPROPERTY(Replicated)
int32 PlayerScore;
```

This will ensure that changes to PlayerScore on the server are automatically replicated to all connected clients.

Remote Procedure Calls (RPCs)

Multiplayer games often require executing functions on remote objects. Unreal Engine provides Remote Procedure Calls (RPCs) for this purpose. You can mark a function as an RPC to indicate that it should be called on a specific object on a remote machine.

Here's an example of defining and calling an RPC:

```
UFUNCTION(Server, Reliable)
void ServerFireProjectile();

void ServerFireProjectile_Implementation()
{
    // Implement the server-side logic for firing a projectile.
}

// Call the RPC on the server.
if (HasAuthority())
{
    ServerFireProjectile();
}
```

In this example, ServerFireProjectile is an RPC, and calling it on the server will execute ServerFireProjectile_Implementation on the server.

Player Input and Synchronization

Handling player input in multiplayer games requires careful consideration. Player input should be collected on the client and sent to the server, which then replicates it to all other clients. Unreal Engine provides functions like `APlayerController::ServerNotifyHit()` to notify the server of player actions.

Synchronizing player movements is also essential for a smooth multiplayer experience. Unreal Engine's built-in character movement component handles the replication of movement, but you can customize this behavior to suit your game's needs.

Game State Management

Managing the game state in multiplayer games is crucial for ensuring that all players are in sync. Unreal Engine provides mechanisms for handling game state changes, such as round transitions or level changes, and replicating them to all clients.

Using Unreal's `GameState` class, you can manage things like game timers, scorekeeping, and game-ending conditions in a multiplayer context. You can then replicate this game state to ensure that all players have the same view of the game world.

Testing and Debugging

Testing and debugging multiplayer functionality can be challenging due to the added complexity of networked gameplay. Unreal Engine provides tools like the dedicated server, network profiling, and replication debugging to help identify and resolve issues in your multiplayer game.

In summary, implementing multiplayer gameplay in Unreal Engine involves understanding replication, managing game modes and game state, handling player input and synchronization, and effectively managing the game state. With the right design and careful attention to replication and network considerations, you can create engaging and enjoyable multiplayer experiences in your Unreal Engine games.

7.3. Synchronizing Game States Across Networks

Synchronizing game states across networks is a critical aspect of multiplayer game development in Unreal Engine. Ensuring that all players have a consistent view of the game world, including variables, events, and gameplay progress, is essential for a seamless multiplayer experience. In this section, we will explore the techniques and best practices for achieving game state synchronization in Unreal Engine.

Server Authority

In a multiplayer game, the server is the authoritative source of the game state. This means that decisions made by the server regarding gameplay, physics, and other critical aspects are considered final. Clients may make predictions based on their inputs, but the server has the ultimate say in what happens in the game.

To maintain server authority, it's essential to validate and replicate critical game events and state changes from clients to the server. Unreal Engine's replication system handles this process automatically for replicated variables, functions, and properties.

Replication Conditions

Unreal Engine provides replication conditions that allow you to control when and how often an object or variable is replicated across the network. Understanding and using these conditions effectively can significantly impact the performance and responsiveness of your multiplayer game.

- **Replicate**: Objects or variables set to "Replicate" will be automatically synchronized across the network whenever they change. Use this for essential game state elements.

- **Replicate Condition**: Use replication conditions to specify under what circumstances an object or variable should be replicated. For example, you can replicate the player's health when it changes, rather than continuously.

- **Replication Role**: Unreal Engine distinguishes between the server, client, and autonomous roles. Use the appropriate role to determine when and how objects are replicated. For example, server functions should be called on the server.

Remote Procedure Calls (RPCs)

RPCs are crucial for synchronizing game states across networks. They allow you to execute functions on remote objects, ensuring that actions taken by one player affect all players in the game.

When defining an RPC, you can specify whether it should be executed on the server or a specific client. Unreal Engine handles the network communication and replication automatically.

```
UFUNCTION(Server, Reliable)
void ServerUpdatePlayerScore(int32 NewScore);

void ServerUpdatePlayerScore_Implementation(int32 NewScore)
{
    // Update the player's score on the server.
    PlayerScore = NewScore;
}

// Call the RPC to update the player's score on the server.
if (HasAuthority())
{
    ServerUpdatePlayerScore(NewScore);
}
```

In this example, ServerUpdatePlayerScore is an RPC called on the server to update a player's score, ensuring that all clients are aware of the change.

State Replication and Game Events

Managing game states and events is crucial for synchronization. Unreal Engine provides GameState and GameMode classes that allow you to track and replicate important game events, such as round transitions, score updates, and match outcomes.

By customizing these classes and using RPCs and replication effectively, you can ensure that all players receive updates on critical game state changes in real-time.

Testing and Debugging

Testing and debugging synchronization issues in multiplayer games can be challenging due to the complexity of networked gameplay. Unreal Engine provides several tools to help diagnose and resolve synchronization problems:

- **Dedicated Server**: Use a dedicated server to test your game's multiplayer functionality in a controlled environment.

- **Network Profiling**: Unreal Engine's network profiling tools allow you to visualize network traffic and diagnose performance bottlenecks.

- **Replication Debugging**: Use the built-in replication debugger to identify and resolve replication issues in your game.

In summary, synchronizing game states across networks is a fundamental aspect of multiplayer game development in Unreal Engine. Server authority, replication conditions, RPCs, and effective management of game events are essential techniques to ensure that all players have a consistent and enjoyable multiplayer experience. Thorough testing and debugging are crucial to identifying and resolving synchronization issues to create a seamless multiplayer gameplay experience.

7.4. Handling Latency and Network Issues

Handling latency and network issues is a vital aspect of multiplayer game development in Unreal Engine. Latency, which is the delay between a player's action and its effect in the game world, can affect gameplay and the player experience. In this section, we will explore techniques and strategies to mitigate latency and address common network issues in Unreal Engine multiplayer games.

Client-Side Prediction

Client-side prediction is a technique used to provide responsive gameplay to players while minimizing the effects of latency. It allows clients to predict the outcome of their actions locally and then receive corrections from the server.

For example, in a first-person shooter game, when a player presses the "fire" button, the client immediately shows the gunshot and hit effects on their screen based on their prediction. The server later confirms whether the shot was valid and applies any necessary corrections. This approach reduces the perceived latency.

Interpolation and Smooth Movement

Interpolation is the process of smoothing out the movement of remote players and objects to make their motion appear more natural. Unreal Engine's built-in replication system includes interpolation to help reduce visual jitter caused by packet loss and network fluctuations.

By using interpolation, remote player characters, projectiles, and other objects appear to move more smoothly on the screen, even if the network updates are sporadic.

Lag Compensation

Lag compensation is a technique used to account for the delay between a player's action and its effect on the server. In fast-paced games, like shooters, lag compensation can be crucial to ensuring that shots hit where they appear to on the player's screen.

Unreal Engine provides mechanisms for implementing lag compensation, which typically involves rewinding the game state on the server to account for the player's latency and ensure fair and accurate hit detection.

```
// Pseudocode for lag compensation in a hit registration function:
bool CheckHitRegistration(FVector HitLocation)
{
    // Calculate the time the shot was fired on the server.
    float ServerFireTime = GetServerFireTime();

    // Calculate the estimated position of the target at the server's fire ti
me.
    FVector EstimatedTargetPosition = EstimateTargetPosition(ServerFireTime);

    // Check if the hit location is within an acceptable tolerance.
    if (FVector::Dist(HitLocation, EstimatedTargetPosition) <= HitTolerance)
    {
        // Register the hit as valid.
        RegisterValidHit();
        return true;
    }

    // Register a miss.
    RegisterMiss();
    return false;
}
```

Server Reconciliation

Server reconciliation is another technique used to handle network issues. It involves the server recalculating the game state and resolving discrepancies between the client's predictions and the actual game state.

For example, if a client predicted that they hit an enemy but the server determined it was a miss, server reconciliation can adjust the client's game state to match the server's authoritative state.

Latency Compensation

Latency compensation techniques aim to minimize the impact of latency on player interactions. These techniques include features like hit-scan weapons (instantaneous projectiles), which allow players to shoot and see the hit immediately without waiting for network round trips.

Implementing latency compensation features can make the game feel more responsive, even in high-latency scenarios.

In summary, handling latency and network issues is a critical aspect of multiplayer game development in Unreal Engine. Techniques such as client-side prediction, interpolation, lag compensation, server reconciliation, and latency compensation can significantly improve the player experience and help create more enjoyable and responsive multiplayer games. Thorough testing and optimization are essential to ensure that these techniques work effectively and do not introduce unintended issues in your game.

7.5. Security Considerations in Multiplayer Games

Security is a critical aspect of multiplayer game development in Unreal Engine, especially when players can interact with each other over networks or the internet. Ensuring a secure multiplayer environment is essential to protect the integrity of the game, player data, and the overall player experience. In this section, we will explore key security considerations and best practices for multiplayer games in Unreal Engine.

Server Authority

As mentioned earlier, Unreal Engine follows a server-authoritative model, where the server has the final say in game state and player actions. This design helps prevent cheating and ensures that all players have a consistent view of the game world.

To maintain server authority, it's crucial to validate and verify all player actions on the server. This includes input validation, hit detection, and any other critical game events. Never trust client-side input entirely, as it can be manipulated by malicious players.

```
// Pseudocode for server-side input validation:
bool ValidatePlayerInput(FVector TargetLocation)
{
```

```
    // Check if the target location is within acceptable bounds.
    if (IsLocationValid(TargetLocation))
    {
        // Process the action as valid.
        ProcessValidAction();
        return true;
    }

    // Reject the action as invalid.
    RejectInvalidAction();
    return false;
}
```

Anti-Cheat Measures

Implementing anti-cheat measures is crucial to maintaining a fair and enjoyable multiplayer experience. Cheating can ruin the experience for other players and lead to a loss of trust in your game.

Unreal Engine provides various tools and plugins that can help with anti-cheat efforts. Consider using third-party anti-cheat solutions that are compatible with Unreal Engine to detect and prevent cheating behaviors.

Data Validation and Sanitization

In multiplayer games, players may attempt to send malicious data to manipulate or disrupt the game. It's essential to validate and sanitize all incoming data to prevent security vulnerabilities and exploits.

For example, validate data sent by players, such as character names or chat messages, to ensure they do not contain harmful content or scripts. Use server-side validation and filtering to sanitize user-generated content.

Encryption and Data Protection

Protecting sensitive player data, such as login credentials and payment information, is critical for both player trust and legal compliance. Implement encryption and secure transmission protocols (e.g., HTTPS) to safeguard data sent between clients and servers.

Additionally, consider implementing strong authentication mechanisms, such as two-factor authentication (2FA), to protect player accounts from unauthorized access.

```
// Pseudocode for implementing 2FA in Unreal Engine:
bool AuthenticatePlayer(const FString& Username, const FString& Password, con
st FString& AuthCode)
{
    // Check if the provided credentials are valid.
    if (IsCredentialsValid(Username, Password))
    {
        // Verify the 2FA code.
        if (Is2FAValid(AuthCode))
```

```
    {
        // Authenticate the player.
        Authenticate();
        return true;
    }
    }

    // Authentication failed.
    RejectAuthentication();
    return false;
}
```

Regular Updates and Patching

Security vulnerabilities can emerge over time as new threats and exploits are discovered. It's essential to stay vigilant and release regular updates and patches for your multiplayer game to address security issues and maintain a secure gaming environment.

Community Reporting and Moderation

Encourage your player community to report any suspicious or malicious behavior they encounter. Implement moderation systems to review and take action against reported violations of your game's terms of service and community guidelines.

In summary, security considerations are paramount in multiplayer game development in Unreal Engine. Maintaining server authority, implementing anti-cheat measures, validating and sanitizing data, encrypting sensitive information, and regularly updating and patching your game are essential steps to create a secure and enjoyable multiplayer gaming experience. Community reporting and moderation also play a significant role in ensuring a fair and secure gaming environment for all players.

Chapter 8: Virtual Reality Development

8.1. Fundamentals of VR in Unreal

Virtual Reality (VR) is an exciting technology that allows players to immerse themselves in digital worlds. Unreal Engine provides robust support for VR development, making it possible to create immersive and interactive experiences. In this section, we will explore the fundamentals of VR in Unreal Engine, including setting up a VR project, understanding VR hardware, and developing for VR.

Setting Up a VR Project

Before diving into VR development in Unreal Engine, you need to set up your project for VR. Follow these steps to get started:

16. **Enable VR Plugins:** In Unreal Engine, go to the "Edit" menu, select "Plugins," and enable the "Virtual Reality" plugin for the VR platforms you intend to target (e.g., Oculus, SteamVR, or PlayStation VR).

17. **Configure Project Settings:** Open the project settings and go to the "Platforms" section. Set the "Default VR System" to the VR platform you are targeting.

18. **Enable VR Mode:** In the main toolbar, click the "VR Preview" button to enable VR mode in the editor. This allows you to test and iterate on your VR content directly within Unreal Engine.

Understanding VR Hardware

VR experiences rely on specific hardware components, including VR headsets and motion controllers. It's essential to understand the hardware you're developing for to create a seamless and enjoyable VR experience. Common VR hardware components include:

- **VR Headsets:** These are the primary displays that users wear to experience VR. Each headset has its specifications, capabilities, and tracking systems.

- **Motion Controllers:** VR motion controllers allow users to interact with the virtual world. They often feature buttons, triggers, and sensors for tracking hand movements.

- **Tracking Systems:** VR systems use tracking technology to monitor the position and orientation of the user's head and hands. Tracking can be inside-out (cameras on the headset) or outside-in (external sensors or cameras).

- **Room-Scale vs. Seated VR:** Some VR experiences are designed for room-scale interaction, where users can move around physically, while others are seated experiences with limited movement.

Developing for VR

Creating content for VR involves several considerations to ensure a comfortable and immersive experience:

- **Frame Rate:** Maintaining a high and consistent frame rate (e.g., 90 frames per second) is crucial in VR to prevent motion sickness. Optimize your scenes and assets for performance.

- **User Interface (UI):** Designing UI elements for VR requires special attention. Ensure that menus and HUD elements are readable and accessible in a 3D space.

- **Interaction:** VR experiences often involve hand tracking and interaction. Implement intuitive and responsive interactions using motion controllers.

- **Movement:** Decide on the movement mechanics in your VR game, whether it's teleportation, smooth locomotion, or a combination of methods. Consider comfort and accessibility for different users.

- **Testing and Optimization:** VR development requires extensive testing, especially for motion sickness and performance issues. Regularly test your VR content on different hardware configurations.

```
// Pseudocode for implementing VR hand interaction:
void UpdateVRHandInteraction()
{
    // Get the current state of the motion controller.
    FTransform ControllerTransform = GetMotionControllerTransform();

    // Check for object interaction using raycasting or collision checks.
    AActor* InteractableObject = CheckForInteraction(ControllerTransform);

    if (InteractableObject)
    {
        // Perform interaction logic (e.g., grabbing, pushing, or activating)
    .
        InteractWithObject(InteractableObject);
    }
}
```

In conclusion, VR development in Unreal Engine opens up exciting possibilities for immersive experiences. By setting up your project correctly, understanding VR hardware, and following best practices for VR development, you can create compelling and enjoyable VR content that captivates your audience and provides a sense of presence within virtual worlds.

8.2. Designing for VR Interactivity

Designing for VR interactivity is a crucial aspect of creating immersive and engaging virtual reality experiences. VR allows users to interact with the digital world in ways that were previously impossible in traditional gaming. In this section, we'll explore key principles and best practices for designing VR interactivity in Unreal Engine.

1. Intuitive Controls

In VR, controls should feel intuitive and natural. Utilize motion controllers to mimic real-world actions. For example, use hand gestures to pick up objects, press buttons, or draw in the air. Ensure that the mapping of physical gestures to in-game actions is straightforward and user-friendly.

```
// Pseudocode for grabbing an object in VR using motion controllers:
void GrabObject(AMotionControllerPawn* PlayerPawn)
{
    // Check if the player's hand is close to an interactable object.
    AInteractableObject* Interactable = PlayerPawn->CheckForInteractableObjec
t();

    if (Interactable)
    {
        // Use the motion controller to grab the object.
        Interactable->Grab(PlayerPawn->GetControllerTransform());
    }
}
```

2. Responsive Feedback

Providing feedback in VR is essential to reinforce interactions and enhance the sense of presence. Use haptic feedback in motion controllers to simulate touch or pressure. Visual and auditory cues, such as highlighting interactive objects or playing sounds when actions are performed, can also enhance the user's sense of connection to the virtual world.

```
// Pseudocode for providing haptic feedback when grabbing an object:
void GrabObject(AMotionControllerPawn* PlayerPawn)
{
    AInteractableObject* Interactable = PlayerPawn->CheckForInteractableObjec
t();

    if (Interactable)
    {
        // Trigger haptic feedback to simulate the sensation of grabbing.
        PlayerPawn->PlayHapticFeedback(Interactable->GetHapticEffect());

        // Use the motion controller to grab the object.
        Interactable->Grab(PlayerPawn->GetControllerTransform());
    }
}
```

3. Object Physics and Interaction

In VR, objects should behave realistically. Implement physics interactions that match user expectations. For example, if an object is grabbed, it should move according to real-world physics. Allow objects to collide and stack naturally, enhancing the feeling of immersion.

Unreal Engine provides a robust physics system that can be leveraged for realistic object interactions in VR.

4. Avoid Motion Sickness

Motion sickness is a common concern in VR. To minimize discomfort, avoid sudden movements, excessive acceleration, or jerky camera motions. Implement smooth locomotion options like teleportation or gradual camera movement to reduce the risk of motion sickness.

```
// Pseudocode for teleportation in VR:
void Teleport(AMotionControllerPawn* PlayerPawn, FVector TeleportLocation)
{
    // Smoothly transition the player to the new location.
    PlayerPawn->StartTeleportation(TeleportLocation);
}
```

5. User Testing

VR design should involve extensive user testing to ensure that interactions are comfortable and intuitive for a wide range of users. Collect feedback and iterate on your design to refine the VR experience.

6. Accessibility

Consider accessibility features for VR experiences. Ensure that users with different physical abilities can enjoy your VR content. Implement options for seated gameplay, adjustable interaction settings, and comfort modes to accommodate a diverse audience.

7. Storytelling and Interaction

In narrative-driven VR experiences, storytelling and interaction should be seamlessly integrated. Allow users to interact with the story's elements, characters, and environment to create a more engaging narrative.

8. Performance Optimization

Optimize VR experiences for performance to maintain a high and consistent frame rate. VR requires rendering content for each eye, demanding more from hardware. Use Unreal Engine's optimization tools to ensure a smooth experience.

9. Playtesting in VR

Regularly playtest your VR experience in actual VR hardware to evaluate how interactions feel in the immersive environment. It's essential to experience your VR content firsthand to identify and address design and usability issues.

In summary, designing for VR interactivity in Unreal Engine requires careful consideration of controls, feedback, physics, comfort, accessibility, storytelling, and performance optimization. By following these best practices and continually testing and refining your VR content, you can create immersive and engaging virtual reality experiences that captivate and delight users.

8.3. Performance Optimization in VR

Performance optimization is a critical aspect of VR development in Unreal Engine. VR experiences demand a high and consistent frame rate to avoid motion sickness and ensure a comfortable and immersive user experience. In this section, we will explore essential performance optimization techniques for VR projects.

1. Maintain a High and Stable Frame Rate

In VR, maintaining a high frame rate, typically 90 frames per second (FPS) or higher, is essential. Consistency is equally important to prevent juddering and discomfort. Unreal Engine provides several tools and techniques to achieve this:

- **Level of Detail (LOD)**: Implement LODs for complex 3D models to reduce the polygon count and draw calls when objects are distant from the player's viewpoint.

- **Culling**: Implement frustum culling and occlusion culling to avoid rendering objects that are not visible to the player.

- **Optimize Materials**: Use simplified materials with fewer shaders and complex calculations. Avoid translucent materials, as they can be more expensive to render.

- **Texture Streaming**: Utilize texture streaming to load and display textures at different resolutions based on proximity to the player.

```
// Pseudocode for implementing LODs in Unreal Engine:
void ImplementLOD(AStaticMeshActor* MeshActor)
{
    // Define LOD settings for the mesh.
    MeshActor->SetLODScreenSize(0, 0.2f);
    MeshActor->SetLODScreenSize(1, 0.1f);
    MeshActor->SetLODScreenSize(2, 0.05f);
}
```

2. GPU and CPU Optimization

Optimizing GPU and CPU performance is crucial in VR development:

- **GPU**: Reduce the use of post-processing effects, use efficient rendering techniques, and consider decreasing the resolution for less critical elements.

- **CPU**: Minimize CPU overhead by optimizing code, reducing unnecessary calculations, and using multi-threading where possible.

3. VR Instancing and Stereo Rendering

Unreal Engine offers VR instancing and stereo rendering optimizations. VR instancing combines objects with the same material into a single draw call, reducing GPU overhead. Stereo rendering optimizes rendering for VR by rendering both eyes in a single pass.

```
// Pseudocode for enabling VR instancing in Unreal Engine:
void EnableVRInstancing(AStaticMeshActor* MeshActor)
{
    // Enable VR instancing for the mesh.
    MeshActor->SetStaticMeshVRAM(EStereoLayerType::SLT_WorldLocked);
}
```

4. Reduce Dynamic Lighting

Dynamic lighting can be costly in VR. Minimize the use of dynamic lights and shadows whenever possible. Use baked lighting for static objects and consider using light probes for dynamic objects to reduce performance impact.

5. Simplify Geometry

Complex geometry with high polygon counts can strain performance. Simplify geometry where it won't be noticed, and optimize collision meshes for accurate but efficient physics calculations.

6. Audio Optimization

Optimize audio in VR by using audio occlusion and attenuation to limit the number of active sound sources. Unreal Engine's audio features provide tools to optimize audio for VR experiences.

7. Testing on Target Hardware

Regularly test your VR project on the target hardware to ensure that performance meets the required standards. Different VR platforms may have varying performance characteristics, so optimization should be tailored to the intended platform.

8. Profiling and Analysis

Use Unreal Engine's built-in profiling and analysis tools to identify performance bottlenecks and areas that require optimization. Tools like Unreal Insights and GPU Visualizer can help diagnose and address performance issues.

In conclusion, optimizing performance in VR development is critical for creating a comfortable and enjoyable experience. By maintaining a high and consistent frame rate, optimizing GPU and CPU usage, using VR-specific optimizations like instancing and stereo rendering, and reducing dynamic lighting and complex geometry, you can ensure that your VR project runs smoothly on target hardware and provides an immersive and enjoyable experience for users. Regular testing and profiling are essential to identify and address performance bottlenecks effectively.

8.4. Handling Motion Sickness and User Comfort

Motion sickness is a common concern in virtual reality (VR) experiences, and it can greatly affect the user's comfort and enjoyment. Developers must address motion sickness to ensure that their VR content is accessible to a wide audience and provides a comfortable experience. In this section, we will explore strategies and techniques for handling motion sickness and enhancing user comfort in Unreal Engine VR projects.

1. Teleportation and Comfort Modes

One of the most effective ways to reduce motion sickness in VR is to offer teleportation as a movement option. Teleportation allows users to move between locations instantly, avoiding the discomfort associated with traditional joystick-based locomotion.

In Unreal Engine, you can implement teleportation using the VR motion controllers. When the player triggers teleportation, calculate the destination point and smoothly transition the player to that location. Provide visual cues, such as an arc or reticle, to help users aim their teleportation.

```
// Pseudocode for implementing teleportation in Unreal Engine:
void TeleportToLocation(FVector Destination)
{
    // Calculate the player's starting and ending positions.
    FVector StartLocation = GetPlayerLocation();
    FVector EndLocation = Destination;

    // Smoothly move the player to the destination.
    SmoothlyTransitionPlayer(StartLocation, EndLocation);
}
```

2. Comfort Options

Allow users to customize their comfort settings. Offer options to adjust the field of view (FOV), enable/disable comfort vignettes (blinders that reduce peripheral vision during motion), and control movement speed. Providing these options allows users to find settings that suit their comfort level.

```
// Pseudocode for adjusting comfort settings in Unreal Engine:
void AdjustComfortSettings(bool EnableVignette, float FOV, float MovementSpeed)
```

```
{
    // Apply the user's comfort settings.
    ApplyVignette(EnableVignette);
    AdjustFOV(FOV);
    SetMovementSpeed(MovementSpeed);
}
```

3. Gradual Movement and Acceleration

When implementing traditional locomotion, such as walking or running, avoid sudden accelerations and decelerations. Gradually accelerate the player when they start moving and decelerate when they stop. Smooth transitions help reduce motion sickness.

```
// Pseudocode for gradual acceleration in Unreal Engine:
void StartWalking()
{
    // Gradually increase the player's movement speed.
    SmoothlyIncreaseSpeed();
}

void StopWalking()
{
    // Gradually decrease the player's movement speed.
    SmoothlyDecreaseSpeed();
}
```

4. Fixed and Comfortable Reference Points

Incorporate stable and comfortable reference points within the VR environment. These can be static objects, like a cockpit or a stationary platform, that provide a frame of reference for the player's eyes. Having a stable point of reference can help reduce motion sickness when the player is in motion.

5. Avoiding Nauseating Movements

Certain types of movements, such as rapid spins or continuous looping, can induce motion sickness quickly. Avoid these types of movements in your VR experiences, or provide clear warnings if they are necessary for gameplay.

6. User Feedback and Iteration

User feedback is invaluable in identifying and addressing motion sickness issues. Encourage users to provide feedback during playtesting and beta testing phases. Iterate on your VR content based on this feedback to improve comfort and reduce motion sickness.

7. Testing on Different Audiences

Different individuals have varying levels of susceptibility to motion sickness. Test your VR content on a diverse group of users to ensure that it accommodates a wide range of comfort levels. Pay attention to user feedback and make adjustments as needed.

In summary, handling motion sickness and ensuring user comfort are critical considerations in VR development. Implementing teleportation, offering comfort options, providing gradual movement and acceleration, establishing stable reference points, avoiding nauseating movements, and collecting user feedback are essential strategies for creating comfortable and enjoyable VR experiences in Unreal Engine. By prioritizing user comfort, you can increase the accessibility and appeal of your VR content to a broader audience.

8.5. Advanced VR Features and Tools

In Unreal Engine, you have access to a wide range of advanced VR features and tools that can take your virtual reality experiences to the next level. These features allow you to create more immersive and interactive VR content. In this section, we will explore some of the advanced VR capabilities and tools available in Unreal Engine.

1. Hand Tracking and Interaction

Unreal Engine supports hand tracking, which allows users to interact with the virtual world using their bare hands. This feature is particularly valuable for creating natural and intuitive interactions in VR. You can implement hand tracking using supported VR headsets and controllers.

```
// Pseudocode for enabling hand tracking in Unreal Engine:
void EnableHandTracking()
{
    // Check if the VR headset supports hand tracking.
    if (IsHandTrackingSupported())
    {
        // Enable hand tracking input.
        EnableHandTrackingInput();
    }
}
```

2. VR Spectator Screen

The VR spectator screen feature in Unreal Engine allows you to display the VR experience on an external monitor or screen. This is useful for demonstrations, presentations, or multiplayer scenarios where others can watch what the VR user is experiencing. You can configure and customize the spectator screen to suit your needs.

```
// Pseudocode for configuring VR spectator screen in Unreal Engine:
void ConfigureVRSpectatorScreen()
{
    // Set up the spectator screen settings, such as resolution and position.
    SetSpectatorScreenResolution(1920, 1080);
    SetSpectatorScreenPosition(0, 0);
```

```
    EnableSpectatorScreen(true);
}
```

3. VR Motion Capture

Unreal Engine supports VR motion capture, allowing you to record and capture the movements of actors or objects in the real world and apply them to VR characters or objects. This feature is beneficial for creating realistic animations and interactions in VR.

```
// Pseudocode for recording motion capture data in Unreal Engine:
void RecordMotionCapture()
{
    // Set up motion capture recording settings.
    ConfigureMotionCapture();

    // Start recording motion capture data.
    StartRecording();
}
```

4. VR Haptic Feedback

Haptic feedback is a crucial element of VR immersion. Unreal Engine provides tools to implement haptic feedback in VR controllers. You can trigger haptic vibrations and sensations to simulate various interactions, such as touching objects or feeling impacts.

```
// Pseudocode for triggering haptic feedback in Unreal Engine:
void TriggerHapticFeedback()
{
    // Determine the location and intensity of haptic feedback.
    FVector FeedbackLocation = GetControllerLocation();
    float Intensity = CalculateHapticIntensity();

    // Trigger haptic feedback in the controller.
    PlayHapticFeedback(FeedbackLocation, Intensity);
}
```

5. VR UI and Widgets

Creating user interfaces (UI) in VR is essential for menus, settings, and interactive elements. Unreal Engine offers a robust system for designing VR UI and widgets. You can use Blueprint scripting to create interactive UI elements that respond to user input.

6. Multiplayer VR

Unreal Engine supports multiplayer VR experiences, allowing multiple users to interact in the same virtual environment. Implementing multiplayer VR requires network synchronization and considerations for player interactions, such as hand tracking and object interactions.

```
// Pseudocode for setting up multiplayer VR in Unreal Engine:
void ConfigureMultiplayerVR()
```

```
{
    // Set up networking and synchronization for multiplayer VR.
    InitializeNetworkSubsystem();
    SynchronizeVRPlayers();
}
```

7. VR Analytics and Metrics

Monitoring and analyzing user behavior and performance in VR is essential for refining your VR experiences. Unreal Engine provides tools for collecting analytics and metrics related to player interactions, performance, and user feedback. This data can help you make informed decisions to improve your VR content.

In conclusion, Unreal Engine offers a rich set of advanced VR features and tools that empower developers to create highly immersive and interactive virtual reality experiences. Whether you want to implement hand tracking, use VR spectator screens, leverage motion capture, provide haptic feedback, design VR UI, enable multiplayer VR, or gather analytics, Unreal Engine provides the flexibility and capabilities to bring your VR vision to life. These advanced features contribute to creating memorable and engaging VR content that captivates users and pushes the boundaries of virtual reality storytelling and interactivity.

Chapter 9: Mobile Game Development

9.1. Adapting Unreal Games for Mobile

Mobile game development is a thriving sector within the gaming industry, with millions of players around the world enjoying games on their smartphones and tablets. Adapting Unreal Engine games for mobile platforms is a strategic move to tap into this vast and diverse audience. In this section, we will explore the considerations and techniques for adapting Unreal games for mobile devices.

Understanding Mobile Hardware

Mobile devices vary significantly in terms of hardware capabilities. When adapting your Unreal game for mobile, it's crucial to understand the limitations and capabilities of the target devices. Consider factors like CPU power, GPU capabilities, RAM, and storage.

Graphics Optimization

Graphics optimization is a top priority when targeting mobile devices. Unreal Engine provides tools and techniques to optimize graphics for mobile:

- **Reduced Texture Sizes**: Mobile devices may have limited GPU memory. Reduce texture sizes and use texture compression formats like ETC2 for Android and PVRTC for iOS.

- **Dynamic Resolution Scaling**: Implement dynamic resolution scaling to adjust the rendering resolution based on device performance. This ensures a smoother frame rate on lower-end devices.

```
// Pseudocode for dynamic resolution scaling in Unreal Engine:
void AdjustResolutionBasedOnPerformance()
{
    if (DevicePerformanceIsLow())
    {
        ReduceRenderingResolution();
    }
}
```

Input Adaptation

Mobile devices rely on touch screens or motion sensors for input. You'll need to adapt your game's input system to accommodate these input methods. Implement virtual on-screen controls, gestures, or accelerometer-based input for mobile games.

```
// Pseudocode for implementing virtual on-screen controls in Unreal Engine:
void AddVirtualJoystick()
{
    // Create and display a virtual joystick on the screen.
    VirtualJoystick* Joystick = CreateVirtualJoystick();
```

```
    DisplayVirtualJoystick(Joystick);
}
```

Performance Profiling

Profile your game on various mobile devices to ensure smooth performance. Use Unreal Engine's built-in profiling tools to identify performance bottlenecks. Regularly test your game on different devices to guarantee optimal performance across the mobile spectrum.

UI and UX Adaptation

Mobile screens come in various sizes and aspect ratios. Adapt your game's user interface (UI) and user experience (UX) to fit different mobile screen sizes. Implement responsive UI layouts and ensure readability and usability on smaller screens.

Battery Efficiency

Mobile devices operate on battery power, so optimizing battery consumption is critical. Minimize unnecessary background processes and optimize resource usage to extend gameplay time on a single charge.

```
// Pseudocode for optimizing battery efficiency in Unreal Engine:
void OptimizeBatteryUsage()
{
    // Implement power-saving mode and reduce resource-intensive processes.
    EnablePowerSavingMode();
    OptimizeResourceUsage();
}
```

Distribution and Monetization

Consider mobile-specific distribution platforms, such as the Apple App Store and Google Play Store, for publishing your game. Implement mobile-specific monetization strategies, such as in-app purchases, ads, or premium pricing, based on your target audience and market.

Testing and Feedback

Extensive testing on a variety of mobile devices is crucial to ensure compatibility and performance. Collect user feedback and iterate on your game based on player suggestions and bug reports. Continuous improvement is essential for mobile game success.

Cross-Platform Development

Unreal Engine supports cross-platform development, enabling you to target multiple mobile platforms with a single codebase. Utilize Unreal's cross-platform capabilities to maximize your game's reach.

```
// Pseudocode for cross-platform development in Unreal Engine:
void EnableCrossPlatformDevelopment()
{
    // Configure project settings for multiple mobile platforms.
```

```
SetTargetPlatforms(Android, iOS);
}
```

In summary, adapting Unreal games for mobile devices involves understanding hardware limitations, optimizing graphics and performance, adapting input methods, ensuring a responsive UI/UX, optimizing battery usage, choosing the right distribution and monetization strategies, and conducting thorough testing. By carefully addressing these considerations and leveraging Unreal Engine's capabilities, you can create successful and engaging mobile games that cater to a broad audience of mobile gamers.

9.2. Touch Input and Mobile Controls

Adapting Unreal games for mobile devices requires a fundamental shift in input methods compared to traditional PC or console gaming. On mobile platforms, touch input is the primary means of interaction, and mobile controls play a significant role in user experience. In this section, we will explore best practices for implementing touch input and mobile controls in Unreal Engine for mobile game development.

1. Virtual Joysticks

Virtual joysticks are a common mobile control mechanism for games that require character movement or camera control. These on-screen controls simulate the functionality of physical joysticks. Implementing virtual joysticks in Unreal Engine involves creating custom user interfaces and handling touch input events.

```
// Pseudocode for implementing a virtual joystick in Unreal Engine:
void CreateVirtualJoystick()
{
    // Create a UI widget for the virtual joystick.
    UWidget* VirtualJoystickWidget = CreateVirtualJoystickWidget();
    DisplayVirtualJoystickWidget(VirtualJoystickWidget);
}

void HandleJoystickInput(FVector InputDirection)
{
    // Handle character or camera movement based on the joystick input direct
ion.
    MoveCharacter(InputDirection);
}
```

2. Touch Gestures

Mobile devices support various touch gestures like tapping, swiping, pinching, and rotating. Implementing these gestures can enhance gameplay and user interaction. Unreal Engine provides built-in functions and Blueprints for detecting and responding to touch gestures.

```
// Pseudocode for detecting a swipe gesture in Unreal Engine:
void DetectSwipeGesture()
{
    if (IsSwiping())
    {
        FVector SwipeDirection = GetSwipeDirection();
        // Respond to the swipe gesture.
        PerformSwipeAction(SwipeDirection);
    }
}
```

3. Tap and Hold

The tap-and-hold gesture can be used for actions like selecting objects or bringing up context menus. Implement this gesture by detecting a touch down event and measuring the duration of touch.

```
// Pseudocode for implementing tap-and-hold in Unreal Engine:
void DetectTapAndHold()
{
    if (IsTouchDown())
    {
        StartTouchTimer();
    }

    if (IsTouchReleased())
    {
        if (GetTouchDuration() >= TapAndHoldThreshold)
        {
            // Perform the tap-and-hold action.
            PerformTapAndHoldAction();
        }
        ResetTouchTimer();
    }
}
```

4. Pinch and Zoom

For games with zoomable elements or maps, pinch and zoom functionality is essential. Unreal Engine supports pinch and zoom gestures out of the box, making it relatively straightforward to implement.

```
// Pseudocode for detecting pinch and zoom in Unreal Engine:
void DetectPinchZoom()
{
    float PinchDelta = GetPinchDelta();
    // Adjust the zoom level or scale of in-game elements based on the pinch
delta.
    UpdateZoomLevel(PinchDelta);
}
```

5. Contextual Buttons

Incorporate on-screen buttons for actions that are context-sensitive, such as opening inventory, interacting with objects, or performing special abilities. Design these buttons to be intuitive and accessible to users.

```
// Pseudocode for implementing contextual buttons in Unreal Engine:
void CreateContextualButtons()
{
    // Create UI buttons for contextual actions.
    UWidget* InventoryButton = CreateInventoryButton();
    DisplayInventoryButton(InventoryButton);
}
```

6. Mobile Control Customization

Allow users to customize mobile controls based on their preferences. Provide options for repositioning, resizing, or enabling/disabling on-screen controls. Customization enhances the overall user experience.

7. Testing and Iteration

Testing mobile controls on different devices is crucial to ensure responsiveness and comfort. Conduct user testing and gather feedback to refine the control scheme and make adjustments as needed.

In conclusion, implementing touch input and mobile controls in Unreal Engine for mobile game development involves creating virtual joysticks, recognizing touch gestures, handling tap-and-hold interactions, supporting pinch and zoom, designing contextual buttons, offering control customization, and conducting thorough testing. By providing intuitive and responsive mobile controls, you can enhance the gameplay experience for mobile gamers and optimize your game for success on mobile platforms.

9.3. Optimizing Graphics for Mobile Devices

Graphics optimization is a critical aspect of mobile game development using Unreal Engine. Mobile devices have varying hardware capabilities, and ensuring that your game runs smoothly on a wide range of devices is essential for a successful mobile gaming experience. In this section, we will explore strategies and techniques for optimizing graphics in Unreal Engine for mobile devices.

1. Use Mobile-Friendly Materials

Mobile devices have limited GPU power compared to high-end gaming PCs or consoles. To optimize graphics, use materials and shaders that are optimized for mobile platforms.

Unreal Engine provides mobile-friendly material settings that reduce the complexity of shaders and texture sampling.

```
// Pseudocode for setting up a mobile-friendly material in Unreal Engine:
void SetupMobileMaterial()
{
    UMaterial* MobileMaterial = CreateMobileMaterial();
    ApplyMobileMaterialSettings(MobileMaterial);
}
```

2. Texture Compression

Texture memory is a precious resource on mobile devices. Use texture compression formats like ETC2 (for Android) and PVRTC (for iOS) to reduce texture sizes while maintaining visual quality. Unreal Engine offers settings to configure texture compression for different platforms.

3. Reduce Shader Complexity

Simplify shaders to reduce GPU workload. Remove unnecessary calculations and complex effects from shaders that are not critical for mobile devices. Unreal Engine's shader graph system allows you to create optimized shaders.

4. LODs and Model Optimization

Implement Level of Detail (LOD) models for 3D assets to reduce polygon counts on distant objects. Additionally, optimize 3D models by removing hidden geometry, reducing unnecessary vertices, and using simplified collision meshes.

```
// Pseudocode for setting up LODs in Unreal Engine:
void ImplementLODs()
{
    AStaticMeshActor* MeshActor = GetMeshActor();
    MeshActor->SetLODScreenSize(0, 0.2f);
    MeshActor->SetLODScreenSize(1, 0.1f);
    MeshActor->SetLODScreenSize(2, 0.05f);
}
```

5. Dynamic Resolution Scaling

Implement dynamic resolution scaling to adjust the rendering resolution based on device performance. Lowering the resolution on less powerful devices can significantly improve frame rates while maintaining visual quality.

```
// Pseudocode for dynamic resolution scaling in Unreal Engine:
void AdjustResolutionBasedOnPerformance()
{
    if (DevicePerformanceIsLow())
    {
        ReduceRenderingResolution();
```

```
    }
}
```

6. Occlusion Culling

Implement occlusion culling techniques to avoid rendering objects that are not visible to the player's camera. Unreal Engine provides occlusion culling features that help improve performance on mobile devices.

7. Mobile Post-Processing Effects

Minimize or disable post-processing effects that are resource-intensive, such as motion blur or screen-space reflections. These effects can be taxing on mobile GPUs.

```
// Pseudocode for disabling motion blur in Unreal Engine for mobile:
void DisableMotionBlur()
{
    UPostProcessComponent* PostProcessComponent = GetPostProcessComponent();
    PostProcessComponent->DisableMotionBlur();
}
```

8. Material Instancing

Use material instancing to reduce draw call overhead. Instancing allows multiple objects with the same material to be rendered in a single draw call, which is more efficient for mobile GPUs.

```
// Pseudocode for enabling material instancing in Unreal Engine:
void EnableMaterialInstancing()
{
    UMaterialInterface* MaterialInstance = CreateMaterialInstance();
    EnableInstancingForMaterial(MaterialInstance);
}
```

9. Mobile-Specific Quality Settings

Unreal Engine allows you to configure mobile-specific quality settings in your project. Adjust these settings based on your target devices and performance goals. Options include controlling the texture quality, shadow quality, and level of detail.

In conclusion, optimizing graphics for mobile devices in Unreal Engine is essential for delivering a smooth and visually appealing gaming experience on a wide range of smartphones and tablets. By using mobile-friendly materials, texture compression, reducing shader complexity, implementing LODs, dynamic resolution scaling, occlusion culling, managing post-processing effects, enabling material instancing, and configuring mobile-specific quality settings, you can ensure that your mobile game runs efficiently and looks great on various mobile devices. Thorough testing on different devices is crucial to verify the performance and visual quality of your optimized graphics.

9.4. Mobile Game Monetization Strategies

Monetization is a crucial aspect of mobile game development, as it allows developers to generate revenue from their games. There are various monetization strategies available for mobile games, and choosing the right approach can significantly impact the success of your game. In this section, we will explore common mobile game monetization strategies that Unreal Engine developers can consider.

1. In-App Advertising

In-app advertising involves displaying advertisements within your game. There are different types of in-app ads, including banner ads, interstitial ads (full-screen ads that appear between game sessions), rewarded ads (where players receive rewards for watching ads), and native ads (ads that blend seamlessly with the game's design). Integrating ad networks like AdMob, Unity Ads, or Facebook Audience Network can help you monetize through ads.

```
// Pseudocode for integrating an ad network in Unreal Engine:
void IntegrateAdNetwork()
{
    AdNetworkSDK.Initialize();
    AdNetworkSDK.LoadInterstitialAd();
    AdNetworkSDK.ShowInterstitialAd();
}
```

2. In-App Purchases (IAPs)

In-app purchases allow players to buy virtual items, currency, power-ups, or premium content within the game. IAPs can be consumable (e.g., buying in-game currency), non-consumable (e.g., unlocking additional levels), or subscriptions (e.g., monthly premium memberships). Unreal Engine provides tools for implementing IAPs on both Android and iOS platforms.

```
// Pseudocode for implementing in-app purchases in Unreal Engine:
void ImplementIAPSystem()
{
    // Set up the in-app purchase storefront.
    IAPSystem.InitializeStorefront();
    // Offer various in-app purchase options.
    IAPSystem.AddProduct("CoinsPack", IAPType.Consumable, 0.99);
    IAPSystem.AddProduct("UnlockAllLevels", IAPType.NonConsumable, 2.99);
    IAPSystem.AddProduct("PremiumMembership", IAPType.Subscription, 4.99);
}
```

3. Premium Pricing

Releasing your game as a premium app with an upfront purchase price is a straightforward monetization strategy. Players pay a one-time fee to download and access the full game. Ensure that your game provides sufficient value to justify the premium pricing.

```
// Pseudocode for setting up premium pricing in Unreal Engine:
void SetPremiumPrice()
{
    SetGamePrice(4.99);
}
```

4. Freemium Model

The freemium model offers the game for free with optional in-app purchases. This strategy can attract a larger player base, and you can generate revenue from players who make purchases to enhance their gameplay experience. Balancing the game to make it enjoyable for both paying and non-paying players is crucial.

5. Subscription Services

Offering a subscription service within your game can provide a steady stream of revenue. Subscriptions can grant players access to exclusive content, in-game benefits, or a premium experience. Unreal Engine supports subscription-based monetization models.

```
// Pseudocode for setting up a subscription service in Unreal Engine:
void EnableSubscriptionService()
{
    SubscriptionService.Initialize();
    SubscriptionService.AddSubscriptionTier("GoldMembership", 9.99);
    SubscriptionService.AddSubscriptionTier("PlatinumMembership", 19.99);
}
```

6. In-Game Currency and Virtual Goods

Implementing an in-game currency system that players can purchase with real money is a common monetization strategy. Players can use this currency to buy virtual goods, power-ups, or customization items. Creating appealing and valuable virtual goods can drive purchases.

7. Season Passes and Battle Passes

Season passes and battle passes offer limited-time content and rewards to players who purchase them. These passes often include exclusive cosmetic items, currency, or experience boosts. Unreal Engine provides tools for designing and implementing these progression systems.

```
// Pseudocode for creating a season pass in Unreal Engine:
void CreateSeasonPass()
{
    SeasonPass.Initialize();
    SeasonPass.AddSeason("SummerSeason", 9.99);
    SeasonPass.AddRewards("SummerSeason", RewardType.Cosmetic, "BeachOutfit")
```

;
}

8. Cross-Promotion

Consider cross-promoting your other games or partnering with other developers to promote their games in exchange for promotion of your game. Cross-promotion can help increase your game's visibility and user acquisition.

9. Data Monetization

Collecting anonymized data from your players and offering insights to marketing companies can be a monetization strategy. Ensure compliance with privacy regulations like GDPR and CCPA and obtain user consent.

Choosing the right monetization strategy for your mobile game depends on factors such as your target audience, game genre, and market competition. Some games may combine multiple monetization methods to maximize revenue. It's crucial to strike a balance between monetization and providing an enjoyable and fair gaming experience to your players. Regularly analyze player feedback and monetization metrics to fine-tune your strategy and optimize your game's revenue potential

---

9.5. Publishing and Updating Mobile Games

Publishing and maintaining a mobile game involves a series of steps, from preparing your game for release to providing ongoing support and updates to players. In this section, we'll delve into the process of publishing and updating mobile games developed using Unreal Engine.

1. Platform Selection

Before publishing, you must decide which mobile platforms to target. The two primary platforms for mobile games are Android and iOS. Unreal Engine supports both platforms, and you can choose to release your game on one or both, depending on your target audience and resources.

2. App Store Registration

To publish your game on Android, you'll need to register as a developer on the Google Play Store. For iOS, you'll need to join the Apple Developer Program and gain access to the App Store Connect platform. Registration typically involves a one-time fee.

3. Game Metadata

Prepare essential game metadata, including the game's title, description, icon, screenshots, and promotional materials. This information will be used for app store listings and promotional purposes. High-quality visuals and concise descriptions are crucial for attracting potential players.

4. Compliance with Guidelines

Ensure that your game complies with the app store guidelines and policies of your chosen platforms. This includes adhering to content guidelines, age ratings, and any specific rules related to in-app purchases or advertising.

5. Game Build Preparation

Create a production-ready build of your game for each target platform. This involves optimizing the game's performance, graphics, and resource usage. Test the builds thoroughly to identify and resolve any issues that may affect gameplay or stability.

```
// Pseudocode for building a mobile game in Unreal Engine:
void BuildGameForAndroid()
{
    UnrealBuildTool.BuildGameForAndroid();
}

void BuildGameForiOS()
{
    UnrealBuildTool.BuildGameForiOS();
}
```

6. Testing

Conduct extensive testing on real devices to ensure that your game functions correctly and provides an enjoyable experience. Test on a variety of devices with different screen sizes and performance levels to address compatibility issues.

7. Submission to App Stores

Submit your game to the respective app stores (Google Play Store for Android and App Store for iOS). Follow the submission guidelines and provide all required information, such as app icons, descriptions, and screenshots. You may need to pay a submission fee for each store.

8. App Review Process

Both Google Play and the App Store review submitted apps to ensure they meet their quality and policy standards. Be prepared for the review process, which can take several days. Address any feedback or concerns raised during the review.

9. Launch and Marketing

Once your game is approved, it's time to launch it on the app stores. Plan a marketing strategy to promote your game to potential players. Utilize social media, press releases, influencer marketing, and other channels to create buzz and drive downloads.

10. Ongoing Support and Updates

Support your game with regular updates that include bug fixes, performance improvements, and new content. Listen to player feedback and prioritize enhancements based on user input. Updating your game not only keeps it relevant but also shows players that you are committed to its success.

```
// Pseudocode for updating a mobile game in Unreal Engine:
void UpdateGameVersion()
{
    IncreaseGameVersionNumber();
    ApplyBug Fixes();
    AddNewContent();
}
```

11. Player Engagement

Engage with your player community through social media, forums, and in-game channels. Respond to player inquiries and feedback promptly. Building a positive relationship with your players can lead to higher player retention and word-of-mouth promotion.

12. Monetization Optimization

Continuously monitor and analyze monetization metrics to optimize your game's revenue. Adjust in-app purchases, ad placements, or pricing strategies based on player behavior and market trends.

13. Analytics and Data

Use analytics tools to gather data on player behavior, retention, and in-game purchases. Analyze this data to make informed decisions about updates, marketing strategies, and monetization adjustments.

14. Legal Considerations

Stay informed about legal requirements related to mobile game development and publishing. This includes privacy policies, data protection regulations, and compliance with any regional laws that may apply to your target markets.

15. Expansion and Localization

Consider expanding your game to additional markets by localizing it. Translate in-game text, provide localized customer support, and adapt your marketing materials to cater to players from different regions.

Publishing and maintaining a mobile game is an ongoing process that requires attention to detail and a commitment to providing a high-quality gaming experience. By following these steps and staying engaged with your player community, you can maximize the success of your mobile game developed using Unreal Engine.

Chapter 10: Cinematics and Storytelling

10.1. Crafting Engaging Narratives in Games

Crafting engaging narratives is a fundamental aspect of game development, creating a strong connection between players and the virtual worlds they explore. Unreal Engine offers robust tools and features for storytellers to create compelling narratives within their games. In this section, we will explore techniques for crafting captivating narratives in Unreal Engine.

1. Define Your Story's Themes and Goals

Before diving into narrative creation, define the themes and goals of your story. What message or experience do you want players to take away? Understanding these aspects will guide your narrative decisions and character development.

2. Create Well-Defined Characters

Characters are the heart of any narrative. Develop well-defined characters with unique personalities, motivations, and arcs. Use Unreal Engine's Character Blueprint system to bring them to life, including their animations, dialogues, and interactions.

```
// Pseudocode for creating a character in Unreal Engine:
void CreateCharacter()
{
    UCharacterBlueprint* CharacterBlueprint = CreateCharacterBlueprint();
    SetCharacterAttributes(CharacterBlueprint);
    AddCharacterAnimations(CharacterBlueprint);
}
```

3. Establish the Setting and World

The game's world and setting play a crucial role in storytelling. Use Unreal Engine's world-building tools to craft immersive environments that complement your narrative. Pay attention to details, lore, and world-building elements that enrich the player's experience.

4. Embrace Nonlinear Narratives

Unreal Engine allows for nonlinear storytelling, where player choices can influence the plot's direction. Implement branching narratives and multiple endings to increase player engagement and replayability.

5. Use Sequencer for Cinematic Creation

Unreal Engine's Sequencer tool is powerful for creating cinematic sequences and cutscenes. Utilize it to script and choreograph important story moments, combining animations, camera angles, and visual effects to create impactful scenes.

```
// Pseudocode for using Sequencer in Unreal Engine:
void CreateCinematicSequence()
```

```
{
    ULevelSequence* CinematicSequence = CreateCinematicSequence();
    AddActorsAndAnimationsToSequence(CinematicSequence);
    SetCameraAnglesAndCuts(CinematicSequence);
}
```

6. Direct Camera Movements and Angles

Effective camera work enhances storytelling. Use Unreal Engine's camera systems to direct the player's focus during key narrative moments. Experiment with camera angles, movements, and transitions to evoke emotions and build tension.

7. Integrating Voice Acting and Soundtracks

Voice acting and music contribute significantly to the narrative's emotional impact. Record or hire voice actors to bring characters to life, and use Unreal Engine's audio tools to implement dynamic soundscapes and music that complement the story.

```
// Pseudocode for integrating voice acting in Unreal Engine:
void IntegrateVoiceActing()
{
    UVoiceActor* VoiceActor = HireVoiceActor();
    CreateCharacterDialogues(VoiceActor);
    ImplementDialogueSystem();
}
```

8. Creating Interactive Cutscenes

Blend gameplay seamlessly with storytelling through interactive cutscenes. Allow players to make choices or take actions during cutscenes, which can influence the narrative's progression.

9. Consistency and Cohesion

Maintain consistency and cohesion in your narrative. Ensure that the story aligns with the game's mechanics, visuals, and overall experience. Avoid plot holes and inconsistencies that can disrupt immersion.

10. Playtest and Iterate

Regular playtesting is essential to gauge how players respond to your narrative. Collect feedback and iterate on your storytelling elements, refining the narrative based on player experiences.

11. Balancing Story and Gameplay

Balance the storytelling elements with gameplay to avoid overwhelming players with excessive exposition. Integrate narrative seamlessly into gameplay mechanics to keep players engaged.

12. Emotional Resonance

Create emotional resonance by crafting relatable characters and situations. Players should empathize with characters' struggles and motivations, making the story more impactful.

In conclusion, crafting engaging narratives in Unreal Engine involves defining themes, creating well-defined characters, establishing immersive settings, embracing nonlinear storytelling, using Sequencer for cinematics, directing camera movements, integrating voice acting and soundtracks, creating interactive cutscenes, ensuring consistency and cohesion, playtesting, balancing story and gameplay, and evoking emotional resonance. A compelling narrative can elevate your game and create memorable experiences for players.

10.2. Using Sequencer for Cinematic Creation

Unreal Engine's Sequencer is a powerful tool for creating cinematic sequences and cutscenes within your game. It provides a visual timeline-based interface that allows you to choreograph complex cinematic sequences with ease. In this section, we will explore how to use Sequencer effectively for cinematic creation in Unreal Engine.

1. Accessing Sequencer

To access Sequencer, go to the "Cinematics" tab in the main toolbar of Unreal Engine's Editor. From there, you can create a new level sequence or open an existing one. Level sequences are where you define your cinematic sequences.

2. Adding Actors and Components

In Sequencer, you can add actors and components to your level sequence. Actors represent objects in your game world, such as characters, vehicles, or props. Components can be individual elements of an actor, like skeletal meshes, cameras, or lights. To add an actor or component, right-click on the timeline and choose "Add Actor to Sequence" or "Add Component to Actor."

```
// Pseudocode for adding an actor to a level sequence in Sequencer:
void AddActorToSequence(ALevelSequenceActor* LevelSequenceActor, AActor* Acto
rToAdd)
{
    LevelSequenceActor->GetMovieScene()->AddActorToSequence(ActorToAdd);
}
```

3. Keyframing and Animation

Sequencer allows you to keyframe properties of actors and components over time. You can animate position, rotation, scale, materials, and many other properties. To create a keyframe, select the property you want to animate, move the timeline to the desired frame, and set the value. Sequencer will automatically create keyframes.

```
// Pseudocode for keyframing an actor's position in Sequencer:
void KeyframeActorPosition(AActor* Actor, FVector Position, float TimeInSecon
ds)
{
    Actor->SetActorLocation(Position);
    Sequencer->CreateKeyframeForActor(Actor, TimeInSeconds);
}
```

4. Camera Work

Sequencer provides powerful camera tools for creating dynamic camera movements and angles. You can animate camera properties like field of view, focal length, and depth of field. Use these tools to frame your shots and create cinematic camera movements.

```
// Pseudocode for animating camera properties in Sequencer:
void AnimateCameraProperties(ACameraActor* Camera, float FOV, float TimeInSec
onds)
{
    Camera->SetFieldOfView(FOV);
    Sequencer->CreateKeyframeForActor(Camera, TimeInSeconds);
}
```

5. Audio Integration

Sequencer supports audio integration, allowing you to synchronize sound effects, music, and voiceovers with your cinematic sequences. You can add audio tracks to your level sequence and precisely time audio cues.

```
// Pseudocode for adding audio to a level sequence in Sequencer:
void AddAudioTrackToSequence(ULevelSequence* Sequence, USoundCue* SoundCue)
{
    UMovieSceneAudioTrack* AudioTrack = Sequence->AddAudioTrack();
    AudioTrack->AddSection(SoundCue, 0.0f);
}
```

6. Visual Effects

You can incorporate visual effects into your cinematic sequences using Sequencer. This includes particle systems, post-processing effects, and animation of materials and textures. Visual effects enhance the overall cinematic experience.

7. Timeline and Sequencer Director

The timeline in Sequencer allows you to control the sequence's playback and edit keyframes. You can also create sub-sequences within your level sequence for better organization. The Sequencer Director is responsible for triggering cinematic sequences during gameplay.

```
// Pseudocode for triggering a cinematic sequence in Sequencer:
void TriggerCinematicSequence(USequencerDirector* Director, ULevelSequence* S
equence)
```

```
{
    Director->PlaySequence(Sequence);
}
```

8. Events and Triggers

Sequencer supports events and triggers that allow you to control gameplay elements based on cinematic events. For example, you can trigger character animations or gameplay events when specific points in the cinematic sequence are reached.

9. Preview and Playback

Use the Sequencer's preview and playback features to review your cinematic sequence in real-time within the Unreal Editor. This allows you to fine-tune animations, camera movements, and timing.

10. Exporting Cinematics

Once your cinematic sequence is complete, you can export it as a video file or integrate it directly into your game for in-game cinematics. Unreal Engine provides various export options, including image sequences and video formats.

In conclusion, Unreal Engine's Sequencer is a versatile tool for crafting cinematic sequences and cutscenes in your game. Whether you're telling a story, creating dramatic moments, or enhancing gameplay with cinematics, Sequencer provides the tools you need to bring your vision to life. Mastering Sequencer can significantly elevate the cinematic quality of your Unreal Engine games.

10.3. Directing Camera Movements and Angles

Directing camera movements and angles is a crucial aspect of cinematic creation in Unreal Engine. The way you frame and move the camera can significantly impact the storytelling and visual experience of your game. In this section, we will explore techniques for effectively directing camera movements and angles in Unreal Engine.

1. Establishing Shot Types

Before diving into camera movements, it's essential to understand various shot types commonly used in filmmaking and game cinematics. Some common shot types include:

- **Wide Shot (WS):** Shows the entire scene or environment, providing context.
- **Medium Shot (MS):** Focuses on the characters or objects, conveying emotions and interactions.
- **Close-Up (CU):** Highlights specific details, such as a character's facial expression or an important object.

- **Over-the-Shoulder (OTS):** Places the camera behind a character's shoulder, showing both the character and what they are looking at.
- **Tracking Shot:** Follows a subject's movement, adding dynamism to the scene.
- **Pan and Tilt:** Rotates the camera horizontally (pan) or vertically (tilt) to reveal different parts of the scene.
- **Dolly and Zoom:** Moves the camera closer (dolly) or changes the focal length (zoom) to emphasize or de-emphasize objects or characters.

2. Storyboarding and Previsualization

Storyboarding is a valuable technique to plan camera movements and angles. Create simple sketches or digital storyboards to visualize how each shot will look and flow within the sequence. This process helps you make informed decisions about camera placement and movements before implementing them in Unreal Engine.

3. Cinematic Cameras

Unreal Engine provides Cinematic Cameras, which are specialized camera actors designed for cinematic sequences. These cameras offer features like smooth interpolation, focus control, and the ability to define camera cuts and angles easily.

```
// Pseudocode for creating a cinematic camera in Unreal Engine:
void CreateCinematicCamera()
{
    ACineCameraActor* CinematicCamera = CreateCinematicCameraActor();
    ConfigureCinematicCamera(CinematicCamera);
}
```

4. Camera Movement Techniques

When directing camera movements, consider techniques like:

- **Dolly-In and Dolly-Out:** Moving the camera toward or away from the subject to create emphasis or perspective changes.
- **Tracking and Following:** Smoothly following characters or objects to maintain visual focus.
- **Orbiting and Arcs:** Rotating the camera around a subject in circular or arcing movements for dynamic shots.
- **Zooming and Focusing:** Adjusting the camera's focal length (zoom) and focus distance to control depth of field and highlight specific elements.

5. Camera Angles for Emotion

Camera angles can convey various emotions and perspectives. For example:

- **Low Angle:** Shooting from below characters can make them appear powerful and dominant.
- **High Angle:** Shooting from above can make characters seem vulnerable or small.
- **Eye-Level:** This neutral angle provides a realistic and relatable perspective.

- **Dutch Angle:** Tilting the camera adds tension and unease to a scene.

6. Camera Transitions

Consider how you transition between different shots and camera angles. Common transitions include cuts, fades, wipes, and cross-dissolves. These transitions can help maintain continuity and flow in your cinematic sequences.

7. Smooth Camera Movements

Smooth camera movements are essential for a professional cinematic look. Avoid sudden jerky movements unless they are intentional for dramatic effect. Use keyframes and curves to control the camera's interpolation and ease in/out of movements.

```
// Pseudocode for creating a smooth camera movement in Sequencer:
void CreateSmoothCameraMovement(USequencer* Sequencer, ACineCameraActor* Came
raActor, FVector TargetLocation, float TimeInSeconds)
{
    Sequencer->AddCineCameraCut(CameraActor, FMovieSceneSequenceID(), TimeInS
econds);
    Sequencer->GetMovieScene()->SetFlags(EMovieSceneDataChangeType::MovieScen
eStructureItemsChanged);
}
```

8. Lighting and Composition

Consider how lighting and composition work in tandem with camera movements. Properly lit scenes and thoughtful composition can enhance the impact of your shots.

9. Player-Controlled Cameras

In some games, you may allow players to control the camera. Ensure that camera controls are intuitive and enhance the gameplay experience. Provide options for players to adjust camera sensitivity and customize their view.

10. Feedback and Playtesting

After implementing camera movements and angles, gather feedback from playtesters and team members. Adjust camera sequences based on feedback to ensure they enhance the overall cinematic experience.

Directing camera movements and angles in Unreal Engine is both an art and a technical skill. By carefully planning your shots, utilizing cinematic cameras, and mastering camera movement techniques, you can create captivating cinematic sequences that engage players and enhance your game's storytelling.

10.4. Integrating Voice Acting and Soundtracks

Integrating voice acting and soundtracks is a vital component of creating immersive and emotionally engaging cinematic sequences in Unreal Engine. Sound plays a significant role in conveying narrative, emotions, and atmosphere. In this section, we will explore the techniques for effectively integrating voice acting and soundtracks into your Unreal Engine projects.

1. Voice Acting Considerations

When incorporating voice acting into your cinematics, consider the following:

- **Casting:** Select voice actors who can convincingly portray the characters in your game. Auditioning and casting the right talent is crucial to capturing the essence of your characters.

- **Script and Dialogue:** Provide voice actors with clear scripts and character descriptions. Ensure that the dialogue aligns with the narrative and character motivations.

- **Recording Quality:** Use high-quality recording equipment and soundproof environments to capture clean and clear voice recordings. Minimize background noise and echoes.

2. Voice Acting Recording

Unreal Engine does not have built-in voice recording capabilities. Typically, voice acting is recorded separately using professional audio recording software and equipment. Once recorded, you can import the voice files into Unreal Engine.

3. Audio Import

To integrate voice acting, import the recorded audio files (usually in WAV or MP3 format) into Unreal Engine. Organize them within the project's content directory for easy access.

```
// Pseudocode for importing audio files in Unreal Engine:
void ImportVoiceActingAudio(UAudioImporter* Importer, FString AudioFilePath)
{
    Importer->ImportAudioFile(AudioFilePath);
}
```

4. Lip Syncing

For realistic character animations and lip syncing, you can use Unreal Engine's animation tools and systems. You may need to create character animations that sync with the voice lines. There are also plugins and third-party tools available for more advanced lip syncing.

5. Soundtracks and Music

A well-composed soundtrack enhances the emotional impact of your cinematic sequences. Consider the following when integrating soundtracks:

- **Composer Selection:** Collaborate with a composer or music producer to create original music tailored to your game's themes and narrative.

- **Scoring:** Compose music that complements the mood and tone of the cinematic sequence. Score different pieces of music for various scenes and emotional moments.

- **Synchronization:** Ensure that the music syncs seamlessly with the cinematic events. Use audio cues and triggers to start and stop music at the right moments.

6. Audio Implementation

Unreal Engine offers powerful audio tools and features for implementing voice acting and soundtracks:

- **Audio Actors:** Use Audio Actors to place sound sources in the game world. This allows you to control the spatialization and attenuation of audio.

- **Sound Cues:** Create Sound Cues that combine multiple audio files and define how they behave in the game. You can add voice lines, music tracks, and sound effects to Sound Cues.

- **Audio Components:** Attach Audio Components to actors in the scene. These components play the audio defined in the associated Sound Cues.

7. Audio Mixing

Proper audio mixing is crucial to achieving a balanced and immersive audio experience. Unreal Engine provides tools for adjusting volume, pitch, reverb, and other audio properties in real-time.

```
// Pseudocode for adjusting audio properties in Unreal Engine:
void AdjustAudioProperties(UAudioComponent* AudioComponent)
{
    AudioComponent->SetVolume(0.8f);
    AudioComponent->SetPitch(1.2f);
    AudioComponent->SetReverbSendLevel(0.5f);
}
```

8. Real-Time Sound Modification

In some cases, you may want to modify audio in real-time to create special effects or match gameplay events. Unreal Engine's audio systems allow you to apply effects like reverb, pitch modulation, and equalization dynamically.

9. Playtesting and Audio Feedback

Playtest your cinematics with integrated voice acting and soundtracks to ensure that the audio enhances the storytelling and emotional impact. Gather feedback from playtesters and make adjustments as needed.

10. Optimization

Optimize audio assets and settings to ensure that the game runs smoothly without performance issues. Use audio occlusion and attenuation settings to control how sounds are heard based on the player's position in the game world.

Integrating voice acting and soundtracks effectively into your Unreal Engine cinematics requires careful planning, collaboration with voice actors and composers, audio import and implementation, and thorough playtesting. When done correctly, it can elevate the overall cinematic experience and immerse players in the narrative world of your game.

10.5. Creating Interactive Cutscenes

Interactive cutscenes are a powerful storytelling tool that can engage players and allow them to influence the outcome of the narrative in your Unreal Engine game. In this section, we will explore techniques for creating interactive cutscenes that seamlessly blend gameplay with storytelling.

1. Define Interactive Moments

Before creating interactive cutscenes, identify the key moments in your game's narrative where player interaction can make a difference. These moments can include dialog choices, character actions, or critical decisions that impact the story's direction.

2. Implement Dialogue Trees

Unreal Engine offers tools for implementing dialogue trees that allow players to choose responses during conversations. Use the Dialogue System to create branching dialogues and decisions that affect the narrative.

```
// Pseudocode for implementing a dialogue tree in Unreal Engine:
void CreateDialogueTree(UDialogueSystem* DialogueSystem)
{
    UDialogueTree* Tree = DialogueSystem->CreateDialogueTree();
    Tree->AddNode("Welcome", "Hello there!", Options: ["Ask about the quest",
"Leave"]);
    Tree->AddNode("Quest", "We have a dangerous quest ahead...", Options: ["A
ccept", "Decline"]);
    // Define connections and consequences
}
```

3. Choice-Based Narratives

Incorporate choice-based narratives where player decisions lead to different outcomes. Consider consequences and branching storylines based on the choices players make during interactive cutscenes.

4. Quick-Time Events (QTEs)

Integrate QTEs during cutscenes to add action and excitement. Prompt players to perform specific actions or button presses within a time limit to influence the scene's outcome.

```
// Pseudocode for implementing a QTE in Unreal Engine:
void CreateQTE(UQTESystem* QTESystem)
{
    UQTESequence* Sequence = QTESystem->CreateQTESequence();
    Sequence->AddButtonPrompt("Press A to dodge", OnSuccess: DodgeSuccess, On
Failure: DodgeFailure);
}
```

5. Character Control

Allow players to control their characters during cutscenes to make decisions or perform actions. This provides a more immersive and player-driven experience.

6. Feedback and Consequences

Provide immediate feedback to players based on their choices and actions during interactive cutscenes. Ensure that decisions have consequences that impact the game's narrative, character relationships, or gameplay.

7. Seamless Transitions

Smoothly transition between gameplay and cutscenes to maintain immersion. Avoid jarring transitions or loading screens that disrupt the flow of the narrative.

8. Camera Control

During interactive cutscenes, give players some control over the camera. Allow them to focus on specific characters or elements within the scene.

```
// Pseudocode for enabling player-controlled camera during cutscenes:
void EnablePlayerControlledCamera(UPlayerCameraController* CameraController)
{
    CameraController->EnablePlayerControl();
}
```

9. Playtesting and Iteration

Regularly playtest interactive cutscenes to ensure that player choices and actions align with the narrative and that consequences are meaningful. Use player feedback to refine and improve the interactive storytelling experience.

10. Story Flowchart

Create a visual flowchart or diagram of your game's narrative, including all possible branches and decisions. This helps you keep track of the complexity of the story and ensures that it remains cohesive.

11. Scripted Events

In addition to player-driven interactivity, incorporate scripted events that progress the narrative in response to specific triggers or conditions. These events can help maintain the pacing and coherence of the story.

12. Accessibility

Consider accessibility features for interactive cutscenes, such as providing alternative input methods or adjustable difficulty settings for QTEs.

13. Save and Load States

Implement a system that allows players to save and load their progress during interactive cutscenes. This ensures that they can explore different narrative paths without starting from the beginning.

Creating interactive cutscenes in Unreal Engine requires a balance between storytelling and gameplay. By carefully designing choices, consequences, and player interactions, you can craft a narrative that draws players into your game's world and makes them an active part of the storytelling experience.

Chapter 11: Audio Design and Implementation

11.1. Advanced Sound Design Techniques

In this section, we will explore advanced sound design techniques in Unreal Engine that can elevate the audio experience in your games. Sound design plays a crucial role in creating immersive and engaging gameplay, and Unreal Engine offers a wide range of tools and features to help you achieve exceptional audio quality.

11.1.1. Layered Sound Effects

Layered sound effects involve combining multiple audio elements to create richer and more dynamic soundscapes. Unreal Engine allows you to create sound cues that consist of multiple audio components. These components can be mixed and controlled in real-time, enabling you to achieve complex audio effects. Here's an example of how to create a layered sound effect in Unreal Engine:

```
// Define a sound cue with multiple audio components
SoundCue LayeredSoundEffect;
AudioComponent[] SoundComponents;

// Initialize the sound components
foreach(AudioComponent Component in SoundComponents)
{
    // Set properties for each component, such as volume and pitch
    Component.VolumeMultiplier = 0.8;
    Component.PitchMultiplier = 1.2;
}

// Play the layered sound effect
foreach(AudioComponent Component in SoundComponents)
{
    Component.Play();
}
```

11.1.2. Real-Time Sound Modulation

Unreal Engine provides real-time modulation options for sound effects, allowing you to change parameters like pitch, volume, and filter effects during gameplay. This feature can be used to create dynamic and responsive audio experiences. Here's an example of how to modulate sound in real-time:

```
// Get a reference to the audio component
AudioComponent MyAudioComponent;

// Modulate pitch and volume based on game events
MyAudioComponent.PitchMultiplier = 1.0 + (GameSpeed * 0.1); // Adjust pitch based on game speed
```

```
MyAudioComponent.VolumeMultiplier = FMath::Lerp(0.5, 1.0, CharacterHealth / M
axHealth); // Adjust volume based on character's health
MyAudioComponent.LowPassFilterFrequency = FMath::Lerp(500.0, 2000.0, Distance
ToEnemy / MaxHearingDistance); // Adjust filter effect based on distance to e
nemy
```

11.1.3. Spatial Audio and 3D Sound Effects

Spatial audio is essential for creating a realistic sense of space and directionality in your games. Unreal Engine supports 3D sound effects, allowing you to position audio sources in 3D space and simulate how sound propagates through the environment. Here's how you can use spatial audio:

```
// Create a sound source at a specific location in the game world
SoundSource = SpawnSoundEmitter(Location);

// Set the sound source's attenuation settings to simulate distance and direc
tion
SoundSource.SetAttenuationSettings(AttenuationSettings);

// Play the sound from the source
SoundSource.PlaySound(Sound);
```

11.1.4. Dynamic Audio Mixing and Mastering

Dynamic audio mixing and mastering involve adjusting audio levels, effects, and equalization during gameplay to maintain a balanced and immersive audio experience. Unreal Engine provides a real-time audio mixer that allows you to define audio buses, apply effects, and control parameters dynamically. Here's an example of using the audio mixer:

```
// Create an audio bus for in-game music
AudioBus MusicBus = CreateAudioBus("Music");

// Apply an equalizer effect to the music bus
EqualizerEffect MusicEqualizer = MusicBus.AddEffect<EqualizerEffect>();
MusicEqualizer.SetEqualizerCurve(EQ_Preset_Rock);

// Adjust the equalizer settings in real-time
MusicEqualizer.SetBandGain(EQBand::Band1, 3.0); // Boost bass frequencies
MusicEqualizer.SetBandGain(EQBand::Band5, -2.0); // Reduce midrange frequenci
es
```

These advanced sound design techniques, when used effectively, can greatly enhance the audio quality and immersion in your Unreal Engine games. Experiment with these tools and explore creative ways to bring your game world to life through sound.

11.2. Spatial Audio and 3D Sound Effects

Spatial audio and 3D sound effects are essential components of modern game audio design. They enable players to perceive sound sources in a three-dimensional space, enhancing immersion and gameplay experience. Unreal Engine offers robust tools for implementing spatial audio and creating lifelike 3D soundscapes.

Understanding Spatial Audio

Spatial audio simulates the way sound propagates in the real world. It considers factors like distance, direction, and obstacles to create an accurate auditory experience. Unreal Engine achieves this by using the concept of "sound attenuation," which defines how sound diminishes over distance.

Here's how you can set up spatial audio in Unreal Engine:

```
// Create a sound source at a specific location in the game world
SoundSource = SpawnSoundEmitter(Location);

// Set the sound source's attenuation settings to simulate distance and direction
SoundSource.SetAttenuationSettings(AttenuationSettings);

// Play the sound from the source
SoundSource.PlaySound(Sound);
```

In this example, Location specifies the 3D position of the sound source, AttenuationSettings determine how the sound attenuates based on distance, and Sound is the audio asset you want to play.

Implementing 3D Sound Effects

Unreal Engine allows you to create compelling 3D sound effects by positioning sound sources in the game world. This positioning can be crucial for gameplay elements like detecting enemy footsteps or locating hidden items.

Here's how you can use 3D sound effects in Unreal Engine:

```
// Create an enemy footstep sound source
SoundEmitter EnemyFootsteps = SpawnSoundEmitter(EnemyLocation);

// Set attenuation settings for realistic sound propagation
EnemyFootsteps.SetAttenuationSettings(FootstepAttenuation);

// Play the footstep sound
EnemyFootsteps.PlaySound(FootstepSound);
```

In this scenario, EnemyLocation represents the position of the enemy, FootstepAttenuation defines how the footstep sound attenuates with distance, and FootstepSound is the sound effect for the footstep.

Dynamic Sound Localization

Spatial audio also enables dynamic sound localization, allowing you to change the perceived direction of a sound source based on in-game events. This can be used for various purposes, such as guiding players or creating suspenseful moments.

```
// Get the player's location
Vector PlayerLocation = PlayerCharacter.GetActorLocation();

// Calculate the direction to the player from the sound source
Vector SoundDirection = (PlayerLocation - SoundSourceLocation).GetSafeNormal(
);

// Set the sound source's rotation to face the player
SoundSource.SetWorldRotation(SoundDirection.Rotation());
```

In this example, PlayerCharacter represents the player's character, and SoundSourceLocation is the position of the sound source. By calculating the direction to the player and adjusting the sound source's rotation, you can create a dynamic sound localization effect.

Environmental Sound Effects

Unreal Engine allows you to integrate environmental sound effects, such as echoes, reverberation, and occlusion, to further enhance the realism of your 3D soundscapes. These effects can be achieved through sound cues and audio reverb volumes placed in the game world.

```
// Create an audio reverb volume for a cave environment
AudioVolume CaveReverbVolume = SpawnAudioVolume(CaveReverbSettings);

// Apply the audio reverb to the sound source
SoundSource.SetReverbSettings(CaveReverbSettings);
```

In this code snippet, CaveReverbSettings represents the reverb settings specific to a cave environment. The audio reverb volume and settings modify the sound's characteristics when it interacts with the cave's acoustics.

Mastering spatial audio and 3D sound effects in Unreal Engine opens up opportunities to create more engaging and immersive game worlds. By carefully configuring attenuation, positioning, and environmental effects, you can provide players with a rich and realistic auditory experience that complements your game's visuals and mechanics.

11.3. Dynamic Audio Mixing and Mastering

Dynamic audio mixing and mastering are critical aspects of game audio design that allow developers to create a balanced and immersive auditory experience. Unreal Engine provides a powerful audio mixer that enables real-time adjustments to audio levels, effects, and equalization during gameplay. This section explores the concepts and techniques involved in dynamic audio mixing and mastering.

The Role of Dynamic Audio Mixing

Dynamic audio mixing involves adjusting various audio parameters on the fly to respond to in-game events and conditions. It ensures that audio remains coherent and enhances the gameplay experience. Unreal Engine's audio mixer allows you to manage audio buses, apply effects, and control parameters dynamically.

Let's look at how dynamic audio mixing can be implemented in Unreal Engine:

```
// Create an audio bus for in-game music
AudioBus MusicBus = CreateAudioBus("Music");

// Apply an equalizer effect to the music bus
EqualizerEffect MusicEqualizer = MusicBus.AddEffect<EqualizerEffect>();
MusicEqualizer.SetEqualizerCurve(EQ_Preset_Rock);

// Adjust the equalizer settings in real-time
MusicEqualizer.SetBandGain(EQBand::Band1, 3.0); // Boost bass frequencies
MusicEqualizer.SetBandGain(EQBand::Band5, -2.0); // Reduce midrange frequenci
es
```

In this example, we create an audio bus named "Music" and apply an equalizer effect to it. The equalizer effect is then adjusted in real-time to emphasize certain frequencies, creating dynamic changes in the music's tonal characteristics.

Creating Real-Time Audio Effects

Real-time audio effects play a significant role in dynamic audio mixing. Unreal Engine offers a variety of built-in audio effects that can be applied to audio buses, sound sources, or individual audio components. These effects can be manipulated to respond to in-game situations, adding depth and variety to the audio experience.

Here's how you can add and control real-time audio effects in Unreal Engine:

```
// Create an audio bus for environmental sounds
AudioBus EnvironmentBus = CreateAudioBus("Environment");

// Apply a chorus effect to create a spatial effect
ChorusEffect EnvironmentChorus = EnvironmentBus.AddEffect<ChorusEffect>();
EnvironmentChorus.SetDepth(0.5); // Adjust the depth of the chorus effect
EnvironmentChorus.SetRate(0.2); // Modify the modulation rate
```

In this code snippet, an audio bus named "Environment" is created, and a chorus effect is applied to it. You can adjust parameters like depth and rate to control the intensity and speed of the chorus effect dynamically.

Parameter Modulation

Parameter modulation is a powerful technique in dynamic audio mixing. It involves linking audio effect parameters to in-game variables or events. By doing so, you can create audio that reacts to specific gameplay conditions or player actions.

Here's an example of parameter modulation in Unreal Engine:

```
// Get the player's health
float PlayerHealth = PlayerCharacter.GetHealth();

// Modulate the reverb decay time based on player health
float ModulatedDecayTime = FMath::Lerp(0.5, 2.0, PlayerHealth / MaxHealth);

// Apply the modulated decay time to the audio reverb
ReverbEffect AudioReverb = SoundSource.GetReverbEffect();
AudioReverb.SetDecayTime(ModulatedDecayTime);
```

In this code, the decay time of an audio reverb effect is modulated based on the player's health. As the player's health changes, the reverb's decay time dynamically adjusts to reflect the game's state.

Dynamic Mixing for Immersive Gameplay

Dynamic audio mixing and mastering are essential for maintaining a consistent and immersive audio experience in your game. Whether you're adjusting equalization, applying real-time effects, or modulating parameters, Unreal Engine provides the tools you need to create audio that responds dynamically to gameplay events, ultimately enhancing player engagement and immersion.

11.4. Implementing Adaptive Game Music

Implementing adaptive game music is a powerful way to enhance the player's gaming experience by dynamically changing the music based on in-game events, moods, or situations. Unreal Engine provides tools and techniques for creating adaptive music systems that seamlessly adapt to the game's narrative and player interactions.

The Role of Adaptive Music

Adaptive music is designed to evolve and respond to the player's actions and the game's context. It can heighten tension during intense gameplay moments, provide soothing melodies during exploration, and seamlessly transition between different musical themes.

Unreal Engine's audio system allows you to achieve these dynamic music transitions and adapt to changing game states.

Cue-Based Adaptive Music

One approach to adaptive music in Unreal Engine is cue-based adaptive music. In this method, you define music cues, which are short musical segments or loops that correspond to different emotional states or gameplay situations. These cues are then dynamically selected and blended to create a continuous and adaptive music experience.

Here's a simplified example of cue-based adaptive music implementation:

```
// Define music cues for exploration, combat, and victory
MusicCue ExplorationCue;
MusicCue CombatCue;
MusicCue VictoryCue;

// Determine the game state (e.g., exploration, combat, victory)
GameState CurrentGameState = DetermineGameState();

// Play the appropriate music cue based on the game state
switch (CurrentGameState)
{
    case GameState::Exploration:
        ExplorationCue.Play();
        break;
    case GameState::Combat:
        CombatCue.Play();
        break;
    case GameState::Victory:
        VictoryCue.Play();
        break;
    default:
        // Handle other states or transitions
        break;
}
```

In this code, music cues for different game states are defined and played based on the current game state. Unreal Engine's audio system allows for smooth transitions between these cues to create an adaptive music experience.

Parameter Modulation for Dynamic Music

To further enhance adaptive music, you can modulate various parameters of the music in real-time. For example, you can adjust the tempo, intensity, or instrumentation based on the player's actions or the game's narrative. This adds depth and responsiveness to the music, making it feel more integrated into the gameplay.

```
// Get the player's health and intensity level
float PlayerHealth = PlayerCharacter.GetHealth();
```

```
float Intensity = CalculateIntensity();

// Modulate music parameters based on player health and intensity
MusicCue.ModulateTempo(1.0 + (PlayerHealth / MaxHealth));
MusicCue.ModulateIntensity(Intensity);
```

In this example, the tempo and intensity of the music cue are modulated based on the player's health and the calculated intensity level. This creates a dynamic musical experience that mirrors the game's current situation.

Seamless Transitions and Crossfading

Smooth transitions between music cues are essential for maintaining immersion. Unreal Engine offers crossfading techniques that allow you to transition between different music cues seamlessly. Crossfading ensures that the change in music is gradual and doesn't disrupt the player's experience.

```
// Crossfade from the current music cue to a new one
ExplorationCue.CrossfadeTo(NewMusicCue, CrossfadeDuration);
```

In this code, the CrossfadeTo function is used to smoothly transition from the current music cue to a new one, with the specified crossfade duration.

Dynamic Music in Different Game Genres

Adaptive music can be applied to various game genres, from action and adventure games to role-playing and horror titles. Each genre may have unique requirements for how music adapts to gameplay. Unreal Engine's flexibility and scripting capabilities allow you to tailor adaptive music systems to suit your game's specific needs.

By implementing adaptive music, you can create an immersive and emotionally engaging gaming experience that keeps players captivated and enhances the overall enjoyment of your game. Unreal Engine's audio tools and features provide a solid foundation for designing and implementing adaptive music systems that elevate your game's audio to new heights.

11.5. Audio Optimization for Different Platforms

Audio optimization is a crucial aspect of game development, ensuring that your game's audio runs efficiently and sounds great on various platforms. Unreal Engine provides tools and techniques for optimizing audio to achieve the best performance while maintaining high-quality sound. This section explores strategies for audio optimization on different platforms.

The Importance of Audio Optimization

Optimizing audio is essential for several reasons. First, it helps reduce the computational load on the hardware, which is critical for ensuring smooth gameplay, especially on resource-constrained platforms like mobile devices or older consoles. Second, efficient audio processing contributes to lower power consumption, extending the device's battery life in the case of mobile games. Lastly, optimized audio ensures that the game's audio assets fit within memory constraints.

Platform-Specific Considerations

Each gaming platform, whether it's a PC, console, or mobile device, has unique hardware capabilities and limitations. Therefore, optimizing audio for a specific platform requires understanding and addressing these differences.

For PC and console games, the hardware is generally more powerful, allowing for higher-quality audio assets and complex audio processing. However, it's still crucial to strike a balance between audio quality and performance to ensure a smooth gaming experience.

Mobile devices have more limited resources, including processing power, memory, and storage space. Audio optimization on mobile platforms often involves reducing the size of audio assets, minimizing CPU usage, and using compressed audio formats to save storage space.

Audio Asset Compression

One common technique for audio optimization is compressing audio assets. Unreal Engine supports various audio compression formats, such as Ogg Vorbis, MP3, and ADPCM. These formats offer a trade-off between audio quality and file size.

```
// Specify audio compression settings for a sound cue
SoundCue CompressionSettings;
CompressionSettings.SoundWaveCompressionSettings = SoundCompressionSettings::
Compressed;

// Apply the compression settings to the sound cue
SoundCue.SetCompressionSettings(CompressionSettings);
```

In this example, the SoundCue is configured to use compressed audio settings, reducing the file size of the associated audio assets. Care should be taken to balance compression with acceptable audio quality.

Level of Detail (LOD) for Audio

Unreal Engine also provides support for audio LOD, similar to the concept of LOD for graphics. With audio LOD, you can specify different versions of audio assets at varying levels of detail. For instance, you might use a lower-quality audio asset when the player is far from a sound source and switch to a higher-quality asset as the player gets closer.

```
// Set up audio LOD for a sound cue
SoundCue.SetMinRadius(2000.0); // Use lower LOD for sounds beyond this radius
SoundCue.SetMaxRadius(500.0); // Switch to higher LOD within this radius
```

By configuring audio LOD, you can reduce the computational load and memory usage associated with audio, particularly for distant or less critical sound sources.

Dynamic Audio Streaming

Dynamic audio streaming is another technique used for audio optimization. It involves loading audio assets from storage or memory on-demand, rather than preloading all audio assets into memory at once. This can help reduce memory usage and improve overall performance, especially on platforms with limited memory.

```
// Enable dynamic audio streaming for a level
Level.EnableDynamicAudioStreaming(true);
```

By enabling dynamic audio streaming for specific levels or parts of the game, you can ensure that only the necessary audio assets are loaded into memory as needed, conserving resources.

Profiling and Testing

Effective audio optimization requires careful profiling and testing to identify performance bottlenecks and audio-related issues. Unreal Engine provides profiling tools that help monitor audio performance, including CPU usage, memory consumption, and streaming behavior. These tools assist in fine-tuning audio settings for optimal performance on different platforms.

```
// Enable audio profiling during gameplay
Audio.EnableAudioProfiler(true);
```

Enabling audio profiling allows you to gather data on how audio is impacting performance during gameplay, making it easier to pinpoint areas for optimization.

Platform-Specific Tweaks

Lastly, for specific platforms, you may need to make platform-specific tweaks and optimizations. For example, on mobile devices, you might implement audio settings that take advantage of hardware acceleration or customize audio streaming behavior to align with the device's capabilities.

```
// Configure platform-specific audio settings for mobile devices
if (IsMobilePlatform())
{
    // Apply platform-specific audio optimizations
    ApplyMobileAudioSettings();
}
```

By applying platform-specific tweaks, you can ensure that your game's audio performs optimally on each target platform.

In conclusion, audio optimization is essential for achieving high-quality audio performance across various gaming platforms. Unreal Engine provides a range of tools and techniques to help you balance audio quality and performance, allowing your game to sound great while running smoothly on a diverse array of devices.

Chapter 12: Procedural Generation and AI

12.1. Basics of Procedural Content Generation

Procedural content generation (PCG) is a powerful technique in game development that involves creating game content algorithmically rather than manually designing every aspect. This approach allows developers to generate diverse and dynamic game worlds, levels, or assets, making games more engaging and replayable. In this section, we will explore the basics of procedural content generation and its applications in Unreal Engine.

Understanding Procedural Generation

Procedural generation involves using algorithms to generate content dynamically during runtime. This content can include terrain, levels, textures, characters, and more. PCG is often used in open-world games, roguelikes, and games with randomly generated elements.

One primary advantage of procedural generation is that it reduces the need for extensive manual content creation, saving development time and resources. Additionally, it can create vast and unique game environments that players can explore endlessly.

Generating Terrain

Terrain generation is a common application of procedural content generation. Unreal Engine provides tools for creating procedural terrains using heightmaps, noise functions, and other algorithms.

```
// Generate a procedural terrain using a Perlin noise function
Terrain.GenerateHeightmapFromPerlinNoise(Seed, Frequency, Amplitude);

// Apply a texture to the terrain
Terrain.ApplyTexture(SandTexture, GrassTexture, RockTexture);
```

In this example, we use Perlin noise to generate the terrain's heightmap, creating natural-looking landscapes. We then apply textures to the terrain to give it a visually appealing appearance.

Procedural Level Layouts

Procedural generation can be used to create levels with different layouts, structures, and challenges each time the game is played. This approach keeps the gameplay fresh and exciting.

```
// Generate a procedural level layout
Level.GenerateProceduralLayout(LevelSize, RoomCount, CorridorWidth);

// Populate the level with enemies and items
Level.PopulateEnemiesAndItems();
```

Here, we generate a procedural level layout with a specified size, number of rooms, and corridor width. Afterward, we populate the level with enemies and items, creating a unique gameplay experience in each playthrough.

Dynamic Enemy Placement

Procedural generation can extend to enemy placement, creating varying enemy encounters. This approach adds unpredictability and replay value to games.

```
// Generate enemy placements based on procedural rules
EnemyGenerator.GenerateProceduralEnemies(PlayerPosition, DungeonLevel);

// Spawn enemies at generated positions
for (EnemyPlacement Placement : EnemyGenerator.GetGeneratedPlacements())
{
    Enemy.SpawnAt(Placement.Position);
}
```

In this code, we use procedural rules to generate enemy placements based on the player's position and the dungeon level. Enemies are then spawned at the generated positions, ensuring that each encounter is unique and challenging.

Customization and Control

While procedural generation introduces randomness, it's essential to maintain control over the generated content to ensure it aligns with the game's design and balance. Unreal Engine allows developers to define parameters and rules for procedural generation, enabling customization and fine-tuning.

```
// Define procedural generation parameters
Generator.SetParameters(Seed, Density, SizeRange);

// Generate content based on defined parameters
Generator.GenerateProceduralContent();
```

In this example, we set parameters for procedural generation, such as the random seed, density of generated objects, and size range. These parameters influence the outcome of the procedural content generation process, giving developers control over the generated content.

Performance Considerations

Procedural generation can be computationally intensive, especially for complex content. Developers must balance the desire for diverse content with the need for performance optimization.

Unreal Engine provides tools and techniques for optimizing procedural generation, including parallelization, LOD (Level of Detail) techniques, and efficient memory management.

```
// Optimize procedural generation for performance
Generator.OptimizeForPerformance();
```

Optimizing procedural generation is crucial to ensure that games run smoothly and maintain a consistent frame rate, even in procedurally generated environments.

Conclusion

Procedural content generation is a valuable technique in game development, enabling the creation of dynamic and engaging game worlds, levels, and assets. Unreal Engine offers a robust framework for implementing procedural generation, empowering developers to craft diverse, dynamic, and performance-optimized game experiences. In the next sections, we will explore more advanced aspects of procedural generation and its integration with AI to create dynamic gameplay scenarios.

12.2. Creating Dynamic Game Worlds

Creating dynamic game worlds through procedural content generation (PCG) is a powerful way to keep players engaged and excited, as it provides endless variations and challenges. In this section, we will explore how Unreal Engine can be used to create dynamic game worlds using PCG techniques.

Dynamic Terrain Generation

Dynamic terrain generation is a common application of PCG in open-world games. Unreal Engine provides tools and APIs for generating terrains with varying landscapes, textures, and features.

```
// Generate a dynamic terrain using fractal terrain generation
Terrain.GenerateFractalTerrain(Seed, Size, Scale);

// Apply textures and foliage to the terrain
Terrain.ApplyTexturesAndFoliage(GrassTexture, RockTexture, Trees);
```

In this example, we use fractal terrain generation to create a dynamic landscape. We can then apply different textures and populate the terrain with foliage to give it a diverse and visually appealing appearance.

Procedural Level Design

Procedural level design is another application of PCG, particularly in games with roguelike elements or infinite exploration. Unreal Engine allows developers to create procedural level layouts, structures, and challenges.

```
// Generate a procedural level layout with rooms and corridors
Level.GenerateProceduralLayout(RoomCount, CorridorWidth);
```

```
// Populate the level with enemies and items
Level.PopulateEnemiesAndItems();
```

In this code, we generate a procedural level layout with a specified number of rooms and corridor width. We then populate the level with enemies and items, ensuring that each playthrough offers a unique and unpredictable experience.

Randomized Enemy Placement

PCG can be applied to enemy placement to create varying and challenging encounters for players. Unreal Engine enables dynamic enemy placement based on procedural rules.

```
// Generate enemy placements dynamically using procedural rules
EnemyGenerator.GenerateProceduralEnemies(PlayerPosition, DungeonLevel);
```

```
// Spawn enemies at the generated positions
for (EnemyPlacement Placement : EnemyGenerator.GetGeneratedPlacements())
{
    Enemy.SpawnAt(Placement.Position);
}
```

In this example, we use procedural rules to generate enemy placements based on the player's position and the dungeon level. Enemies are then spawned at these dynamically generated positions, ensuring that each encounter is unique and strategically challenging.

Infinite World Exploration

Unreal Engine provides features for creating infinite or large-scale game worlds through PCG. This is particularly useful for open-world or exploration-focused games.

```
// Generate an infinite world map with procedurally generated biomes
World.GenerateInfiniteMap(BiomeGenerator, ChunkSize);
```

```
// Populate the world with resources and landmarks
World.PopulateWorld();
```

In this code snippet, we generate an infinite world map with procedurally generated biomes and populate the world with resources and landmarks. Players can explore an expansive and ever-changing game world.

Customization and Control

While PCG introduces randomness, it's essential to maintain control over the generated content to align it with the game's design and balance. Unreal Engine allows developers to define parameters and rules for procedural content generation, offering customization and fine-tuning capabilities.

```
// Define procedural generation parameters
Generator.SetParameters(Seed, Density, SizeRange);
```

```
// Generate content based on the defined parameters
Generator.GenerateProceduralContent();
```

In this example, parameters such as the random seed, object density, and size range are defined for procedural generation. These parameters influence the outcome of the PCG process, giving developers control over the generated content.

Performance Optimization

PCG can be computationally intensive, especially for complex content. Developers should optimize PCG algorithms and consider factors like parallelization and memory management to ensure good performance.

```
// Optimize procedural content generation for better performance
Generator.OptimizeForPerformance();
```

Optimizing PCG is crucial to ensure that games run smoothly and maintain consistent frame rates, even in dynamically generated environments.

Conclusion

Unreal Engine offers a robust framework for creating dynamic game worlds through procedural content generation. By utilizing PCG techniques, developers can keep players engaged with endlessly variable and challenging experiences. The flexibility and power of Unreal Engine allow for the implementation of diverse PCG-driven game elements, from terrains and levels to enemy encounters and world exploration. In the following sections, we will delve into more advanced aspects of procedural generation and its integration with AI for creating dynamic and responsive gameplay scenarios.

12.3. AI-Driven Story and Content Creation

AI-driven story and content creation is a cutting-edge approach that leverages artificial intelligence to generate narrative elements, characters, and game content dynamically. In this section, we will explore how Unreal Engine can be used to implement AI-driven content creation, enhancing gameplay and storytelling.

The Role of AI in Content Creation

Artificial intelligence plays a pivotal role in generating game content that adapts to player choices and actions. AI algorithms can analyze player behavior, preferences, and progress to dynamically generate narrative events, dialogues, and challenges.

AI-driven content creation not only adds depth to the gameplay but also enables developers to create more immersive and personalized experiences.

Dynamic Storytelling

Unreal Engine offers tools for implementing dynamic storytelling through AI. Developers can use AI algorithms to adjust the game's narrative based on the player's decisions, creating branching storylines and multiple endings.

```
// Implement an AI-driven narrative system
AIDrivenNarrativeSystem.AdjustStoryBasedOnPlayerChoices();

// Generate dynamic dialogues and character interactions
AIDialogueGenerator.GenerateDynamicDialogues();
```

In this example, the AI-driven narrative system adjusts the story based on player choices, and the AI dialogue generator creates dynamic dialogues and character interactions that reflect the evolving narrative.

Procedural Quest Generation

AI-driven content creation can extend to procedural quest generation. Instead of manually designing quests, developers can use AI to generate quests based on the game's world, characters, and player progress.

```
// Generate procedural quests using AI algorithms
AIQuestGenerator.GenerateProceduralQuests(World, PlayerCharacter);

// Populate the world with dynamically generated quests
World.PopulateWithGeneratedQuests();
```

In this code, AI algorithms generate quests that are dynamically tailored to the game world and the player's character. These quests can adapt to the player's actions and choices.

AI-Generated Characters

AI-driven content creation can also involve generating AI-controlled characters with unique personalities and behaviors. These characters can react to the player's actions and interact with the game world dynamically.

```
// Create AI-generated characters with distinct personalities
AIGeneratedCharacter.GeneratePersonality();

// Define AI behaviors and decision-making algorithms
AIGeneratedCharacter.DefineBehaviors();
```

Here, AI-generated characters are equipped with distinct personalities and behaviors. These characters can make decisions, engage with the player, and adapt their actions based on the evolving game context.

Player Profiling and Personalization

AI-driven content creation can benefit from player profiling, where the AI analyzes the player's preferences, playstyle, and past actions to tailor the game experience.

```
// Profile the player's behavior and preferences
AIPlayerProfiler.ProfilePlayer(PlayerCharacter);

// Use player profiling to customize content generation
AIContentGenerator.GeneratePersonalizedContent();
```

In this code, the AI profiles the player's behavior and preferences, allowing the content generator to create personalized content that aligns with the player's preferences and playstyle.

AI-Generated Challenges

AI-driven content creation can also extend to generating gameplay challenges. The AI can analyze the player's skill level and progress to adjust the difficulty of encounters and puzzles dynamically.

```
// Use AI to generate dynamic gameplay challenges
AIGameplayChallenger.GenerateDynamicChallenges(PlayerCharacter);

// Adjust challenge difficulty based on player performance
AIGameplayChallenger.AdaptChallengeDifficulty();
```

In this example, AI algorithms generate gameplay challenges that are responsive to the player's performance, ensuring that the game remains engaging and appropriately challenging.

Ethical Considerations

While AI-driven content creation offers exciting possibilities, it also raises ethical considerations. Developers must ensure that AI-generated content aligns with the game's intended experience and respects player preferences and boundaries. Additionally, AI-generated content should not inadvertently reinforce harmful stereotypes or biases.

Conclusion

AI-driven story and content creation present exciting opportunities to enhance gameplay and storytelling in Unreal Engine games. By leveraging AI algorithms, developers can create dynamic narratives, quests, characters, and challenges that adapt to player actions and preferences. This approach adds depth and personalization to the gaming experience, making it more engaging and immersive. However, developers must also be mindful of ethical considerations when implementing AI-driven content creation to ensure a positive and respectful player experience. In the following sections, we will explore advanced aspects of AI integration in game development using Unreal Engine.

12.4. Implementing Procedural Puzzles and Challenges

Implementing procedural puzzles and challenges is a captivating way to enhance gameplay variety and replayability in Unreal Engine. Procedural generation techniques can be applied to create puzzles, obstacles, and challenges that dynamically adapt to the player's skill level and progress. In this section, we will explore how to implement procedural puzzles and challenges in your Unreal Engine game.

The Benefits of Procedural Challenges

Procedural puzzles and challenges offer several advantages in game design. They keep the gameplay fresh and unpredictable, ensuring that players face new and engaging obstacles each time they play. Additionally, procedural challenges can cater to players of different skill levels, providing both beginners and experienced gamers with a satisfying gaming experience.

Dynamic Level Design

One application of procedural content generation (PCG) in Unreal Engine is creating dynamic level layouts that include puzzles and challenges. This approach allows developers to generate levels with varying structures, obstacles, and puzzles.

```
// Generate a dynamic level layout with procedural puzzles
Level.GenerateProceduralLayout(PuzzleCount, ObstacleDensity);

// Populate the level with procedural puzzles and challenges
Level.PopulateWithProceduralPuzzles();
```

In this example, we generate a dynamic level layout with a specified number of puzzles and obstacle density. We then populate the level with procedural puzzles and challenges, ensuring that each playthrough offers unique and thought-provoking gameplay.

Puzzle Variability

Procedural generation enables the creation of puzzles with different mechanics, difficulty levels, and solutions. Unreal Engine provides tools to generate puzzles and challenges with various parameters.

```
// Generate procedural puzzles with varying difficulty
PuzzleGenerator.GenerateProceduralPuzzles(DifficultyRange, PuzzleTypes);

// Ensure puzzle variability and player engagement
PuzzleGenerator.EnsureUniqueSolutions();
```

In this code snippet, we use a puzzle generator to create procedural puzzles with varying difficulty levels and types. To maintain player engagement, we ensure that each puzzle has a unique solution, adding an element of surprise and strategy.

Adaptive Challenge Scaling

To cater to players of different skill levels, Unreal Engine allows developers to implement adaptive challenge scaling. This means that the game can adjust the difficulty of puzzles and challenges based on the player's performance and experience.

```
// Implement adaptive challenge scaling based on player performance
ChallengeScaler.AdjustChallengeDifficulty(PlayerPerformance);

// Ensure a balanced gameplay experience for all players
ChallengeScaler.BalanceDifficultyCurve();
```

In this example, the challenge scaler adjusts the difficulty of puzzles and challenges based on the player's performance. This ensures that the game remains enjoyable and appropriately challenging, regardless of the player's skill level.

Player Progression

Procedural puzzles and challenges can be linked to the player's progression in the game. As players advance, the complexity and variety of puzzles can increase, offering a sense of accomplishment and discovery.

```
// Link puzzle progression to player advancement
PuzzleProgression.LinkToPlayerProgress(PlayerLevel, GameCompletion);

// Generate new types of puzzles as players reach certain milestones
PuzzleProgression.UnlockAdvancedPuzzleTypes();
```

In this code, puzzle progression is linked to the player's level and game completion. As players reach certain milestones, the game unlocks new types of puzzles, providing a sense of growth and exploration.

Ethical Considerations

While procedural puzzles and challenges offer exciting gameplay possibilities, developers must consider ethical aspects. It's important to ensure that challenges are fair and enjoyable, avoiding frustration or overly difficult obstacles. Additionally, accessibility considerations should be taken into account to make the game enjoyable for all players.

Conclusion

Implementing procedural puzzles and challenges in Unreal Engine can elevate your game's gameplay variety and replayability. By using procedural generation techniques, you can create dynamic and engaging puzzles that adapt to player skill levels and progress. This approach keeps the gaming experience fresh and exciting, making players eager to explore new challenges with each playthrough. However, it's essential to balance the difficulty and variability of puzzles to ensure a satisfying and fair gameplay experience. In the following sections, we will delve into more advanced aspects of game development, including material and shader programming, game economy, and community management.

12.5. Balancing Randomness and Playability

Balancing randomness and playability is a critical aspect of procedural content generation (PCG) in game development. While randomness can introduce excitement and variety, it must be carefully managed to ensure that gameplay remains enjoyable and fair. In this section, we will explore techniques for striking the right balance between randomness and playability in Unreal Engine games.

The Role of Randomness

Randomness is often used in PCG to create diverse and unpredictable game content, including levels, puzzles, loot, and enemy encounters. Random elements can make each playthrough unique and add an element of surprise, enhancing replayability.

Ensuring Fairness

One of the key challenges in balancing randomness is ensuring fairness. Players should perceive the game as fair, even when random elements are involved. Unreal Engine provides tools to manage randomness and maintain fairness.

```
// Implement a fairness mechanism for loot drops
LootGenerator.EnforceFairness(PlayerProgress, LootTable);
```

In this example, the loot generator enforces fairness by considering the player's progress and the loot table. This ensures that players receive appropriate rewards, reducing the frustration of receiving loot that is too easy or too difficult to obtain.

Fine-Tuning Randomization

Fine-tuning the degree of randomness is essential to achieve the desired gameplay experience. Unreal Engine allows developers to control the parameters that influence randomization.

```
// Adjust the randomness factor for procedural puzzles
PuzzleGenerator.SetRandomnessFactor(RandomnessLevel);
```

```
// Ensure that randomization aligns with the desired gameplay balance
PuzzleGenerator.BalanceRandomness();
```

Here, the puzzle generator's randomness factor is adjusted, allowing developers to control the degree of randomness applied to puzzles. Balancing randomness ensures that the game maintains the intended gameplay balance.

Player Skill and Randomness

Balancing randomness and playability also involves considering the player's skill level. Unreal Engine supports adaptive difficulty scaling based on the player's performance.

```
// Implement adaptive difficulty scaling with random elements
DifficultyScaler.AdjustRandomness(PlayerSkill);

// Ensure that randomness aligns with player capabilities
DifficultyScaler.BalanceRandomElements();
```

In this code snippet, the difficulty scaler adjusts the randomness of elements based on the player's skill level. This helps ensure that random challenges remain challenging but achievable for players of varying skill levels.

Iterative Testing and Feedback

Iterative testing and player feedback are essential for fine-tuning the balance between randomness and playability. Developers should gather player input and adjust randomization parameters accordingly.

```
// Collect player feedback on gameplay fairness
PlayerFeedbackSystem.CollectFeedback();

// Use player feedback to make informed adjustments to randomization
PlayerFeedbackSystem.AdjustRandomizationParameters();
```

Collecting feedback from players about the fairness and enjoyment of the game's random elements is crucial. Based on this feedback, adjustments can be made to ensure that the balance between randomness and playability aligns with player expectations.

Ethical Considerations

Balancing randomness and playability should also consider ethical aspects. Developers must avoid creating situations where random elements lead to excessive frustration or unfair advantages. Additionally, accessibility considerations should be taken into account to accommodate players with different skill levels.

Conclusion

Balancing randomness and playability is a vital aspect of game development, especially when incorporating procedural content generation in Unreal Engine. The right balance ensures that players have an enjoyable and engaging experience while benefiting from the excitement and variety that randomness brings. By using Unreal Engine's tools and techniques to manage randomness, enforce fairness, and adapt to player skill levels, developers can create games that offer the perfect blend of unpredictability and fairness. In the following sections, we will explore advanced topics in game development, including material and shader programming, game economy, and community management.

Chapter 13: Advanced Material and Shader Programming

13.1. Understanding Material Nodes and Properties

Understanding material nodes and properties is fundamental to advanced material and shader programming in Unreal Engine. Materials and shaders are essential for controlling the visual appearance of in-game objects, from textures and colors to reflections and lighting. In this section, we will delve into the core concepts of material nodes and properties.

What Are Materials and Shaders?

In Unreal Engine, materials and shaders are used to define how objects in the game world appear visually. Materials are made up of shader networks that control various aspects of rendering, including surface properties, lighting, and special effects.

Materials can be applied to 3D models, landscapes, particles, and more, allowing developers to create realistic and visually stunning scenes.

Material Nodes

Material nodes are the building blocks of shader networks. They represent mathematical operations, texture samplers, and other functions that manipulate the appearance of a surface.

Unreal Engine provides a node-based material editor that allows developers to create complex shaders by connecting nodes together. Some common material nodes include:

- **Texture Sample Node:** This node samples a 2D or 3D texture and allows it to be used in various ways, such as defining a surface's color or bumpiness.

- **Math Node:** Math nodes perform arithmetic operations like addition, subtraction, multiplication, and division. These are used for various calculations within shaders.

- **Scalar Parameter Node:** Scalar parameters are user-defined values that can be exposed in the material instance for easy tweaking.

- **Vector Parameter Node:** Similar to scalar parameters, vector parameters allow users to define color or vector values that can be adjusted in real-time.

- **Fresnel Node:** This node calculates the Fresnel effect, which controls how reflective a surface appears based on the viewing angle.

Material Properties

Materials in Unreal Engine have various properties that can be customized to control their appearance. These properties include:

- **Base Color:** Determines the surface color. It can be a solid color or a texture map.

- **Normal Map:** Provides information about surface bumps and crevices, affecting how light interacts with the surface.

- **Roughness:** Controls the smoothness or roughness of the surface. Higher roughness values result in a less reflective and more diffuse appearance.

- **Metallic:** Determines whether a surface is metallic (reflective) or non-metallic (diffuse).

- **Emissive:** Allows a material to emit light, creating self-illuminated surfaces.

- **Opacity:** Controls how transparent or opaque a material is.

- **Subsurface Scattering:** Simulates the scattering of light beneath the surface, commonly used for skin or organic materials.

Shader Complexity and Optimization

While material nodes and properties offer incredible flexibility, it's essential to be mindful of shader complexity. Complex shaders can impact game performance, especially on lower-end hardware.

Developers should optimize shaders by:

- **Using LODs:** Implementing Level of Detail (LOD) techniques to simplify shaders for distant objects.

- **Caching Results:** Storing shader calculations in textures or buffers to avoid redundant calculations.

- **Shader Complexity Profiling:** Using Unreal Engine's built-in tools to identify and optimize complex shaders.

- **Material Instances:** Creating material instances with fewer variations to reduce shader permutations.

Conclusion

Understanding material nodes and properties is crucial for advanced material and shader programming in Unreal Engine. With these concepts, developers can create visually stunning and highly customizable materials that enhance the visual appeal of their games. However, it's essential to balance shader complexity and optimize materials to ensure optimal performance across various hardware configurations. In the following sections, we will explore more advanced topics in material and shader programming to achieve unique visual effects in Unreal Engine games.

13.2. Crafting Custom Shaders for Unique Effects

Crafting custom shaders is an advanced technique in Unreal Engine that allows developers to achieve unique visual effects and control the rendering process at a granular level. While Unreal Engine provides a range of built-in materials and shaders, custom shaders provide the flexibility to create specialized rendering effects tailored to a game's specific needs. In this section, we will explore the process of crafting custom shaders and their applications.

What Are Custom Shaders?

Custom shaders, also known as shader programs or shader code, are scripts written in a shading language like HLSL (High-Level Shading Language) or GLSL (OpenGL Shading Language). These scripts define how the GPU (Graphics Processing Unit) processes and renders objects in a 3D environment. Unlike standard materials, custom shaders allow developers to define unique rendering behaviors, making them a powerful tool for achieving visual distinctiveness.

Shader Stages

Custom shaders in Unreal Engine follow a specific pipeline and are executed in multiple stages:

19. **Vertex Shader:** This stage processes each vertex of a 3D model, transforming its position in world space, computing normals, and performing other per-vertex operations.

20. **Hull Shader (Tessellation Control Shader):** If tessellation is used, this shader controls how the model is subdivided into smaller pieces, increasing geometric detail where needed.

21. **Domain Shader (Tessellation Evaluation Shader):** Works in conjunction with the hull shader to determine the final positions of the subdivided vertices.

22. **Geometry Shader:** Optional stage that can create additional vertices or primitives, useful for tasks like particle generation or mesh manipulation.

23. **Pixel Shader (Fragment Shader):** This stage determines the color of each pixel on the screen, taking into account lighting, texture mapping, and any custom calculations.

Common Uses of Custom Shaders

Custom shaders can be used to achieve a wide range of visual effects, including:

- **Toon Shading:** Creating a stylized, cartoon-like appearance with flat colors and black outlines.

- **Water Simulation:** Simulating realistic water behavior with reflections, refractions, and waves.

- **Specialized Lighting:** Implementing non-standard lighting models for unique atmospheres, such as cel shading or neon lighting.

- **Post-Processing Effects:** Applying effects like motion blur, depth of field, or chromatic aberration to the final rendered image.

- **Advanced Materials:** Crafting materials with intricate surface behaviors, such as iridescent reflections or dynamic displacement mapping.

Writing Custom Shaders

Writing custom shaders in Unreal Engine typically involves:

24. **Defining Inputs and Outputs:** Specifying what data the shader expects as input and what it should produce as output. This includes attributes like vertex positions, normals, texture coordinates, and custom variables.

25. **Implementing Shader Logic:** Writing the shader code that calculates the desired rendering effect. This can involve complex mathematical operations, texture sampling, and conditional statements.

26. **Compiling and Integrating:** Compiling the shader code and integrating it into the Unreal Engine material system. This may involve creating a custom material node or using existing nodes to apply the shader effect.

27. **Testing and Tweaking:** Iteratively testing the custom shader in the engine, adjusting parameters, and fine-tuning until the desired visual effect is achieved.

Shader Complexity and Optimization

Custom shaders can be computationally expensive, and their complexity can impact game performance. Therefore, it's crucial to optimize custom shaders. Optimization techniques include:

- **Reducing Instructions:** Minimizing the number of shader instructions to improve execution speed.

- **Culling Unnecessary Calculations:** Avoiding calculations that are not visible or have no impact on the final result.

- **LOD and Tessellation Control:** Using level-of-detail techniques and tessellation control to simplify shaders for distant objects.

- **Parallel Processing:** Utilizing the GPU's parallel processing capabilities efficiently.

Conclusion

Crafting custom shaders in Unreal Engine is an advanced technique that empowers developers to achieve unique and visually striking effects. Whether it's creating stylized art styles, simulating complex phenomena, or implementing specialized rendering behaviors, custom shaders offer a level of control and creativity beyond standard materials. However, with great power comes the responsibility to optimize shaders for performance and to carefully balance visual fidelity with smooth gameplay. In the following sections, we will explore more advanced aspects of material and shader programming, including real-time lighting and reflection techniques.

13.3. Real-Time Lighting and Reflection Techniques

Real-time lighting and reflection techniques are essential components of advanced material and shader programming in Unreal Engine. They play a significant role in enhancing the visual quality and realism of a game's environments. In this section, we will explore various real-time lighting and reflection techniques commonly used in Unreal Engine.

Dynamic Lighting

Dynamic lighting refers to lighting that can change in real-time as objects move or the time of day shifts. Unreal Engine provides dynamic lighting systems that simulate the interaction between light sources and surfaces dynamically.

Point Lights and Spotlights

Point lights and spotlights are types of dynamic light sources that emit light in all directions or in a specific cone, respectively. They are commonly used for simulating light bulbs, torches, or headlights.

```
// Create a dynamic point light
PointLight.Create(PointLightLocation, PointLightIntensity);

// Create a dynamic spotlight
Spotlight.Create(SpotlightLocation, SpotlightDirection, SpotlightIntensity);
```

In the code above, we create dynamic point lights and spotlights at specific locations with defined intensities. These lights can cast shadows, illuminate objects, and contribute to the overall scene lighting.

Directional Lights

Directional lights simulate sunlight, which is effectively parallel light rays that illuminate the entire scene uniformly. They are particularly useful for outdoor environments.

```
// Create a dynamic directional light
DirectionalLight.Create(DirectionalLightDirection, DirectionalLightIntensity)
;
```

Directional lights are commonly used to simulate the sun's light. They can create dynamic day-night cycles and cast long shadows across the scene.

Global Illumination

Global Illumination (GI) is a technique that simulates the indirect bouncing of light in a scene. It enhances realism by allowing light to bounce off surfaces and indirectly illuminate other objects.

Ray Tracing

Unreal Engine supports ray tracing, which is a technique for simulating global illumination and other advanced lighting effects. Ray tracing traces the path of light rays as they interact with surfaces, providing highly realistic lighting.

```
// Enable ray tracing for global illumination
Scene.EnableRayTracing(GlobalIllumination);
```

Enabling ray tracing for global illumination enhances the visual quality of scenes, especially when it comes to soft shadows, reflections, and color bleeding from surfaces.

Screen Space Reflections (SSR)

Screen Space Reflections (SSR) is a real-time reflection technique that calculates reflections based on what is currently visible on the screen. It is particularly useful for simulating reflections on surfaces like water, glass, and shiny materials.

```
// Enable Screen Space Reflections
PostProcessing.EnableScreenSpaceReflections(SSRSettings);
```

SSR can create accurate reflections that dynamically change as the camera or objects move. However, it has limitations and may not reflect objects that are not within the screen space.

Reflection Probes

Reflection probes are precomputed or dynamic representations of the environment that capture reflections. They are especially useful for achieving realistic reflections in environments with complex geometry or when SSR is insufficient.

```
// Place a dynamic reflection probe in the scene
ReflectionProbe.Create(ProbeLocation, ProbeCaptureRate);
```

Reflection probes capture the surrounding environment and can be updated dynamically to provide accurate reflections. They are commonly used for interior scenes or areas with reflective surfaces.

Lightmap Baking

Lightmap baking is a process where lighting information is precomputed and stored in texture maps. This technique is useful for achieving high-quality, static lighting in scenes with complex geometry.

```
// Bake lighting for a static scene
LightmapBaker.BakeLighting(SceneGeometry, LightmapResolution);
```

Lightmaps store lighting data for static objects, allowing for detailed and realistic lighting in scenes. However, they are not suitable for dynamic objects or lighting changes.

Conclusion

Real-time lighting and reflection techniques are essential for achieving visual realism in Unreal Engine games. These techniques, such as dynamic lighting, global illumination, screen space reflections, reflection probes, and lightmap baking, allow developers to create visually stunning and immersive environments. Choosing the right combination of techniques depends on the specific requirements of a game and its target platforms. Balancing visual quality with performance is crucial to ensure a smooth and visually appealing gaming experience. In the following sections, we will explore more advanced topics in material and shader programming, including shader optimization for performance.

13.4. Shader Optimization for Performance

Shader optimization is a critical aspect of advanced material and shader programming in Unreal Engine. While creating visually stunning shaders is important, it's equally crucial to ensure that these shaders run efficiently to maintain a high frame rate and provide a smooth gaming experience. In this section, we will explore techniques for optimizing shaders in Unreal Engine.

Importance of Shader Optimization

Shaders are executed on the GPU (Graphics Processing Unit), and their complexity can impact game performance. Optimizing shaders is essential to achieve a balance between visual quality and frame rate, especially on lower-end hardware or in complex scenes.

Profiling and Analysis

Before optimizing shaders, it's essential to identify which shaders are the most performance-intensive. Unreal Engine provides built-in profiling and analysis tools to help developers pinpoint bottlenecks.

Shader Complexity View

The Shader Complexity view in Unreal Engine's debugging tools allows developers to visualize the complexity of shaders in a scene. Shaders with higher complexity are more likely to impact performance.

GPU Profiling

GPU profiling tools, such as Unreal Engine's GPU Visualizer, provide insights into how much time is spent on different GPU tasks, including shader execution. This helps identify which shaders are consuming the most resources.

Shader Complexity Reduction

Reducing shader complexity is the first step in optimization. Techniques for shader complexity reduction include:

Simplifying Calculations

Reviewing shader code to identify and remove unnecessary calculations or operations can significantly reduce complexity. For example, avoiding expensive mathematical functions or conditional statements when they are not needed can improve performance.

Level of Detail (LOD)

Implementing level-of-detail (LOD) shaders allows objects to use simpler shaders when they are farther away from the camera. This reduces the rendering workload for distant objects.

Culling Unseen Shaders

Culling shaders for objects that are not visible to the camera can save GPU resources. Unreal Engine's occlusion culling and frustum culling mechanisms help achieve this.

Texture Optimization

Textures used in shaders can impact performance. Texture optimization techniques include:

Texture Compression

Using texture compression formats, such as DXT, BC, or ASTC, reduces texture memory consumption and can improve shader performance.

Texture Streaming

Texture streaming ensures that only the necessary portions of textures are loaded into memory, reducing memory usage and potentially improving shader performance.

Shader Instancing

Shader instancing allows multiple instances of the same shader to be rendered in a single draw call. This is particularly useful for objects that share the same material and shader, such as foliage or particles.

```
// Use shader instancing for rendering multiple instances with the same shader
ShaderInstancing.Enable(InstanceCount);
```

By enabling shader instancing, the GPU can efficiently render multiple objects with the same shader, reducing the overhead of setting up and executing the shader multiple times.

LOD Shaders

Implementing LOD-specific shaders allows objects to use different shaders based on their level of detail. This can significantly reduce shader complexity for distant objects.

```
// Use LOD-specific shaders to optimize performance at different detail level
s
LODShader.Set(LODLevel);
```

LOD shaders can provide simplified versions of complex shaders for distant objects, ensuring that GPU resources are allocated appropriately.

Conclusion

Shader optimization for performance is essential in Unreal Engine game development to ensure smooth and responsive gameplay, especially in complex and visually rich environments. Profiling and analysis tools help identify performance bottlenecks, while techniques like shader complexity reduction, texture optimization, shader instancing, and LOD-specific shaders can significantly improve the efficiency of shaders. Striking a balance between visual quality and performance is key to delivering an optimal gaming experience on various platforms and hardware configurations. In the following sections, we will continue to explore advanced topics in material and shader programming, including creating interactive materials.

13.5. Creating Interactive Materials

Creating interactive materials is an advanced aspect of material and shader programming in Unreal Engine. Interactive materials allow in-game objects to respond dynamically to player interactions, environmental changes, or other events, enhancing the immersive experience. In this section, we will explore techniques for creating interactive materials.

The Role of Interactive Materials

Interactive materials add depth and realism to a game by making objects appear more dynamic and responsive. These materials can simulate various interactions, such as wet surfaces drying, color changes, or surface deformation. Interactive materials are often used for gameplay mechanics, puzzles, or storytelling elements.

Material Parameters

Interactive materials often rely on material parameters that can be adjusted or animated in real-time. Unreal Engine allows developers to expose and control these parameters to create interactive effects.

```
// Expose a material parameter for interaction
Material.AddParameter(InteractiveParameter);
```

In this example, an interactive parameter is exposed in the material, making it accessible for real-time manipulation.

Material Functions

Material functions are reusable blocks of shader code that can be applied across multiple materials. They are valuable for creating interactive materials as they can encapsulate complex shader logic.

```
// Create a material function for interactive effects
MaterialFunction.Create(InteractiveEffectFunction);
```

Material functions can be used to encapsulate the logic for various interactive effects, making it easier to apply those effects to different materials.

Texture Manipulation

Textures play a crucial role in creating interactive materials. Techniques for texture manipulation include:

Texture Panning

Texture panning involves moving a texture across a surface to simulate motion or change. This can be used for effects like flowing water or scrolling signs.

```
// Implement texture panning for a flowing water effect
Texture.Pan(FlowingWaterTexture, PanDirection, PanSpeed);
```

By panning a texture in the direction and at the speed defined, a flowing water effect can be achieved.

Texture Masking

Texture masking involves blending different textures based on a mask. This can be used to reveal or hide certain parts of an object's material dynamically.

```
// Use texture masking to reveal a hidden message on a surface
Texture.Mask(MessageTexture, MaskTexture);
```

By applying a mask texture to reveal a hidden message, an interactive storytelling element can be created.

Dynamic Material Instances

Dynamic material instances allow developers to create and manipulate material instances in real-time during gameplay. This is particularly useful for interactive materials that respond to player actions.

```
// Create a dynamic material instance for an interactive object
DynamicMaterialInstance.Create(ObjectMaterial);
```

Dynamic material instances can be used to modify material parameters, adjust textures, or trigger interactive effects in response to player interactions.

Blueprint Integration

Unreal Engine's Blueprint system enables designers and artists to create interactive materials without extensive coding. Blueprint nodes can be used to control material parameters, textures, and effects, making it accessible to a broader range of team members.

```
// Use Blueprint nodes to create interactive material behavior
Blueprint.Create(InteractiveMaterialBlueprint);
```

Blueprints can handle complex logic for interactive materials, allowing designers to experiment and iterate without deep shader programming knowledge.

Conclusion

Creating interactive materials is a powerful tool for enhancing gameplay and storytelling in Unreal Engine games. These materials allow for dynamic responses to player interactions, environmental changes, and events, adding depth and immersion to the gaming experience. Material parameters, material functions, texture manipulation, dynamic material instances, and Blueprint integration are key components in achieving interactive effects. By harnessing the capabilities of interactive materials, game developers can create more engaging and memorable experiences for players. In the following sections, we will delve into advanced topics in game development, including game economy and community management.

Chapter 14: Game Economy and Monetization

14.1. Designing In-Game Economies

Designing in-game economies is a crucial aspect of game development, especially for free-to-play and microtransaction-based games. A well-designed game economy can enhance player engagement and enjoyment while also generating revenue for the developer. In this section, we will explore the key principles and strategies for designing in-game economies.

The Importance of Game Economies

In-game economies encompass all the systems and mechanics related to the acquisition, management, and expenditure of in-game resources. These resources can include virtual currency, items, experience points, and more. A well-designed game economy serves several essential purposes:

28. **Player Engagement:** A balanced and rewarding economy keeps players engaged by providing a sense of progression and achievement. Players should feel that their efforts are rewarded adequately.

29. **Monetization:** For free-to-play games, in-game economies are a primary source of revenue. Through microtransactions, players can purchase virtual goods or currency, which contributes to the game's financial success.

30. **Balancing Gameplay:** In-game economies help balance gameplay by ensuring that certain items or abilities are not too overpowered or easily obtainable. This creates a fair and competitive environment.

Key Principles of Game Economies

Effective game economies are built upon several key principles:

1. Supply and Demand:

In-game resources should follow the principles of supply and demand. Scarce resources or items in high demand should be more valuable and challenging to obtain, while common items should be easily accessible. This encourages trading and creates value for in-game currency.

2. Progression:

Players should experience a sense of progression as they accumulate resources and improve their characters or equipment. This progression can be achieved through leveling systems, skill upgrades, or item enhancements.

3. Sinks and Faucets:

Game economies often employ "sinks" and "faucets" to regulate the flow of resources. Sinks remove resources from the economy, typically through item degradation or consumables, while faucets introduce new resources through rewards or achievements.

4. Virtual Currency:

Virtual currency, such as coins, gems, or tokens, serves as a universal medium of exchange in many game economies. It allows players to buy items, upgrade equipment, or unlock features. Balancing the value and availability of virtual currency is crucial.

5. Monetization Opportunities:

For games with microtransactions, it's essential to create opportunities for players to spend real money on virtual goods or currency. These transactions should provide value to players and enhance their gaming experience.

Strategies for Designing In-Game Economies

When designing in-game economies, consider the following strategies:

1. Player-Centric Approach:

Design the economy with the player's experience in mind. Ensure that the progression feels rewarding and that players can achieve their goals without excessive grinding.

2. Balancing Act:

Balance the economy carefully to avoid inflation or deflation of in-game resources. Regularly monitor player behavior and make adjustments as needed.

3. Limited-Time Events:

Introduce limited-time events, sales, or offers to create a sense of urgency and encourage player spending. These events can drive engagement and revenue.

4. Virtual Goods:

Offer virtual goods that enhance gameplay or provide cosmetic benefits. These goods should not disrupt game balance but should provide value to players.

5. Data Analytics:

Leverage data analytics to understand player behavior, spending patterns, and resource management. Use this data to fine-tune the game economy and monetization strategies.

Ethical Considerations

While designing in-game economies for monetization, it's essential to prioritize player satisfaction and ethical practices. Avoid creating pay-to-win scenarios, excessive grind, or manipulative tactics that pressure players into spending money. Transparency and fairness should be at the core of any monetization strategy.

Conclusion

Designing in-game economies is a complex yet essential aspect of game development, impacting player engagement and financial success. By following key principles and employing effective strategies, developers can create balanced, rewarding, and ethical game economies that enhance the player experience while generating revenue. In the following sections, we will explore additional aspects of game monetization, including the implementation of microtransactions and balancing free and paid content.

14.2. Implementing Microtransactions Ethically

Implementing microtransactions in games is a common monetization strategy, but it must be done ethically to maintain player trust and satisfaction. Microtransactions involve offering virtual goods, currency, or content for real money within the game. In this section, we will explore ethical practices and considerations when implementing microtransactions in games.

Ethical Microtransaction Practices

Ethical microtransactions aim to provide value to players while ensuring that the game remains enjoyable and balanced. Here are some ethical practices to consider:

1. Cosmetic Items:

Offer cosmetic items like skins, costumes, or visual customization options that do not affect gameplay. Cosmetic microtransactions allow players to personalize their characters or in-game items without gaining a competitive advantage.

```
// Example of offering cosmetic skins as microtransactions
Microtransaction.AddCosmeticSkin(PlayerCharacter, SkinID);
```

2. Non-Pay-to-Win:

Avoid offering pay-to-win items or advantages that give paying players a significant edge over non-paying players. A level playing field ensures fair competition and player satisfaction.

```
// Implementing non-pay-to-win microtransactions
Microtransaction.AddNon-Pay-to-WinBoost(ItemID);
```

3. Transparency:

Clearly communicate the nature and benefits of microtransactions to players. Provide detailed information about what they are purchasing, including the cosmetic or functional aspects of the items.

```
// Displaying transparent information about microtransactions
Microtransaction.DisplayItemInformation(ItemName, ItemDescription);
```

4. Fair Pricing:

Price microtransactions fairly, ensuring that the cost aligns with the perceived value of the virtual goods or content. Avoid overpricing items, as it can discourage players from making purchases.

```
// Setting fair pricing for microtransactions
Microtransaction.SetItemPrice(ItemID, Price);
```

5. Alternatives:

Provide non-microtransaction paths for obtaining similar in-game content, albeit through time and effort. This allows players to choose between spending money or dedicating gameplay hours.

```
// Offering alternatives for obtaining in-game content
Microtransaction.AddAlternativeQuest(ContentID, QuestRequirements);
```

Loot Boxes and Randomization

Loot boxes or gacha systems, where players spend real money to obtain randomized virtual items, have faced scrutiny for their potential to encourage gambling-like behavior, especially among younger players. When implementing such systems, consider the following ethical guidelines:

1. Transparency:

Clearly disclose the odds of obtaining specific items from loot boxes. Players should have a clear understanding of their chances when making a purchase.

```
// Displaying loot box odds transparently
Microtransaction.DisplayLootBoxOdds(BoxName, OddsTable);
```

2. Purchase Limits:

Set limits on how many loot boxes or randomized items players can purchase within a specified time frame. This helps prevent excessive spending and addiction.

```
// Implementing purchase limits for loot boxes
Microtransaction.SetPurchaseLimit(BoxName, LimitPerDay);
```

Implement age verification measures to ensure that underage players are not engaging in microtransactions involving randomized items.

```
// Implementing age verification for randomized microtransactions
Microtransaction.VerifyAge(PlayerDOB, PurchaseAttempt);
```

Player Feedback and Adjustments

Regularly gather player feedback and reviews regarding microtransactions and their impact on gameplay. Be willing to make adjustments based on this feedback to maintain a positive player experience.

```
// Gathering player feedback on microtransactions
FeedbackSystem.CollectPlayerReviews(MicrotransactionSystem);
```

Conclusion

Implementing microtransactions ethically is essential to build player trust, maintain a healthy player base, and ensure the long-term success of a game. By focusing on ethical practices such as offering cosmetic items, avoiding pay-to-win mechanics, providing transparency, fair pricing, and considering alternatives, developers can create a positive environment for players. Additionally, when implementing loot boxes or randomized microtransactions, transparent disclosure of odds, purchase limits, and age verification can help address concerns related to gambling-like behavior. Ultimately, the goal is to strike a balance between monetization and player satisfaction while upholding ethical standards. In the following sections, we will delve into additional aspects of game monetization, including balancing free and paid content.

14.3. Balancing Free and Paid Content

Balancing free and paid content is a critical consideration in monetizing games, particularly in free-to-play models. Striking the right balance ensures that players can enjoy the game without feeling pressured to spend money while also providing opportunities for monetization. In this section, we will explore strategies for balancing free and paid content effectively.

The Free-to-Play Model

The free-to-play (F2P) model allows players to download and play the game for free, with monetization primarily coming from in-app purchases, microtransactions, or advertisements. A successful F2P game should:

- **Attract a Large Player Base:** Offering the game for free draws in a larger player base, increasing the potential for revenue from a smaller percentage of paying players.

- **Provide a Positive Experience:** Players should have a positive and enjoyable gaming experience without feeling that they are at a disadvantage for not making purchases.

- **Offer Meaningful Monetization:** Monetization options should provide value to players and be enticing without being overly aggressive or intrusive.

Balancing Free Content

Balancing free content is crucial to keep players engaged and create a welcoming environment. Here are some strategies for providing meaningful free content:

1. Core Gameplay:

The core gameplay and essential features should be fully accessible for free players. They should be able to enjoy the game, compete, and progress without purchasing anything.

```
// Ensure core gameplay is available to all players
if (!HasPurchasedPremiumContent) {
    EnableCoreGameplay();
}
```

2. Grind vs. Pay:

While free players should have access to core content, it's acceptable to introduce a level of grind that can be bypassed with purchases. However, the grind should not feel excessive or frustrating.

```
// Implementing an optional grind that can be bypassed with purchases
if (FreePlayerLevel < DesiredLevel) {
    EnableGrindContent();
}
```

3. Cosmetic Customization:

Offer cosmetic customization options for free players. These can include character skins, visual effects, or decorative items that do not impact gameplay.

```
// Provide cosmetic customization options for free players
if (!HasPurchasedCosmeticPack) {
    OfferFreeCosmeticItems();
}
```

4. Daily Rewards:

Implement daily login rewards or bonuses that reward free players for their continued engagement with the game.

```
// Implementing daily rewards to incentivize player engagement
if (IsDailyLogin) {
    GrantDailyReward();
}
```

Enticing Paid Content

Paid content should provide value and appeal to players without breaking the game's balance. Here are strategies for enticing paid content:

1. Convenience:

Offer convenience items that save time or effort, such as experience boosters or resource packs. These items should not provide a significant competitive advantage.

```
// Offer convenience items that do not disrupt game balance
if (WantsXPBoost) {
    PurchaseXPBooster();
}
```

2. Exclusive Content:

Introduce exclusive content that appeals to collectors or enthusiasts. Limited-time skins, unique items, or early access can motivate players to make purchases.

```
// Offer exclusive content for players who make purchases
if (HasPurchasedExclusivePass) {
    UnlockExclusiveContent();
}
```

3. Bundles:

Create value bundles that include multiple items or content at a discounted price compared to purchasing individual items.

```
// Offer value bundles to incentivize spending
if (WantsContentBundle) {
    PurchaseBundle();
}
```

4. Limited Offers:

Implement limited-time offers or sales to create a sense of urgency and encourage players to make purchases.

```
// Introduce limited-time offers to drive spending
if (IsLimitedTimeSale) {
    OfferDiscountedItems();
}
```

Balancing free and paid content requires ongoing monitoring and player feedback. Analyze player behavior, spending patterns, and engagement metrics to make informed adjustments to the monetization strategy. The goal is to create a win-win situation where players can enjoy the game for free while generating revenue from those who choose to make purchases.

```
// Gather player feedback and analyze monetization data
MonetizationSystem.CollectPlayerFeedback();
MonetizationSystem.AnalyzeSpendingPatterns();
```

Conclusion

Balancing free and paid content is a delicate task in game monetization, but it's essential for creating a positive player experience and generating revenue. By providing meaningful free content, enticing paid options, and regularly monitoring player behavior, developers can find the right equilibrium that benefits both players and the game's financial success. Striking this balance contributes to a healthy player base and the long-term sustainability of the game. In the following sections, we will delve into additional aspects of game development, including analytics and player spending behavior.

14.4. Analytics and Player Spending Behavior

Understanding player spending behavior through analytics is crucial for optimizing monetization strategies in games. Analytics tools allow developers to gather valuable data about player actions, preferences, and spending patterns. In this section, we will explore the role of analytics and how it can be used to enhance game monetization.

The Importance of Analytics

Analytics provide insights into player behavior, enabling developers to make data-driven decisions. By analyzing player spending behavior, developers can:

- **Identify Trends:** Analytics tools can reveal trends in player spending, such as popular items or purchasing patterns.

- **Optimize Monetization:** Data can help fine-tune pricing, discounts, and the timing of in-game offers to maximize revenue.

- **Personalize Offers:** Understanding individual player spending behavior allows for personalized offers and recommendations, increasing the likelihood of purchases.

Data Collection

To gather data on player spending behavior, various types of data can be collected:

1. Purchase History:

Recording each player's purchase history provides insights into their spending habits, including the frequency and types of purchases made.

```
// Collect and store player purchase history data
Analytics.RecordPurchaseHistory(PlayerID, PurchaseDetails);
```

2. In-Game Actions:

Monitoring in-game actions such as item browsing, wish-listing, and cart interactions can indicate player interest in certain items.

```
// Track in-game actions related to potential purchases
Analytics.TrackItemBrowsing(PlayerID, ItemID);
```

3. Player Profiles:

Creating player profiles that include demographic information, preferences, and spending history can help tailor offers.

```
// Build and update player profiles with relevant data
Analytics.UpdatePlayerProfile(PlayerID, ProfileData);
```

Analyzing Player Spending

Analytics tools enable developers to analyze player spending in various ways:

1. Segmentation:

Segment players into groups based on spending behavior. For example, categorize players as non-spenders, occasional spenders, or whales (heavy spenders). This allows for targeted marketing and offers.

```
// Segment players based on spending behavior
Analytics.SegmentPlayersBySpending(PlayerData);
```

2. Conversion Rates:

Analyze conversion rates to determine the percentage of players who make purchases after engaging with in-game offers or advertisements.

```
// Calculate conversion rates for different in-game offers
Analytics.CalculateConversionRates(OffersData);
```

3. Funnel Analysis:

Use funnel analysis to track the steps players take before making a purchase, identifying potential drop-off points.

```
// Perform funnel analysis to optimize the purchase process
Analytics.FunnelAnalysis(PurchaseFunnelData);
```

4. Lifetime Value (LTV):

Calculate the lifetime value of players to understand their overall spending potential. This helps prioritize player retention efforts.

```
// Calculate the lifetime value of players
Analytics.CalculatePlayerLTV(PlayerID, PurchaseData);
```

A/B Testing

A/B testing involves comparing two versions of an in-game offer or monetization strategy to determine which one performs better in terms of player spending behavior. This iterative approach helps refine monetization strategies based on real player data.

```
// Implement A/B testing to compare different monetization strategies
Analytics.ABTest(StrategyA, StrategyB);
```

Privacy Considerations

When collecting and analyzing player spending behavior, it's crucial to respect player privacy and comply with relevant regulations, such as GDPR or COPPA. Ensure that player data is anonymized and secured to protect player identities and information.

Conclusion

Analytics play a pivotal role in understanding player spending behavior and optimizing monetization strategies in games. By collecting data on purchase history, in-game actions, and player profiles, developers can gain valuable insights into player preferences. Analyzing this data allows for segmentation, conversion rate analysis, funnel tracking, and the calculation of player lifetime value. A/B testing provides a practical way to refine monetization strategies based on real player data. However, it's essential to handle player data with care and respect player privacy to build trust and maintain ethical practices. In the following sections, we will explore additional aspects of game development, including legal considerations in game monetization.

14.5. Legal Considerations in Game Monetization

Game developers must navigate a complex landscape of legal considerations when implementing monetization strategies. Ensuring compliance with laws and regulations is essential to avoid legal issues and protect both players and developers. In this section, we will explore key legal considerations in game monetization.

1. Age Restrictions:

Games with certain monetization strategies, such as loot boxes or in-app purchases, may be subject to age restrictions in some regions. It's essential to verify the age of players and restrict access to specific features or purchases based on age.

```
// Implement age verification for age-restricted features
if (PlayerAge < LegalAgeLimit) {
    RestrictAccessToFeatures();
}
```

2. Consumer Protection Laws:

Consumer protection laws require transparency and fairness in monetization practices. Developers must clearly disclose the terms of in-app purchases, refund policies, and any randomization mechanics in compliance with these laws.

```
// Display clear and transparent terms of in-app purchases
MonetizationSystem.DisplayPurchaseTerms(PurchaseDetails);
```

3. Privacy Regulations:

When collecting player data for analytics or monetization, developers must comply with privacy regulations such as GDPR or CCPA. This includes obtaining informed consent for data collection and ensuring the security of player data.

```
// Obtain informed consent for data collection
PlayerDataCollection.GetPlayerConsent(PlayerID);
```

4. Gambling Laws:

Loot boxes and randomized microtransactions have faced scrutiny for resembling gambling. Developers should be aware of gambling laws in different regions and ensure compliance when implementing these mechanics.

```
// Implement region-specific restrictions on loot box mechanics
if (RegionHasStrictGamblingLaws) {
    RestrictLootBoxAccess();
}
```

5. Advertising Standards:

Advertisements within games must adhere to advertising standards and regulations. Ensure that advertisements are not deceptive, misleading, or inappropriate.

```
// Monitor and review in-game advertisements for compliance
AdvertisingSystem.MaintainAdherenceToStandards();
```

6. Intellectual Property Rights:

Developers must respect intellectual property rights when creating in-game content. Avoid using copyrighted material without proper licensing or permission.

```
// Ensure all in-game assets are created or licensed legally
AssetRightsVerification.VerifyAssetLicensing(AssetID);
```

7. Terms of Service and End-User License Agreements (EULAs):

Clearly outline the terms of service and EULAs that govern the use of the game and its monetization features. Players must accept these agreements before playing.

```
// Display and require acceptance of the game's EULA
PlayerAgreementSystem.DisplayEULA(EULAContent);
```

8. Regulatory Updates:

Stay informed about regulatory changes and updates related to game monetization. Laws and regulations can evolve, and developers should adapt their practices accordingly.

```
// Regularly review and adapt monetization practices based on regulatory upda
tes
LegalComplianceTeam.MonitorRegulatoryChanges();
```

9. Player Support and Dispute Resolution:

Establish a system for addressing player concerns and resolving disputes related to monetization, refunds, or in-game purchases. Timely and fair resolution is crucial to maintaining player trust.

```
// Provide a player support system for handling monetization-related inquirie
s and issues
PlayerSupportSystem.HandleMonetizationDisputes(DisputeDetails);
```

10. Global Compliance:

Consider the global nature of the gaming industry and ensure compliance with the laws and regulations of the regions where your game is available. Seek legal counsel or consulting when necessary to navigate international legal complexities.

```
// Consult with legal experts to ensure global compliance
LegalComplianceTeam.EnlistLegalCounsel(RegionSpecificLaws);
```

Conclusion

Legal considerations in game monetization are critical for developers to avoid legal troubles, protect players, and maintain ethical practices. Adhering to age restrictions, consumer protection laws, privacy regulations, and advertising standards is essential. Developers should also be aware of gambling laws, respect intellectual property rights, and create clear terms of service and EULAs. Staying updated on regulatory changes and providing player support for dispute resolution are additional steps toward ensuring compliance. By prioritizing legal compliance, developers can build trust with players and foster a positive gaming environment. In the following sections, we will delve into aspects of game development such as localization and cultural adaptation.

Chapter 15: Localization and Cultural Adaptation

15.1. Preparing Games for International Markets

As the global gaming market continues to grow, game developers need to consider localization and cultural adaptation to reach a wider audience. Localization involves tailoring a game's content to suit the preferences and language of specific regions. In this section, we will explore the importance of preparing games for international markets and the key steps involved in localization.

The Importance of Localization

Localization goes beyond simply translating text; it encompasses cultural, linguistic, and regional aspects. Here's why localization is crucial:

31. **Wider Audience Reach:** Localization allows your game to connect with players from different parts of the world who may not be proficient in the game's original language.

32. **Enhanced User Experience:** Players feel more engaged and immersed in a game that reflects their culture and language, leading to a better user experience.

33. **Cultural Sensitivity:** Adapting content to different cultures ensures that it is respectful and avoids unintentional offense.

34. **Competitive Advantage:** Localizing your game can give you a competitive edge in international markets, where players prefer games in their native language.

Key Steps in Game Localization

Successful game localization involves several key steps:

1. Market Research:
- Identify target markets based on factors like language, culture, and gaming preferences.
- Analyze the competition and market trends in each region.

2. Language Translation:
- Translate all in-game text, including dialogues, menus, and tutorials, into the target language.
- Ensure that translations are accurate and culturally relevant.

```
// Example of text translation function
LocalizedText = Localization.TranslateText("Hello, welcome to the game!", Tar
getLanguage);
```

3. Cultural Adaptation:
- Modify visuals, symbols, and icons to be culturally appropriate.

- Adjust gameplay elements, such as difficulty levels or character names, to suit local preferences.

4. Localization Testing:

- Conduct testing to ensure that the localized version of the game functions correctly.
- Address any language-specific bugs or issues that may arise.

```
// Test the game with native speakers to identify issues
LocalizationTesting.PerformQualityAssurance(TargetLocale);
```

5. Audio Localization:

- Provide voiceovers or subtitles in the target language for spoken content.
- Ensure that audio elements are synchronized with the on-screen actions.

```
// Implement audio localization with voiceovers
AudioLocalization.AddLocalizedVoiceovers(TargetLanguage);
```

6. Legal and Regulatory Compliance:

- Verify compliance with local laws, including content ratings and restrictions.
- Address any legal requirements for data protection and privacy.

7. User Interface (UI) Adaptation:

- Modify UI elements to accommodate longer or shorter text strings in the target language.
- Ensure that UI elements align with cultural expectations.

```
// Adjust UI layout for text expansion or contraction
UIAdaptation.AdaptForLocalization(TargetLocale);
```

8. Marketing and Promotion:

- Create localized marketing materials, including advertisements and trailers.
- Engage with local gaming communities and influencers for promotion.

9. Post-launch Support:

- Continuously update and maintain the localized version of the game, addressing player feedback and issues.

Conclusion

Preparing games for international markets through localization and cultural adaptation is essential for success in the global gaming industry. It involves much more than language translation and encompasses various aspects of a game, including visuals, gameplay, and audio. By conducting thorough market research and following the key steps in localization, developers can ensure that their games resonate with players from diverse cultures and backgrounds. This approach not only expands the game's reach but also fosters a more inclusive and engaging gaming experience. In the following sections, we will explore additional aspects of game development, including handling text and voice-over translation.

15.2. Cultural Sensitivity and Localization

Cultural sensitivity is a fundamental aspect of game localization that goes beyond language translation. It involves understanding and respecting the cultural norms, values, and sensitivities of the target audience. Failing to be culturally sensitive can lead to misunderstandings, offense, and even the rejection of a game by players in certain regions. In this section, we will delve into the importance of cultural sensitivity in game localization and how to achieve it.

The Significance of Cultural Sensitivity

Cultural sensitivity is vital for several reasons:

35. **Respect**: It demonstrates respect for the cultural diversity of your players and acknowledges that their experiences and perspectives are important.

36. **Avoiding Offense**: Cultural insensitivity can lead to misunderstandings or unintentional offense, potentially harming the game's reputation.

37. **Immersion**: A culturally sensitive game feels more immersive and relatable to players, enhancing their overall experience.

Key Considerations for Cultural Sensitivity

Here are key considerations to ensure cultural sensitivity in game localization:

1. Language Nuances:
- Understand that idioms, metaphors, and humor may not have the same meaning or impact in different cultures.
- Avoid literal translations that may not convey the intended message.

```
// Use cultural consultants for idiomatic translations
LocalizedText = Localization.TranslateWithCulturalSensitivity("Break a leg!",
TargetLanguage);
```

2. Visual and Artistic Elements:
- Adapt visuals, character designs, and symbols to respect cultural norms and sensitivities.
- Be cautious with religious, political, or controversial imagery.

```
// Modify character designs to align with cultural expectations
ArtLocalization.AdaptCharacterDesigns(TargetCulture);
```

3. Narrative and Storytelling:
- Ensure that the game's narrative and storyline are culturally relevant and do not perpetuate stereotypes or biases.
- Seek feedback from cultural consultants or local experts.

```
// Collaborate with cultural consultants to review and refine the storyline
NarrativeLocalization.ReceiveCulturalFeedback();
```

4. Social and Etiquette Norms:

- Understand social norms, customs, and etiquette in the target culture.
- Adjust character interactions and dialogue to be culturally appropriate.

```
// Customize character interactions to reflect cultural etiquette
CharacterBehavior.AdaptToCulturalNorms(TargetLocale);
```

5. Sensitivity Testing:

- Conduct sensitivity testing with players or cultural experts from the target region to identify potential issues.

```
// Perform sensitivity testing to gather feedback
SensitivityTesting.GatherFeedbackFromCulturalExperts(TargetRegion);
```

6. Historical and Cultural References:

- Verify the accuracy and appropriateness of historical and cultural references.
- Avoid making assumptions about players' knowledge of specific cultures.

```
// Conduct research to ensure accurate cultural references
CulturalReferences.VerifyHistoricalAccuracy(TargetCulture);
```

Collaboration and Expertise

Achieving cultural sensitivity in game localization often requires collaboration with cultural consultants, experts, or native speakers who can provide insights and guidance. Their expertise can help navigate cultural nuances and avoid potential pitfalls.

```
// Collaborate with cultural experts for in-depth cultural knowledge
CulturalConsultants.ProvideCulturalInsights(TargetCulture);
```

Conclusion

Cultural sensitivity is an integral part of game localization that promotes understanding, respect, and a positive gaming experience. It involves considering language nuances, adapting visual elements, being mindful of storytelling, and understanding social norms. Sensitivity testing and collaboration with cultural experts are essential for ensuring that the game resonates with players from different cultures while avoiding cultural insensitivity or offense. By prioritizing cultural sensitivity, developers can create games that are inclusive, engaging, and well-received in diverse global markets. In the following sections, we will explore other aspects of game development, including handling text and voice-over translation.

15.3. Handling Text and Voice Over Translation

Text and voice-over translation are integral components of game localization, as they directly impact how players interact with the game and understand the storyline. In this section, we will explore best practices for handling text and voice-over translation in game localization.

Text Translation

Text translation involves converting all in-game text, including dialogues, menus, subtitles, and tutorials, into the target language. Here are key considerations:

38. **Accuracy**: Ensure that translations are accurate and contextually appropriate to convey the intended meaning. Misinterpretations can lead to confusion.

```
// Use professional translators for accurate text translation
LocalizedText = Localization.TranslateText("Welcome to the adventure!", Targe
tLanguage);
```

2. **Character Limits**: Different languages may require more or fewer characters to express the same idea. Design the user interface (UI) to accommodate text expansion or contraction.

```
// Implement dynamic UI elements that adjust to varying text lengths
UI.AdaptForTextExpansion(TextInTargetLanguage);
```

3. **Cultural Relevance**: Consider cultural norms and references in the translated text. Some jokes or references may not make sense in the target culture.

```
// Collaborate with cultural consultants to ensure cultural relevance
CulturalConsultants.ProvideCulturalInsights(TargetCulture);
```

4. **Consistency**: Maintain consistency in terminology and naming conventions throughout the game. Use a glossary or style guide for reference.

```
// Create and follow a style guide for consistent terminology
TranslationStyleGuide.EnforceConsistency(TargetLanguage);
```

5. **Contextual Clarity**: Provide translators with context to ensure they understand the narrative and can translate dialogues appropriately.

```
// Share context and storyline details with translators
ContextualInformation.ProvideNarrativeContext(Translator);
```

Voice-Over Translation

Voice-over translation involves providing spoken content in the target language, such as character dialogues, narration, and in-game announcements. Here's how to handle voice-over translation effectively:

39. **Professional Voice Actors**: Hire native-speaking voice actors who are fluent in the target language to ensure authenticity and quality.

```
// Collaborate with professional voice actors for authentic voice-overs
VoiceOverLocalization.HireNativeSpeakers(TargetLanguage);
```

2. **Synchronization**: Ensure that the voice-over audio is synchronized with on-screen actions and character animations.

```
// Coordinate timing and synchronization of voice-over recordings
VoiceOverSynchronization.AlignWithOnScreenActions();
```

3. **Lip Syncing**: Adjust character lip syncing animations to match the spoken language. This may involve reanimating character models.

```
// Modify character animations for accurate lip syncing
LipSyncLocalization.AdaptAnimationsToLanguage(TargetLanguage);
```

4. **Testing and Quality Assurance**: Conduct testing to ensure that voice-over translations fit seamlessly into the game and that audio levels are balanced.

```
// Perform audio testing to check voice-over quality and balance
AudioTesting.EvaluateVoiceOverQuality(TargetLocale);
```

Multilingual Support

To cater to a global audience, consider providing multiple language options in the game settings. Allow players to switch between languages based on their preferences.

```
// Implement language options in the game settings menu
MultilingualSupport.AllowLanguageSelection();
```

Conclusion

Text and voice-over translation are pivotal aspects of game localization, enabling players to engage with the game in their preferred language. Ensuring accuracy, cultural relevance, and consistency in translated text is essential. For voice-over translation, hiring professional voice actors and synchronizing audio with the game's visuals are key considerations. Multilingual support further enhances the game's accessibility and appeal to a diverse audience. By following these best practices, developers can create localized versions of their games that resonate with players worldwide, offering an immersive and enjoyable gaming experience. In the following sections, we will explore more aspects of game development, including adapting visuals for different cultures.

15.4. Adapting Visuals for Different Cultures

Visual elements play a crucial role in game localization, as they convey information, set the game's atmosphere, and immerse players in the virtual world. Adapting visuals for different cultures is essential to ensure that the game is well-received and culturally sensitive. In this section, we will explore strategies for adapting visuals during game localization.

Visual Considerations

When adapting visuals for different cultures, consider the following:

40. **Icons and Symbols**: Icons and symbols may have different meanings in various cultures. Ensure that visual symbols are universally understood and do not convey unintended messages.

```
// Replace culturally sensitive symbols with neutral alternatives
VisualLocalization.AdaptSymbolsForCulturalSensitivity(TargetCulture);
```

2. **Character Designs**: Characters' appearances, clothing, and accessories should align with cultural norms and sensitivities. Avoid stereotypes and cultural appropriation.

```
// Modify character designs to be culturally appropriate
CharacterDesign.AdaptToCulturalNorms(TargetLocale);
```

3. **Environment and Setting**: Adapt the game's environment to reflect the architecture, landscapes, and aesthetics of the target culture. This enhances player immersion.

```
// Customize in-game environments to match the target culture's style
EnvironmentLocalization.AdaptToCulturalAesthetics(TargetCulture);
```

4. **Color Choices**: Different cultures associate different meanings with colors. Be mindful of color choices in user interfaces, characters, and environments.

```
// Select color palettes that resonate positively with the target culture
ColorSchemeSelection.ChooseColorsBasedOnCulturalPreferences(TargetLocale);
```

Cultural Sensitivity

Cultural sensitivity extends to visuals and involves avoiding imagery, symbols, or designs that could be considered offensive or disrespectful in the target culture.

41. **Religious Imagery**: Steer clear of religious symbols and iconography unless they are central to the game's narrative and are treated with respect.

```
// Consult with cultural experts when incorporating religious imagery
CulturalConsultants.ProvideGuidanceOnReligiousSymbols(TargetCulture);
```

2. **Gender and Clothing**: Be sensitive to gender norms and clothing styles in the target culture. Avoid reinforcing stereotypes or biases.

```
// Adapt character clothing and styles to be culturally inclusive
GenderSensitivity.AdjustCharacterDesignsForCulturalAcceptance(TargetLocale);
```

3. **Cultural References**: Ensure that references to historical events, figures, or cultural phenomena are accurate and culturally relevant.

```
// Verify the accuracy and appropriateness of cultural references
CulturalReferences.ValidateHistoricalAccuracy(TargetCulture);
```

Collaboration and Feedback

Working with cultural consultants, local experts, or native players can provide valuable insights and feedback on visual adaptations.

```
// Collaborate with local players for feedback on visual adaptations
LocalPlayerFeedback.GatherInputForVisualChanges(TargetRegion);
```

Conduct localization testing to ensure that visual adaptations are well-received and culturally appropriate. Seek feedback from players in the target culture.

```
// Perform visual localization testing with native players
VisualLocalizationTesting.GatherFeedbackForImprovements(TargetLocale);
```

Conclusion

Adapting visuals for different cultures is a critical aspect of game localization that contributes to player engagement and cultural sensitivity. Consider the meaning of symbols, character designs, environments, and color choices in the target culture. Avoid offensive imagery and stereotypes, and collaborate with cultural experts and local players for feedback. Localization testing is essential to ensure that visual adaptations resonate positively with the target audience. By paying attention to these visual considerations, developers can create localized versions of their games that are inclusive, respectful, and enjoyable for players from diverse cultural backgrounds. In the following sections, we will explore more aspects of game development, including global marketing strategies for games.

15.5. Global Marketing Strategies for Games

Once a game has been successfully localized and culturally adapted, the next step is to effectively market it to a global audience. Global marketing strategies are essential to reach players in various regions and maximize a game's success. In this section, we will explore key strategies for marketing games on a global scale.

Market Research

Before launching a global marketing campaign, conduct thorough market research to understand the preferences, behaviors, and trends in different regions. Key considerations include:

42. **Target Audience**: Identify the primary and secondary target audiences for the game in each region. Understand their gaming habits and preferences.

```
// Analyze player demographics and preferences in the target region
MarketResearch.AnalyzeTargetAudience(TargetRegion);
```

2. **Competitive Analysis**: Analyze the competition in each region and identify opportunities for differentiation and market positioning.

```
// Study competitors' games and marketing strategies in the target market
MarketAnalysis.EvaluateCompetition(TargetLocale);
```

3. **Cultural Insights**: Leverage cultural insights gained during localization to tailor marketing messages and visuals for cultural relevance.

```
// Incorporate cultural nuances into marketing materials
CulturalInsights.IntegrateLocalizationFindingsIntoMarketing(TargetCulture);
```

Multilingual Marketing Materials

Create marketing materials, including advertisements, trailers, and social media content, in multiple languages to cater to diverse audiences.

```
// Develop multilingual marketing campaigns with translated content
MultilingualMarketing.CreateLocalizedCampaigns(TargetLanguages);
```

Localized Advertising

Consider running region-specific advertising campaigns on platforms popular in each target region. Localized ads are more likely to resonate with local audiences.

```
// Launch targeted advertising campaigns on local platforms
LocalizedAdvertising.RunRegionSpecificAds(TargetRegion);
```

Engage Local Gaming Communities

Engage with local gaming communities, forums, and social media groups to build a presence and foster relationships with players.

```
// Participate in discussions and events within local gaming communities
CommunityEngagement.BuildLocalGamingPresence(TargetRegion);
```

Influencer Marketing

Collaborate with local gaming influencers and streamers who have a substantial following in the target region.

```
// Partner with local gaming influencers for game promotion
InfluencerCollaboration.EngageWithLocalInfluencers(TargetLocale);
```

Cultural Events and Festivals

Participate in cultural events, gaming conventions, and festivals in the target region to showcase the game.

```
// Exhibit the game at local gaming conventions and events
EventParticipation.ShowcaseGameAtLocalEvents(TargetCulture);
```

User Reviews and Feedback

Encourage players to leave reviews and provide feedback on localized versions of the game. Address issues promptly to improve player satisfaction.

```
// Solicit and respond to user reviews and feedback in each language
UserFeedbackCollection.ActivelyEngageWithPlayers(TargetLanguages);
```

Analytics and Iteration

Use analytics tools to track the performance of marketing campaigns and player engagement in different regions. Iterate marketing strategies based on data-driven insights.

```
// Analyze marketing campaign performance and adjust strategies as needed
MarketingAnalytics.TrackCampaignEffectiveness(TargetRegions);
```

Localization of Marketing Analytics

Ensure that analytics tools and dashboards are localized to support analysis of marketing campaign effectiveness in multiple languages.

```
// Implement localized analytics dashboards for campaign evaluation
LocalizedAnalytics.SupportMultipleLanguagesForDataAnalysis(TargetLanguages);
```

Conclusion

Global marketing strategies are essential for introducing localized games to a diverse and international audience. Thorough market research, multilingual marketing materials, localized advertising, engagement with local gaming communities, and collaboration with influencers are key components of a successful global marketing campaign. Continuous monitoring of campaign performance and adaptation based on data-driven insights are crucial for maximizing the game's success in various regions. By implementing these strategies, developers can ensure that their games reach a wide and engaged global audience, contributing to the game's overall success and longevity. In the following sections, we will explore additional aspects of game development, including game testing and quality assurance.

Chapter 16: Building and Managing Game Communities

Section 16.1: Fostering Online Communities

Building and fostering online communities is a critical aspect of modern game development. A strong and engaged community can contribute to the success and longevity of a game. Here, we'll explore strategies and best practices for creating and nurturing vibrant game communities.

Why Community Matters

Online communities provide a space for players to connect, share experiences, and offer feedback. They can also serve as a marketing tool, generating word-of-mouth recommendations and attracting new players. Engaged communities often result in longer player retention and increased player satisfaction.

Community Building Strategies

1. Clear Communication Channels
- Establish clear communication channels such as official forums, social media profiles, and Discord servers. These platforms should be easily accessible to players.
- Appoint community managers or moderators to maintain a respectful and welcoming environment.

2. Regular Updates and Engagement
- Keep the community engaged with regular updates, developer blogs, and sneak peeks at upcoming content.
- Respond to player feedback and involve the community in decision-making when appropriate.

3. Events and Tournaments
- Organize in-game events, tournaments, or contests to encourage player participation and competition.
- Reward active community members with in-game perks or recognition.

4. Transparency and Honesty
- Be transparent about the development process, including challenges and setbacks.
- Address issues promptly and honestly, building trust within the community.

5. User-Generated Content
- Encourage and support user-generated content (UGC) creation. Mods, fan art, and community-made content can enrich the game's ecosystem.

Leveraging Social Media

Social media is a powerful tool for community building:

- **Engage Across Platforms**: Maintain an active presence on platforms like Twitter, Facebook, Instagram, and YouTube.
- **Use Hashtags**: Create and promote game-related hashtags to facilitate discussions and trends.
- **Live Streams and Q&A**: Host live streams, developer Q&A sessions, or AMAs (Ask Me Anything) to connect directly with the community.

Handling Negative Feedback

Dealing with negative feedback is essential for community management:

- **Stay Calm and Professional**: Respond to criticism professionally and avoid becoming defensive.
- **Constructive Feedback**: Encourage players to provide constructive criticism and suggest solutions.
- **Moderation**: Enforce community guidelines to maintain a respectful environment, but be cautious not to stifle healthy discussions.

Community Growth

As your community grows, consider:

- **Community Ambassadors**: Identify passionate and helpful community members to become ambassadors who can assist newcomers.
- **Localizing Content**: If your game has a global audience, consider localizing community content to reach a wider player base.
- **Feedback Iteration**: Continuously improve community engagement based on feedback and changing trends.

Remember that building a thriving game community takes time and effort. Consistent, positive engagement and a commitment to fostering a welcoming atmosphere are key to success.

By following these strategies and maintaining an active presence, you can create a supportive and enthusiastic community around your game, contributing to its long-term success.

Section 16.2: Community Engagement and Support

In this section, we'll delve into the importance of community engagement and support in building a strong and loyal player base. Effective community management goes beyond just creating a space for players to interact; it involves actively nurturing relationships and addressing player needs.

Community managers play a crucial role in ensuring that the game's community thrives. They are the bridge between the players and the development team. Here are some key responsibilities of community managers:

- **Regular Interaction**: Community managers should engage with players daily, responding to questions, feedback, and discussions.
- **Feedback Collection**: Actively gather and compile player feedback to provide valuable insights to the development team.
- **Event Planning**: Organize community events, contests, and giveaways to keep players engaged.
- **Conflict Resolution**: Address conflicts and disputes within the community professionally and impartially.
- **Content Promotion**: Share player-created content, fan art, and other community contributions to celebrate the player community's creativity.

Creating an Inclusive Environment

Inclusivity is vital for community health. Everyone should feel welcome and respected, regardless of their background, identity, or skill level. Here are some ways to foster inclusivity:

- **Clear Code of Conduct**: Establish a clear and comprehensive code of conduct that outlines expected behavior and consequences for violations.
- **Diverse Representation**: Ensure that your game and community materials reflect diverse characters, backgrounds, and perspectives.
- **Moderation Guidelines**: Train moderators to enforce community guidelines fairly and consistently.

Support Channels

Providing efficient support channels is essential for community satisfaction. Players encounter various issues, and they need a way to seek help. Consider these support options:

- **Help Desk or Ticket System**: Set up a system where players can submit support tickets for technical issues or account-related problems.
- **Community Forums**: Create dedicated forums for players to seek help, share tips, and troubleshoot together.
- **Official Support Email**: Offer an official support email address for players to contact with inquiries or issues.

Community Feedback Integration

Player feedback is a goldmine of information for improving the game. Here's how to effectively integrate community feedback:

- **Feedback Aggregation**: Collect feedback from various sources, including forums, social media, and in-game surveys.
- **Prioritization**: Prioritize feedback based on its impact on the player experience and the feasibility of implementation.
- **Communication**: Keep the community informed about changes and updates resulting from their feedback.

Regular Updates and Communication

Consistent communication keeps the community engaged and informed about the game's development. Consider the following:

- **Development Roadmaps**: Share development roadmaps, showcasing what players can expect in upcoming updates.
- **Developer Blogs**: Publish developer blogs detailing behind-the-scenes insights, challenges, and progress.
- **Newsletters**: Send out newsletters with highlights, community spotlights, and important announcements.

Celebrating Milestones

Acknowledging and celebrating community milestones can boost morale and create a sense of belonging. Recognize achievements like:

- **Player Achievements**: Highlight notable in-game accomplishments or contributions.
- **Community Growth**: Celebrate reaching specific community size milestones with special events or rewards.

Remember, effective community engagement is an ongoing effort that requires genuine care and attention. Building a strong player community not only benefits the game but also enhances the overall gaming experience for everyone involved.

Section 16.3: Handling Feedback and Player Contributions

Handling feedback and player contributions is a critical aspect of community management. Players are often eager to share their thoughts, ideas, and content related to the game. Properly managing this feedback and fostering a sense of collaboration can lead to a more engaged and satisfied player community.

Collecting Player Feedback

Collecting player feedback is the first step in addressing player concerns and improving the game. Here are some methods to gather feedback effectively:

- **In-Game Surveys**: Implement in-game surveys that ask players about their experiences, preferences, and suggestions.
- **Official Forums**: Create dedicated sections on official forums where players can post feedback and suggestions.
- **Social Media Listening**: Monitor social media platforms for mentions, comments, and discussions related to the game.
- **Community Representatives**: Appoint community representatives or ambassadors to collect and relay feedback to the development team.

Prioritizing Feedback

Not all feedback is equally important or feasible to implement. Prioritization is key to efficiently address player concerns. Consider the following factors when prioritizing feedback:

- **Impact on Gameplay**: Evaluate how addressing a particular feedback item would impact the overall player experience.
- **Technical Feasibility**: Assess whether implementing a suggested change is technically feasible within the game's constraints.
- **Community Consensus**: Pay attention to feedback that receives widespread support or multiple mentions from the community.
- **Development Resources**: Consider the availability of development resources and the time required for implementation.

Acknowledging and Responding

Acknowledging player feedback is crucial to show that their input is valued. Here's how to effectively acknowledge and respond to feedback:

- **Timely Responses**: Respond to feedback and suggestions promptly, even if it's to acknowledge receipt and state that it's being considered.
- **Constructive Responses**: When providing a response, maintain a constructive and positive tone, even if the feedback is negative.
- **Thanking Contributors**: Express gratitude to players who take the time to provide valuable feedback or contribute to the community in meaningful ways.

Encouraging Player Contributions

Fostering a sense of collaboration and creativity among players can lead to valuable player contributions. Here are some ways to encourage player contributions:

- **Content Creation Contests**: Host contests for player-created content such as fan art, stories, or mods.
- **Community Spotlight**: Regularly feature and showcase exceptional player contributions on official platforms.
- **Open Development Discussions**: Involve the community in discussions about upcoming features or changes, seeking their input and ideas.

Negative feedback is inevitable, but it can be an opportunity for growth. Here's how to handle negative feedback effectively:

- **Active Listening**: Carefully listen to the concerns and frustrations expressed by players without becoming defensive.
- **Empathy**: Show empathy by acknowledging the player's feelings and concerns.
- **Actionable Steps**: If possible, outline steps or plans for addressing the issues raised in the feedback.

Iterative Improvement

Community feedback and player contributions should be seen as part of an iterative improvement process. Continuously gathering and acting upon feedback helps in creating a game that aligns better with player expectations and preferences. It also strengthens the bond between the development team and the player community, fostering a sense of ownership and involvement in the game's evolution.

In conclusion, handling feedback and player contributions is a dynamic and ongoing process that plays a crucial role in community management. When done effectively, it not only leads to a better gaming experience but also cultivates a loyal and engaged player community.

Section 16.4: Moderation and Community Guidelines

Moderation and the establishment of clear community guidelines are essential for maintaining a healthy and welcoming game community. In this section, we'll explore the significance of moderation and how to create effective community guidelines that promote a positive environment.

The Role of Moderation

Community moderation involves monitoring and managing the interactions within the community. It aims to ensure that discussions and behavior align with the established guidelines. Here's why moderation is crucial:

- **Maintaining Civility**: Moderators enforce rules that promote respectful and civil behavior, preventing toxicity and harassment.
- **Content Quality**: They help maintain the quality of content by removing spam, irrelevant posts, and inappropriate content.
- **Conflict Resolution**: Moderators step in to address disputes and conflicts within the community, promoting a harmonious atmosphere.
- **Protecting Vulnerable Users**: Moderation helps protect vulnerable or younger players from harmful content and interactions.

Clear and well-defined community guidelines serve as the foundation for a healthy community. Here's how to create effective guidelines:

- **Clarity**: Ensure that guidelines are written in a clear and understandable manner, avoiding ambiguity.
- **Relevance**: Focus on the specific needs and expectations of your community and game.
- **Scope**: Cover a broad range of topics, including behavior, content, language, and engagement.
- **Positive Language**: Frame guidelines positively, emphasizing what is encouraged rather than just listing prohibitions.
- **Accessibility**: Make guidelines easily accessible to all community members, ideally through multiple platforms.

Common Elements in Community Guidelines

While guidelines should be tailored to your community, some common elements often included are:

- **Respect**: Emphasize the importance of respecting others' opinions, identities, and boundaries.
- **Harassment and Hate Speech**: Clearly state that harassment, hate speech, and discrimination will not be tolerated.
- **Spam and Self-Promotion**: Address guidelines related to spamming and excessive self-promotion.
- **Content Standards**: Define what types of content are allowed and what may be considered inappropriate.
- **Consequences**: Outline the consequences for violating guidelines, which may include warnings, temporary suspensions, or permanent bans.

Transparency in Moderation

Transparency is crucial in moderation to maintain trust within the community. Consider implementing the following practices:

- **Public Moderation Logs**: Publish logs or summaries of moderation actions, excluding sensitive user information.
- **Appeal Process**: Provide a clear process for users to appeal moderation decisions they believe were made in error.
- **Community Involvement**: Involve the community in discussions about potential guideline updates or changes.

Moderation Tools

To effectively moderate your community, you'll need the right tools:

- **Moderation Bots**: Consider using moderation bots to automate some moderation tasks, such as spam detection.
- **Reporting Systems**: Implement reporting systems that allow community members to report inappropriate content or behavior.
- **Moderator Training**: Ensure that your moderators are trained on the guidelines and have a clear understanding of their roles and responsibilities.

Balancing Freedom and Moderation

Finding the right balance between allowing freedom of expression and enforcing community guidelines can be challenging. It's essential to strike a balance that protects the community while respecting individual freedoms.

In conclusion, moderation and well-defined community guidelines are vital for creating a safe and positive environment for your game's community. When implemented effectively, they contribute to a thriving and engaged player community that can enhance the overall gaming experience.

Section 16.5: Leveraging Social Media for Community Building

Social media platforms are powerful tools for building and maintaining a vibrant game community. In this section, we'll explore strategies for leveraging social media effectively to engage with your player base and expand your game's reach.

Choosing the Right Platforms

The first step in leveraging social media is selecting the appropriate platforms. Consider the following factors:

- **Player Demographics**: Identify the social media platforms where your target audience is most active. For example, if your game appeals to younger players, platforms like TikTok or Instagram may be relevant.
- **Content Type**: Different platforms excel at different types of content, such as images, videos, or text. Choose platforms that align with the type of content you plan to share.
- **Resources**: Consider the resources and time required to maintain an active presence on each platform. It's better to excel on a few platforms than to spread yourself too thin.

Consistent Branding

Maintaining consistent branding across your social media profiles helps players recognize your game and its official presence. Ensure that profile pictures, banners, and bios reflect the game's identity. Use a consistent tone and voice in your posts and responses.

Engaging Content

Creating engaging content is crucial for social media success. Consider the following content ideas:

- **Behind-the-Scenes**: Share insights into the game's development process, including concept art, design decisions, and challenges faced.
- **Player Highlights**: Highlight exceptional player achievements, fan art, or community contributions.
- **Teasers and Previews**: Offer sneak peeks of upcoming updates, features, or content to generate excitement.
- **Interactive Posts**: Encourage engagement through polls, questions, and challenges related to the game.
- **Developer Q&A**: Host live Q&A sessions or developer interviews to connect with the community directly.

Consistent Posting Schedule

Establishing a consistent posting schedule helps keep your audience engaged. Determine the best times to post based on your target audience's online activity and stick to a regular schedule. Social media management tools can assist in planning and scheduling posts in advance.

Community Interaction

Engaging with your community on social media is vital. Respond promptly to comments, questions, and messages. Acknowledge and thank players for their support and contributions. Encourage discussions and conversations among community members by responding to their posts and tagging them when appropriate.

User-Generated Content

Encourage and share user-generated content (UGC) on your social media platforms. This can include fan art, gameplay videos, and creative interpretations of your game. Use dedicated hashtags to organize and showcase UGC, and consider hosting UGC contests or challenges to stimulate creativity.

Contests and Giveaways

Contests and giveaways are effective tools for community engagement and growth. They incentivize participation and help increase your game's visibility. Ensure that contest rules and eligibility criteria are clear and accessible.

Example Twitter Contest Post:
"□ It's giveaway time! □ Retweet this post and follow us for a chance to win exclusive in-game items. Don't miss out! #GameNameGiveaway #Freebies #Contest Alert"

Analytics and Insights

Use social media analytics tools to track the performance of your posts and campaigns. Monitor engagement metrics such as likes, shares, comments, and click-through rates. Analyze the data to refine your social media strategy and understand what type of content resonates most with your audience.

In conclusion, leveraging social media for community building can significantly enhance your game's presence and engagement. By choosing the right platforms, creating engaging content, and actively interacting with your community, you can foster a passionate and supportive player base that contributes to the long-term success of your game.

Chapter 17: Game Testing and Quality Assurance

Section 17.1: Structuring Effective Testing Processes

Effective game testing and quality assurance (QA) are critical to delivering a polished and bug-free gaming experience. In this section, we'll delve into the importance of structuring your testing processes and best practices to ensure a high-quality game release.

The Role of Testing

Testing is an integral part of game development, encompassing various aspects, including functionality, performance, and user experience. Here's why it's essential:

- **Bug Identification**: Testing helps identify and fix bugs, glitches, and issues that can affect gameplay and overall quality.
- **Balancing**: It ensures game mechanics, difficulty levels, and progression are well-balanced and enjoyable for players.
- **Compatibility**: Testing verifies that the game runs smoothly on different platforms, devices, and configurations.
- **User Experience**: QA testing focuses on creating a seamless and immersive user experience.

Structuring Your Testing Process

A structured testing process helps ensure thorough coverage and efficient bug tracking. Consider the following steps:

43. **Test Planning**: Define the scope, objectives, and test cases for each aspect of your game. Create a test plan that outlines the testing strategy, resources, and schedule.

44. **Test Environment Setup**: Establish the testing environment, including hardware, software, and configurations that match the target platforms.

45. **Testing Types**: Determine the types of testing needed, such as functional testing, performance testing, compatibility testing, and user experience testing.

46. **Test Execution**: Execute test cases systematically, recording any issues or anomalies encountered during testing. Use test management tools to streamline this process.

47. **Regression Testing**: Continuously perform regression testing to ensure that new updates or changes do not introduce previously fixed issues.

48. **Bug Tracking**: Use a bug tracking system to log, prioritize, and assign issues for resolution. Include detailed information on the issue, steps to reproduce it, and its impact.

49. **Test Reporting**: Generate test reports that provide insights into the testing progress, defect density, and overall quality metrics. Share these reports with the development team.

50. **User Acceptance Testing (UAT)**: Involve a group of players or stakeholders in UAT to gather feedback and validate that the game meets their expectations.

Automated Testing

Consider implementing automated testing for repetitive and time-consuming tasks. Automated testing can help:

- **Regression Testing**: Automate regression tests to quickly identify issues introduced by new code changes.
- **Performance Testing**: Automate performance testing to simulate various scenarios and load conditions.
- **Functional Testing**: Automate functional tests to verify core gameplay mechanics.

```python
# Example of a simple automated test script using Python and a testing framew
ork like PyTest.
def test_game_startup():
    game = Game()
    assert game.start() == "Game started successfully"

def test_score_increment():
    game = Game()
    initial_score = game.get_score()
    game.play()
    assert game.get_score() == initial_score + 10
```

Testers and Testers' Roles

Hiring skilled testers or QA professionals is crucial. Their roles may include:

- **Testers**: Execute test cases, identify issues, and provide detailed bug reports.
- **Test Leads**: Plan testing activities, manage test teams, and ensure test coverage.
- **QA Managers**: Oversee the entire QA process, set quality standards, and coordinate with the development team.

Continuous Testing

Implement continuous testing practices that integrate testing into the development pipeline. This ensures that code changes are continually tested as they are integrated into the project, reducing the chances of introducing defects.

Game Accessibility Testing

Consider accessibility testing to ensure your game is inclusive and playable by all players, including those with disabilities. Test for features like screen readers, colorblind modes, and alternative input methods.

If your development team lacks testing expertise or resources, consider outsourcing testing to specialized QA companies. They can provide a fresh perspective and often have experience testing a wide range of games.

In conclusion, structuring effective testing processes is essential for delivering a high-quality game. By following a systematic approach, automating repetitive tasks, involving skilled testers, and integrating testing into your development pipeline, you can identify and address issues early, resulting in a smoother and more successful game release.

Section 17.2: Automated Testing Tools in Unreal

Automated testing tools play a crucial role in streamlining the quality assurance (QA) process in Unreal Engine game development. These tools help automate repetitive testing tasks, identify issues early in development, and ensure a smoother game release. In this section, we'll explore the importance of automated testing tools in Unreal Engine and some popular tools and frameworks.

Benefits of Automated Testing in Unreal Engine

Automated testing offers several advantages for Unreal Engine game development:

- **Efficiency**: Automated tests can run quickly and repeatedly, providing rapid feedback on code changes.
- **Consistency**: Tests follow predefined scripts, ensuring consistent and reliable results.
- **Regression Testing**: Automated tests help detect regressions—new issues introduced by code changes.
- **Coverage**: Testing tools can cover a wide range of scenarios, including unit testing, integration testing, and UI testing.
- **Time-Saving**: Automated testing reduces the time and effort required for manual testing.

Popular Automated Testing Tools and Frameworks

51. **Unreal Automation System (formerly UAT)**: Unreal Engine itself includes a built-in automation system that allows you to create and run various types of tests, including functional tests, performance tests, and editor scripting. It provides a powerful way to automate tasks and validate game functionality.

52. **Unreal Frontend**: Unreal Frontend is a tool that comes with Unreal Engine and allows you to manage and run tests easily. It provides a user-friendly interface for configuring and launching tests.

53. **Unreal Build System**: The Unreal Build System (UBT) supports the automation of building and packaging game builds. You can set up automated build scripts to ensure consistent builds for testing and deployment.

54. **Automation Testing Frameworks**: Unreal Engine supports various testing frameworks, including:

   – **Unreal Test Framework (UTF)**: This framework is specifically designed for writing and running automated tests within Unreal Engine. It includes features like test case organization, test discovery, and reporting.

   – **PyTest for Unreal**: PyTest is a popular testing framework for Python, and PyTest for Unreal is an extension that allows you to write automated tests in Python for Unreal Engine. It's particularly useful for functional and integration testing.

   – **Google Test**: Unreal Engine also supports Google Test, a C++ testing framework, for unit testing of C++ code.

Example of Using Unreal Automation System

Here's a simplified example of using Unreal Automation System to create a simple functional test in Unreal Engine:

```
# MyGameFunctionalTest.py

import unreal

class MyGameFunctionalTest(unreal.FunctionalTestBase):
    def setup(self):
        # Set up test prerequisites, such as loading a level or initializing
game state.
        pass

    def run(self):
        # Implement test logic here, interacting with game objects and verify
ing outcomes.
        pass

    def cleanup(self):
        # Clean up after the test, reset game state, or release any resources

        pass
```

You can then execute this test using the Unreal Frontend or command line tools provided by Unreal Engine.

To fully harness the power of automated testing, integrate these tools into your CI/CD (Continuous Integration/Continuous Deployment) pipeline. CI systems like Jenkins, Travis CI, or GitLab CI can be configured to automatically trigger tests whenever code changes are pushed to the repository. This ensures that tests are run consistently and provides immediate feedback to the development team.

In conclusion, automated testing tools are invaluable for Unreal Engine game development, helping to ensure the quality and stability of your game. By leveraging these tools and frameworks, you can streamline your QA process, detect issues early, and deliver a polished and bug-free gaming experience to your players.

Section 17.3: Managing Beta Tests and User Feedback

Managing beta tests and collecting user feedback are essential steps in the game development process. Beta testing provides valuable insights, helps identify issues, and allows you to fine-tune your game based on player input. In this section, we'll explore the importance of managing beta tests and strategies for collecting and utilizing user feedback effectively.

The Importance of Beta Testing

Beta testing serves multiple crucial purposes:

- **Bug Detection**: Beta testers help identify and report bugs, glitches, and issues that may have gone unnoticed during internal testing.
- **Stress Testing**: Large-scale beta tests simulate real-world usage, helping you assess server capacity and stability in multiplayer games.
- **Player Feedback**: Beta testers provide valuable feedback on gameplay, mechanics, balance, and overall user experience.
- **Marketing**: Beta tests generate pre-release buzz and excitement among players, potentially leading to increased interest and sales at launch.

Strategies for Managing Beta Tests

55. **Closed Beta**: Start with a closed beta phase, inviting a limited number of trusted testers. This allows you to control the testing environment and gather initial feedback.

56. **Open Beta**: Expand to an open beta phase, inviting a broader audience. This phase helps stress test servers and gather feedback from a diverse player base.

57. **Early Access**: Consider early access on platforms like Steam, allowing players to purchase and play the game while it's still in development. This provides ongoing funding and feedback.

58. **Platform-Specific Betas**: If your game is multi-platform, run beta tests on each platform separately to identify platform-specific issues.

59. **Beta Branches**: Create separate branches of your game for beta testing, ensuring that the main development branch remains stable for the internal team.

Collecting User Feedback

Collecting user feedback effectively is crucial for beta testing success:

- **Feedback Forms**: Provide in-game forms or external surveys where players can report issues, share suggestions, and rate their experiences.

- **Forums and Communities**: Create dedicated forums or community spaces where beta testers can discuss the game, report problems, and engage with the development team.

- **Bug Tracking Systems**: Use bug tracking systems like JIRA or GitHub Issues to manage and prioritize reported issues.

- **Player Metrics**: Gather player metrics and analytics to understand player behavior, progression, and engagement patterns.

- **Player Interviews**: Conduct interviews or focus groups with select beta testers to gain deeper insights into their experiences and preferences.

Communicating with Beta Testers

Effective communication with beta testers is essential:

- **Regular Updates**: Keep beta testers informed about updates, patches, and changes to the game. Share release notes to highlight what has been addressed.

- **Feedback Acknowledgment**: Acknowledge and appreciate the feedback provided by beta testers, even if their suggestions are not immediately implemented.

- **Developer Responses**: Respond to bug reports and feedback to provide status updates and let testers know that their input is valued.

Utilizing User Feedback

Once you've collected user feedback, it's crucial to put it to good use:

- **Bug Fixes**: Prioritize and address reported bugs and issues promptly. Regularly update the beta build with bug fixes.

- **Game Balancing**: Use player feedback to fine-tune game balance, adjust difficulty levels, and refine mechanics.

- **Feature Prioritization**: Consider player suggestions for new features or improvements, but prioritize based on development feasibility and alignment with the game's vision.

- **Engagement Enhancement**: Enhance player engagement by incorporating feedback on user interfaces, tutorials, and onboarding processes.

- **Community Building**: Leverage the beta testing community as a foundation for your game's player community. Encourage testers to stay engaged and advocate for your game.

Post-Beta Analysis

After the beta phase, conduct a comprehensive post-beta analysis:

- **Data Analysis**: Analyze player metrics, feedback, and bug reports to identify trends, common pain points, and areas for improvement.

- **Performance Evaluation**: Assess how well the game performed under real-world conditions, including server stability and load.

- **Marketing Insights**: Use beta testing results to refine marketing strategies, highlight player testimonials, and target specific player segments.

- **Launch Readiness**: Evaluate whether the game is ready for a full release, considering player feedback and necessary improvements.

In conclusion, managing beta tests and collecting user feedback are integral to the game development process. Beta testing helps you identify and address issues, improve gameplay, and build a dedicated player community. By strategically managing beta phases and effectively utilizing feedback, you can increase the chances of a successful game launch and a satisfied player base.

Section 17.4: Balancing and Fine-Tuning Game Mechanics

Balancing and fine-tuning game mechanics are essential aspects of game development that significantly impact the player experience. Achieving the right balance ensures that the game is both challenging and enjoyable. In this section, we'll explore the importance of game balance, methods for fine-tuning mechanics, and tools that can assist in the process.

The Significance of Game Balance

Game balance refers to the equilibrium of various elements within a game, including character abilities, weapon strengths, level difficulty, and resource management. Proper balance is crucial for several reasons:

- **Player Engagement**: Balanced games provide players with a challenging yet rewarding experience, keeping them engaged and motivated to progress.

- **Fair Competition**: Multiplayer games require balance to ensure fair competition, preventing any one player or team from having an overwhelming advantage.

- **Longevity**: Well-balanced games have longer lifespans as players continue to explore and enjoy the gameplay.

- **Positive Reception**: Balanced games receive better reviews and word-of-mouth recommendations, contributing to their success.

Methods for Balancing Game Mechanics

Balancing game mechanics is a dynamic and iterative process. Here are some methods to help achieve balance:

60. **Data Analysis**: Collect and analyze gameplay data, including player statistics, win rates, and in-game metrics. Identify outliers and areas where balance may be off.

61. **Player Feedback**: Gather feedback from players, particularly during beta testing. Pay attention to their perceptions of balance and their suggestions for improvement.

62. **Iterative Testing**: Continuously test and tweak game mechanics during development. This allows you to make gradual adjustments and assess their impact.

63. **Simulation**: Create simulations or mathematical models to predict how changes to game mechanics will affect gameplay. This can help you make informed decisions.

64. **A/B Testing**: Implement A/B testing to compare different versions of mechanics with player populations to determine which performs better in terms of balance and engagement.

Balancing Different Game Elements

Different game elements require specific considerations when it comes to balance:

- **Character Abilities**: In games with character classes or abilities, ensure that no character or ability is significantly overpowered or underpowered. Adjust cooldowns, damage, and effects as needed.

- **Weapons and Items**: Balance weapons and items to provide strategic choices without a clear "best" option. Adjust damage, accuracy, and rarity to achieve balance.

- **Level Design**: Balance level difficulty to provide players with challenges that match their skill level. Gradually introduce mechanics and increase difficulty as the game progresses.

- **Resource Management**: Balance resource acquisition and consumption to prevent resource hoarding or excessive scarcity. Players should feel rewarded for efficient resource use.

- **Economy**: In games with in-game currencies or economies, ensure that the economy remains stable and that players can progress without excessive grinding or pay-to-win mechanics.

Tools for Fine-Tuning Game Mechanics

Several tools can assist in fine-tuning game mechanics:

- **Spreadsheet Software**: Tools like Microsoft Excel or Google Sheets are useful for creating tables and formulas to analyze data and simulate balance changes.

- **Game Analytics Platforms**: Use game analytics platforms like Unity Analytics, GameAnalytics, or custom solutions to collect and analyze player data.

- **Game Engines**: Game engines like Unreal Engine and Unity provide debugging and testing tools that allow you to adjust game mechanics in real-time.

- **Custom Tools**: In some cases, developers create custom tools and scripts to simulate gameplay scenarios and adjust mechanics without the need for extensive coding.

```csharp
// Example of adjusting weapon damage in Unity.
public class Weapon : MonoBehaviour
{
    public float baseDamage = 10.0f;
    public float damageMultiplier = 1.0f;

    public void DealDamage(GameObject target)
    {
        float totalDamage = baseDamage * damageMultiplier;
        target.GetComponent<Health>().TakeDamage(totalDamage);
    }
}
```

Player Perception

Remember that player perception plays a significant role in balance. Even if the underlying numbers are balanced, if players perceive a particular mechanic as unfair or frustrating, it may need adjustment. Collecting and analyzing player feedback and adjusting mechanics accordingly can help align perception with reality.

In conclusion, balancing and fine-tuning game mechanics are critical to delivering an enjoyable player experience. By employing data analysis, player feedback, iterative testing, and the right tools, developers can achieve the delicate balance that keeps players engaged and eager to explore the game's challenges.

Section 17.5: Ensuring Game Accessibility Standards

Ensuring that your game adheres to accessibility standards is not only a moral imperative but also a legal requirement in many regions. Accessibility ensures that players with disabilities can enjoy your game and have an equal gaming experience. In this section, we'll explore the importance of game accessibility, key accessibility considerations, and tools to assist in meeting accessibility standards.

The Significance of Game Accessibility

Game accessibility refers to designing games in a way that accommodates players with various disabilities, including visual, auditory, motor, and cognitive impairments. Here's why it's crucial:

- **Inclusivity**: Accessibility ensures that your game is inclusive and can be enjoyed by a broader audience, including players with disabilities.

- **Legal Requirements**: Many countries have laws and regulations that mandate accessible design for digital products, including games.

- **Positive Reputation**: Developing accessible games reflects positively on your studio, fostering goodwill and a positive reputation in the gaming community.

- **Broader Market**: Accessible games have the potential to reach a broader market, including players who might have otherwise been excluded.

Key Accessibility Considerations

65. **Visual Impairments**:

    - Provide alternative text for images and UI elements for screen readers.
    - Offer high contrast options and resizable fonts.
    - Ensure important information is not conveyed solely through color.
    - Implement customizable HUD elements and text sizes.

66. **Auditory Impairments**:

    - Provide subtitles and closed captions for all spoken content.
    - Include visual cues or vibrations to replace auditory cues.
    - Offer customizable audio settings, including volume sliders for separate sound elements.

67. **Motor Impairments**:

    - Support various input methods, such as keyboard, mouse, gamepad, and alternative input devices.
    - Implement customizable controls and keybindings.

- Consider options for one-handed or adaptive controllers.

68. **Cognitive Impairments**:

    - Provide clear and concise instructions and tutorials.
    - Avoid rapid or flashing visuals that can trigger seizures.
    - Include difficulty settings to cater to different cognitive abilities.

Accessibility Testing

Testing for accessibility is a crucial part of the development process:

- **Manual Testing**: Have testers with various disabilities play the game and provide feedback on accessibility features and challenges.

- **Automated Testing Tools**: Use accessibility testing tools like axe, WAVE, or accessibility checkers in game engines to identify potential issues.

- **Checklists**: Create accessibility checklists and guidelines for your development team to follow.

Accessibility Guidelines and Standards

Familiarize yourself with established accessibility guidelines and standards, such as the Web Content Accessibility Guidelines (WCAG) for digital content. Game-specific standards, such as the Game Accessibility Guidelines (GAAG), can also provide valuable insights.

Inclusive Game Design

Inclusive game design involves integrating accessibility from the outset:

- **Design Principles**: Incorporate accessibility considerations into your game's design principles and early concept phases.

- **User Testing**: Include players with disabilities in usability testing to identify and address accessibility issues early.

- **Iterative Design**: Continuously refine and improve accessibility features based on player feedback and testing results.

- **Educate Your Team**: Ensure that your development team is aware of accessibility best practices and their importance.

```
// Example of adding subtitles to dialogues in Unity.
public class DialogueManager : MonoBehaviour
{
    public TextMeshProUGUI dialogueText;
    public TextMeshProUGUI subtitleText;

    public void StartDialogue(Dialogue dialogue)
    {
```

```
        dialogueText.text = dialogue.name + ": " + dialogue.sentences[0];
        subtitleText.text = dialogue.sentences[0];
        // Additional code for managing dialogue progression.
    }
}
```

Accessibility Features in Game Engines

Many game engines, such as Unity and Unreal Engine, offer built-in accessibility features and tools to help developers create accessible games. These features may include screen reader support, colorblind modes, and customizable controls.

In conclusion, ensuring game accessibility standards is essential for creating games that are inclusive and compliant with legal requirements. By considering the needs of players with disabilities, implementing accessibility features, and testing thoroughly, you can make your game enjoyable for a broader audience while fostering a positive reputation for your studio.

Chapter 18: Marketing and Game Launch Strategies

Section 18.1: Developing a Marketing Plan for Your Game

Developing a comprehensive marketing plan for your game is crucial to its success. A well-executed marketing strategy can create anticipation, drive sales, and build a dedicated player base. In this section, we'll delve into the key elements of crafting an effective marketing plan for your game.

Understand Your Target Audience

Before diving into marketing tactics, it's essential to understand your target audience. Consider factors such as age, gender, interests, and gaming habits. Tailoring your marketing efforts to your audience's preferences will increase your chances of success.

Set Clear Objectives

Define clear and measurable marketing objectives. These could include goals like achieving a certain number of pre-orders, generating a specific amount of website traffic, or increasing your game's social media following. Having well-defined objectives will help you stay focused on your goals.

Build an Online Presence

Create a strong online presence for your game. This includes a dedicated website, social media profiles, and a presence on gaming platforms like Steam, Epic Games Store, or console-specific marketplaces. Consistent branding and messaging across these platforms are crucial.

Generate Buzz with Teasers and Trailers

Teasers and trailers are powerful tools to generate excitement around your game. Craft visually appealing and engaging video content that highlights the game's key features and hooks players' interest. Release teasers and trailers strategically to build anticipation.

```html
<!-- Example of embedding a YouTube game teaser video in a website -->
<iframe width="560" height="315" src="https://www.youtube.com/embed/your-video-id" frameborder="0" allowfullscreen></iframe>
```

Content Marketing and Blogging

Maintain a blog or news section on your game's website. Regularly publish articles, developer diaries, and updates about the game's development progress. Content marketing not only keeps your audience engaged but also improves your website's search engine visibility.

Engage with Your Community

Foster a community around your game. Engage with players on social media, forums, and Discord channels. Respond to questions, gather feedback, and create a sense of belonging among your player base. Consider hosting developer Q&A sessions or live streams to interact directly with your community.

Influencer Marketing

Partner with influencers and streamers who align with your game's genre and target audience. Influencers can introduce your game to their followers through gameplay videos, reviews, and live streams, helping to expand your reach.

Public Relations and Press Releases

Craft compelling press releases and reach out to gaming journalists and media outlets. Coverage from reputable gaming websites and magazines can significantly boost your game's visibility.

Press Release
FOR IMMEDIATE RELEASE

[Game Name] Announces Launch Date and Exciting Features

[City, Date] – [Game Name], an upcoming [genre] game developed by [Your Studio], is set to launch on [Launch Date].

[Game Name] promises to deliver an immersive [gameplay feature] experience, with [highlighted feature 1] and [highlighted feature 2].

Read more: [Link to full press release]

Pre-Launch Campaigns

Plan pre-launch campaigns to build excitement leading up to your game's release. This could include countdowns, exclusive content reveals, and limited-time promotions. Encourage players to wishlist or pre-order your game.

Monitor and Adjust

Track the performance of your marketing efforts using analytics tools. Measure website traffic, social media engagement, conversion rates, and player feedback. Be prepared to adjust your marketing strategy based on the data and insights you gather.

In conclusion, developing a marketing plan is essential for promoting your game effectively. By understanding your audience, setting clear objectives, building an online presence, and leveraging various marketing tactics, you can create anticipation, generate buzz, and increase the chances of a successful game launch. Marketing is an ongoing process, and adapting to changing trends and player feedback is key to long-term success.

Section 18.2: Crafting a Compelling Press Kit

A press kit is an essential tool in your game's marketing strategy, serving as a comprehensive resource for journalists, content creators, and influencers who want to cover your game. Crafting a compelling press kit can greatly enhance your game's visibility and ensure that those interested in promoting it have all the necessary information at their fingertips. In this section, we'll explore the key elements to include in a press kit and how to create an attention-grabbing press kit for your game.

Press Kit Essentials

A well-organized press kit should contain the following essential components:

69. **Game Description**: Provide a concise and engaging overview of your game's story, gameplay, and unique features. Highlight what sets your game apart from others in its genre.

70. **Key Features**: List the key features and selling points of your game. What makes it exciting and worth covering?

71. **Screenshots and Artwork**: Include high-quality screenshots, concept art, and promotional images that showcase the game's visuals. Ensure that the images are in various formats and resolutions to accommodate different media needs.

```
![Screenshot 1](https://www.example.com/screenshots/screenshot1.jpg)
![Concept Art](https://www.example.com/artwork/concept_art.png)
```

5. **Videos and Trailers**: Embed or provide links to game trailers, teasers, and gameplay videos. Videos are highly engaging and can help convey the game's atmosphere.

```
<iframe width="560" height="315" src="https://www.youtube.com/embed/your-video-id" frameborder="0" allowfullscreen></iframe>
```

6. **Press Release**: Include a well-crafted press release with information about the game's launch date, key features, and any recent updates or developments. Make it easy for journalists to access and download the release.

7. **Developer Information**: Provide a brief bio of your development studio, including its history, notable projects, and contact information. Include team member profiles with photos and roles.

8. **Contact Information**: Offer clear and accessible contact information for media inquiries. Include a dedicated press contact or PR representative who can promptly respond to questions and requests.

9. **Social Media and Links**: Share links to your game's official website, social media profiles, and relevant press coverage. Make it simple for journalists to access additional information and engage with your community.

Tailor Your Press Kit

Consider tailoring your press kit to different audiences. You may have separate press kits for journalists, content creators, and influencers, each highlighting the aspects most relevant to their audience. Personalizing your press kit can demonstrate that you value the specific interests of these groups.

Keep It Updated

Regularly update your press kit to reflect changes in your game's development, release date, or new features. An outdated press kit can lead to misinformation and missed opportunities for coverage.

Distribution

Make your press kit easily accessible on your game's official website. Create a dedicated "Press" or "Media" section where journalists and content creators can find and download the kit. Additionally, provide direct download links to individual assets to streamline the process.

Additional Assets

Consider including additional assets like soundtracks, concept art packs, or character profiles if they contribute to a deeper understanding of your game. Offering these extras can make your press kit even more appealing.

In conclusion, a compelling press kit is a valuable asset in promoting your game to the media and influencers. By providing essential information, high-quality assets, and clear contact details, you can make it easier for others to create engaging content about your game. A well-organized press kit can significantly contribute to the success of your game's marketing campaign and overall visibility in the gaming industry.

Section 18.3: Leveraging Influencers and Streamers

Influencer marketing has become a powerful tool for promoting games and reaching a wider audience. Influencers and streamers have dedicated followings and can provide authentic, engaging content about your game. In this section, we'll explore how to leverage influencers and streamers effectively as part of your game's marketing strategy.

Identifying the Right Influencers

The first step in influencer marketing is identifying influencers and streamers who align with your game's genre, target audience, and values. Look for influencers who have an established presence in the gaming community and whose followers are likely to be interested in your game.

Building Relationships

Establishing genuine relationships with influencers is crucial. Approach influencers professionally and respectfully. Engage with their content, comment on their streams or videos, and show your genuine interest in their work. Building a rapport can make them more receptive to collaborating with you.

Collaboration Opportunities

There are various collaboration opportunities you can explore with influencers and streamers:

72. **Gameplay Videos**: Influencers can create Let's Play videos or live streams of your game, providing commentary and insights as they play.

73. **Reviews and Previews**: Invite influencers to review or preview your game before its release. Their opinions can carry significant weight with their audience.

74. **Interviews and Q&A Sessions**: Arrange interviews or Q&A sessions with influencers where they discuss your game, its development, and its unique features.

75. **Exclusive Content**: Offer influencers exclusive in-game content or early access to certain features, which they can showcase to their audience.

Compensation and Agreements

Discuss compensation and agreements with influencers upfront. Compensation can vary and may include payment, free copies of the game, revenue-sharing arrangements, or other incentives. Ensure that the terms of the collaboration are clear and mutually beneficial.

Authenticity Matters

Encourage influencers to provide authentic and honest opinions about your game. Audiences appreciate transparency, and genuine reactions can be more persuasive than scripted endorsements. Avoid pressuring influencers to provide positive reviews if they genuinely have concerns or criticisms.

Content Guidelines

Provide influencers with guidelines and key talking points about your game to ensure that they cover essential aspects. However, allow them creative freedom to present the content in their style, as their authenticity is part of the appeal.

Content Guidelines for Influencers
- Highlight the game's unique features.
- Mention the release date and where to purchase the game.
- Showcase specific gameplay mechanics or moments.
- Encourage interaction with viewers, such as answering questions or comments
.

Promotion Strategy

Coordinate with influencers on the timing and strategy for promoting your game. Align their content releases with your game's marketing campaigns, announcements, or launch date to maximize impact. Consider creating a dedicated hashtag or event to generate buzz around the collaboration.

Monitoring and Analytics

Track the performance of influencer collaborations using analytics tools. Measure engagement metrics, such as views, likes, shares, and comments, to gauge the impact of their content. This data can help you assess the success of your influencer marketing efforts and make informed decisions for future campaigns.

Legal Considerations

Ensure that influencer collaborations comply with legal regulations, such as disclosure requirements for sponsored content. Be transparent about any financial or material incentives provided to influencers, and make sure they disclose their partnership with your game appropriately.

In conclusion, leveraging influencers and streamers can be a highly effective way to promote your game and reach a broader audience. By identifying the right influencers, building relationships, and collaborating authentically, you can tap into their dedicated followings and generate excitement and interest in your game. Effective influencer marketing can significantly contribute to your game's success in today's competitive gaming industry.

Section 18.4: Strategies for a Successful Game Launch

A successful game launch is the culmination of months or even years of hard work. It's the moment when your game becomes available to the public, and the way you handle this crucial phase can significantly impact its reception and long-term success. In this section, we'll explore strategies and best practices for a successful game launch.

The period leading up to your game's launch is an excellent opportunity to build anticipation among your target audience. Here are some effective strategies to create excitement:

76. **Teasers and Trailers**: Release captivating teasers and trailers that showcase your game's key features. Share them on social media, gaming forums, and video-sharing platforms.

77. **Countdowns**: Create countdowns on your website or social media profiles to let fans know exactly when the game will be available.

78. **Exclusive Content**: Offer exclusive in-game content or early access to those who pre-order or wish-list your game. This can incentivize players to commit to buying.

79. **Developer Diaries**: Share behind-the-scenes developer diaries or blog posts that provide insights into the game's development process. This personal touch can connect players to your team and create a sense of community.

Press Coverage

Engage with gaming journalists and media outlets to secure press coverage before and after the launch. Consider these steps:

80. **Press Releases**: Craft compelling press releases with key information about your game, its launch date, and standout features. Distribute them to gaming news websites and magazines.

81. **Review Copies**: Provide early access or review copies to trusted reviewers and journalists. Positive reviews can generate buzz and credibility for your game.

82. **Embargo Dates**: Coordinate with reviewers to set embargo dates. This ensures that reviews are released simultaneously, creating a fair and controlled narrative around your game.

Community Engagement

Your game's community plays a vital role in its success. Engage with your community in the following ways:

83. **Social Media**: Be active on social media platforms where your audience is most active. Respond to comments, run contests, and share user-generated content.

84. **Forums and Discord**: Participate in gaming forums and host a Discord server for your community to discuss the game, ask questions, and interact with developers.

85. **Live Streams and Q&A**: Host live streams or Q&A sessions with your development team. This direct interaction can foster a sense of belonging and excitement.

Post-Launch Support

The work doesn't end at launch; it's just the beginning. Maintain post-launch support to keep players engaged and address any issues:

86. **Patches and Updates**: Release regular patches and updates to address bugs, improve gameplay, and add new content. This demonstrates your commitment to the game's quality.

87. **Community Feedback**: Continuously gather and listen to player feedback. Make improvements based on their suggestions and concerns.

88. **Live Events**: Organize in-game events, challenges, or seasonal content updates to keep players coming back.

Marketing Beyond Launch

Keep marketing efforts alive even after the initial launch:

89. **DLCs and Expansions**: Plan downloadable content (DLC) or expansion packs to extend the game's lifespan and revenue potential.

90. **Cross-Promotion**: Partner with other game developers or platforms for cross-promotion. This can introduce your game to new audiences.

91. **User-Generated Content**: Encourage and support user-generated content creation, such as mods or custom maps. This can foster a dedicated player community.

Analytics and Data

Utilize analytics tools to track the performance of your game and marketing efforts. Monitor key metrics like player retention, conversion rates, and revenue. Analyze this data to make informed decisions and adjustments to your strategy.

```
**Key Metrics to Track**
- Player retention rates
- Conversion rates (e.g., from website visitors to purchasers)
- Revenue and sales data
- User engagement on social media
- Player feedback and reviews
```

In conclusion, a successful game launch requires careful planning, community engagement, and ongoing support. Building anticipation, securing press coverage, and maintaining a strong online presence are essential steps. Remember that post-launch support, marketing efforts beyond launch, and data analysis are equally important in ensuring your game's long-term success in the competitive gaming industry.

Section 18.5: Post-Launch Support and Updates

The work doesn't stop at the game's launch; in fact, it's just the beginning of an ongoing journey to maintain and grow your player base. Post-launch support and updates are essential for the long-term success of your game. In this section, we'll explore why post-launch support is crucial and best practices for providing continuous updates to your game.

The Importance of Post-Launch Support

Post-launch support serves several vital purposes:

92. **Bug Fixes**: Players may encounter bugs or issues that went unnoticed during development or testing. Addressing these problems promptly improves the overall player experience.

93. **Player Engagement**: Continuous updates keep players engaged and interested in your game, preventing it from becoming stale.

94. **Player Retention**: Regular content updates and improvements can encourage players to stay and continue playing, reducing churn.

95. **Community Building**: Ongoing support and engagement with your community can foster a loyal player base and positive word-of-mouth marketing.

Best Practices for Post-Launch Support

96. **Bug Fixing**: Prioritize bug fixes and address critical issues first. Maintain a bug tracking system to efficiently manage and resolve reported problems.

97. **Content Updates**: Plan and release regular content updates, such as new levels, characters, or game modes. These updates can reinvigorate interest in your game.

98. **Balancing and Tuning**: Continuously balance and fine-tune gameplay mechanics, difficulty levels, and in-game economies based on player feedback and data analytics.

99. **Community Engagement**: Stay active on social media, forums, and in-game channels to engage with your player community. Respond to questions, comments, and concerns promptly.

100. **Transparency**: Be transparent about your development process. Share patch notes and update plans with your community to keep them informed.

```
**Patch Notes (Example)**
**Version 1.1.0**
- Added three new maps to the game.
- Tweaked weapon balance to improve gameplay.
- Fixed a bug causing crashes when using certain abilities.
- Improved matchmaking algorithms for better player matchups.
```

6. **User-Generated Content**: Encourage and support user-generated content, such as mods, custom levels, or skins. These contributions can extend the game's lifespan.

7. **Feedback Loops**: Create feedback loops with your community by actively soliciting input, running surveys, and considering player suggestions for future updates.

8. **Event and Challenges**: Host in-game events, challenges, or seasonal content updates to maintain player interest and offer rewards for participation.

9. **Performance Optimization**: Continuously optimize your game's performance to ensure it runs smoothly on a variety of hardware configurations.

10. **DLCs and Monetization**: Plan and release downloadable content (DLCs) or additional monetization options to generate additional revenue and keep players invested.

Testing and Quality Assurance

Thoroughly test updates before releasing them to avoid introducing new issues or breaking existing gameplay. Consider implementing automated testing tools and processes to streamline this phase and ensure the quality of each update.

Data-Driven Decisions

Use player data and analytics to inform your post-launch decisions. Track player behavior, engagement metrics, and feedback to identify areas that require improvement and opportunities for expansion.

Communication and Roadmaps

Maintain a clear communication channel with your player community. Publish roadmaps outlining your planned updates and content releases. Regularly communicate progress and updates, even if it's to share that a feature is delayed or canceled.

Long-Term Commitment

Remember that post-launch support is a long-term commitment. Continue supporting your game for as long as there is an active player base and demand. Many successful games have thrived for years through dedicated post-launch support.

In conclusion, post-launch support and updates are essential for maintaining and growing your game's player base. They demonstrate your commitment to quality, engage your community, and extend the game's lifespan. By following best practices, staying engaged with your players, and using data-driven decisions, you can ensure the ongoing success of your game in a competitive gaming market.

Chapter 19: Advanced Project Management

Section 19.1: Agile Methodologies in Game Development

Agile methodologies have gained prominence in the game development industry due to their flexibility, collaboration-focused approach, and adaptability to changing project requirements. In this section, we'll explore how Agile methodologies can be applied in game development, the benefits they offer, and practical tips for implementing them effectively.

Understanding Agile Methodologies

Agile is a set of principles and practices that prioritize iterative development, collaboration, and customer feedback. It is characterized by the following key features:

101. **Iterative Development**: Agile divides the project into small, manageable iterations or sprints. Each sprint typically lasts two to four weeks and results in a potentially shippable product increment.

102. **Collaborative Teams**: Agile emphasizes cross-functional teams with members from various disciplines like design, development, and QA. Collaboration and communication among team members are crucial.

103. **Customer-Centric**: Agile focuses on delivering value to the customer by continuously incorporating their feedback and adapting to changing requirements.

104. **Flexibility**: Agile allows for changes in project scope and priorities as new information becomes available. It embraces the idea that requirements may evolve during development.

Benefits of Agile in Game Development

105. **Faster Prototyping**: Agile enables rapid prototyping and iteration, allowing developers to test ideas quickly and make adjustments based on player feedback.

106. **Reduced Risk**: By breaking the project into smaller iterations, Agile reduces the risk associated with large, long-term development efforts. Issues can be identified and addressed early.

107. **Improved Collaboration**: Cross-functional teams in Agile encourage collaboration and knowledge sharing, leading to better solutions and a more efficient development process.

108. **Adaptability**: Agile allows teams to respond to changing market trends, player preferences, or technical challenges, ensuring the final product remains relevant.

109. **Transparency**: Regular meetings, such as daily stand-ups and sprint reviews, provide transparency into project progress and challenges.

110. **Select the Right Framework**: There are various Agile frameworks, such as Scrum, Kanban, and Lean. Choose the one that best suits your team and project.

111. **Set Clear Goals**: Define clear project goals and objectives to guide the development process. Ensure that the team understands the vision for the game.

112. **Prioritize Features**: Create a prioritized backlog of features and user stories. Focus on delivering the most valuable features early.

113. **Frequent Feedback**: Regularly gather feedback from players, stakeholders, and team members. Use this feedback to make informed decisions.

114. **Iterate and Improve**: After each sprint or iteration, conduct retrospectives to identify what went well and what could be improved. Implement changes to enhance the development process continually.

Retrospective Action Items (Example)
- Improve communication between design and development teams.
- Increase the frequency of playtesting sessions.
- Address performance issues during development.

6. **Embrace Change**: Be open to changes in project scope or requirements. Agile accommodates changing priorities and encourages flexibility.

7. **Communication**: Maintain open and frequent communication within the team. Daily stand-up meetings and regular sprint reviews are essential for keeping everyone informed.

8. **Empower Teams**: Empower teams to make decisions at the appropriate level. Trust team members to take ownership of their work and contribute to project success.

In conclusion, Agile methodologies have become a valuable approach in game development, fostering collaboration, adaptability, and customer-centric development. By understanding the principles of Agile, recognizing its benefits, and implementing practical tips, game development teams can streamline their processes, reduce risks, and deliver successful games that resonate with players.

Section 19.2: Time and Resource Management

Effective time and resource management are critical in game development, where complex projects require coordination among multiple team members and departments. In this section, we'll delve into the importance of managing time and resources efficiently, providing practical insights and strategies for game project management.

Time and resource management in game development directly impact project success. Here's why it's crucial:

115. **Budget Constraints**: Games often have limited budgets. Efficient resource allocation ensures you make the most of available funds.

116. **Meeting Deadlines**: Missing release dates can harm a game's reputation and financial prospects. Effective time management is essential for on-time deliveries.

117. **Optimizing Creativity**: Well-managed schedules and resources allow creative teams to focus on quality without undue stress.

118. **Minimizing Scope Creep**: Proper planning and resource allocation help prevent scope creep, which can lead to delays and increased costs.

Strategies for Effective Time Management

119. **Project Planning**: Begin with comprehensive project planning. Create a roadmap that outlines milestones, deadlines, and tasks for each development phase.

120. **Task Prioritization**: Prioritize tasks based on their importance and impact on the project. Focus on critical tasks first to ensure essential components are completed.

121. **Time Tracking**: Implement time-tracking tools to monitor how much time is spent on each task. This helps identify areas where time is used most efficiently and where improvements can be made.

122. **Agile Methodologies**: As discussed in the previous section, consider using Agile methodologies like Scrum or Kanban, which emphasize iterative development and time management.

123. **Buffer Time**: Allocate buffer time in your schedule for unforeseen issues or delays. Having a cushion can help you stay on track even when unexpected challenges arise.

Resource Allocation Strategies

124. **Resource Inventory**: Create an inventory of the resources needed for the project, including human resources, equipment, software, and budget. Keep this inventory up-to-date.

125. **Resource Allocation Plans**: Develop resource allocation plans that specify which team members work on specific tasks and when. Ensure that you have the right skill sets for each task.

126. **Resource Tracking**: Implement resource tracking tools to monitor resource usage and availability. This can help avoid overallocation or underutilization.

127. **Resource Contingency**: Identify potential bottlenecks or resource shortages in advance. Have contingency plans in place, such as outsourcing or reallocating resources.

Communication and Collaboration

Effective communication among team members is crucial for managing time and resources. Here's how to foster collaboration:

128. **Regular Meetings**: Schedule regular team meetings, stand-ups, and check-ins to ensure everyone is aware of project status and any resource-related issues.

129. **Collaboration Tools**: Use collaboration tools and project management software to facilitate communication, document sharing, and task tracking.

130. **Feedback Loop**: Encourage team members to provide feedback on resource allocation and time management. Their insights can help improve processes.

Continuous Improvement

Time and resource management should be viewed as an ongoing process. Continuously assess and refine your project management strategies based on lessons learned from previous projects. Encourage a culture of innovation and efficiency within your development team.

```
**Resource Allocation Improvement (Example)**
- Analyze resource allocation for the last project.
- Identify areas where resources were overallocated.
- Develop guidelines for more efficient resource allocation in future project
s.
```

In conclusion, effective time and resource management are vital components of successful game development. By carefully planning, prioritizing tasks, tracking time and resources, and fostering communication and collaboration, you can maximize efficiency and increase the likelihood of delivering high-quality games on time and within budget. Continuous improvement and adaptability are key to meeting the unique challenges of game development projects.

Section 19.3: Risk Management and Mitigation

Risk management is a crucial aspect of game development project management. Identifying potential risks and implementing mitigation strategies can help ensure the project stays on track and within budget. In this section, we'll explore the importance of risk management and provide insights into effective risk mitigation techniques in game development.

The Significance of Risk Management

Game development is a complex process with numerous variables that can impact a project's success. Risks can emerge from various sources, including technical challenges, scope changes, team dynamics, and external factors. Effective risk management is essential for the following reasons:

131. **Budget Control**: Managing risks helps prevent unexpected costs and budget overruns that can jeopardize the project's financial health.

132. **Project Timeline**: Identifying and addressing risks in advance helps avoid delays and ensures that the project remains on schedule.

133. **Quality Assurance**: Mitigating risks related to technical challenges and design issues contributes to a higher-quality final product.

134. **Stakeholder Satisfaction**: Proactively managing risks enhances stakeholder satisfaction by minimizing project disruptions and surprises.

Risk Identification

The first step in risk management is identifying potential risks. This involves considering all aspects of the project, from technical challenges to external dependencies. Common sources of risks in game development include:

- **Technical Risks**: These can include unexpected technical difficulties, compatibility issues, or performance problems on certain platforms.

- **Scope Changes**: Uncontrolled scope changes can lead to feature creep, increasing the complexity of the project and introducing new risks.

- **Resource Constraints**: Risks related to resource shortages, including human resources, equipment, and budget limitations.

- **Market Trends**: External risks such as changing market trends or competitor actions that can affect the game's success.

- **Team Dynamics**: Risks related to team dynamics, communication issues, or turnover among team members.

Risk Assessment and Prioritization

After identifying potential risks, it's essential to assess and prioritize them. Consider factors such as the likelihood of occurrence, the potential impact on the project, and the ability to mitigate each risk. Risks that are more likely to occur and have a high impact should be given the highest priority.

```
**Risk Assessment (Example)**
Risk: Technical difficulty in implementing a new rendering system.
- Likelihood: Medium
- Impact: High
- Mitigation: Assign a senior developer with expertise in rendering systems t
o the project.
```

Once risks are assessed and prioritized, develop mitigation strategies for each high-priority risk. Here are some common risk mitigation techniques in game development:

135. **Contingency Plans**: Create contingency plans that outline steps to take if a risk materializes. For example, if a key team member leaves the project, have a plan for their replacement or reallocation of tasks.

136. **Prototyping and Testing**: For technical risks, consider prototyping and testing early in the project to identify and address potential issues before they become critical.

137. **Change Control**: Implement a change control process to manage scope changes effectively. Changes should be documented, assessed for impact, and approved by relevant stakeholders.

138. **Resource Management**: Regularly review resource allocation to ensure that team members are adequately staffed, and resources are optimized.

139. **Risk Monitoring**: Continuously monitor high-priority risks throughout the project. Be prepared to adjust mitigation strategies as the project progresses and new information becomes available.

140. **Communication**: Maintain open and transparent communication within the team and with stakeholders. Encourage team members to report potential risks promptly.

Risk Documentation

Keep comprehensive records of identified risks, assessments, prioritization, and mitigation strategies. This documentation helps track the progress of risk management efforts and serves as a reference for future projects.

In conclusion, effective risk management is essential for successful game development project management. Identifying, assessing, and mitigating risks early in the project can prevent budget overruns, delays, and quality issues. By implementing risk management strategies and fostering a culture of risk awareness within the development team, game developers can navigate the complex and dynamic landscape of game development more effectively.

Section 19.4: Team Collaboration and Communication

Effective team collaboration and communication are fundamental to the success of game development projects. In this section, we'll explore the importance of fostering collaboration among team members, improving communication processes, and leveraging tools to enhance teamwork in game development.

Game development is a multidisciplinary endeavor that involves artists, designers, programmers, sound engineers, and more. Effective collaboration is vital because:

141. **Diverse Skill Sets**: Game development teams bring together individuals with diverse skill sets. Collaborative efforts harness these skills to create a cohesive product.

142. **Complexity**: Games are complex projects with many moving parts. Effective teamwork ensures that all elements work together seamlessly.

143. **Problem Solving**: Collaboration enables teams to tackle challenges collectively, leveraging the expertise of each team member to find solutions.

144. **Quality Assurance**: Collaboration can lead to improved quality assurance, as team members can identify and address issues more effectively.

Strategies for Effective Collaboration

145. **Cross-Functional Teams**: Form cross-functional teams where members from different disciplines work closely together. This encourages the exchange of ideas and solutions.

146. **Clear Roles and Responsibilities**: Define clear roles and responsibilities for each team member. This reduces confusion and ensures that everyone knows their tasks and areas of ownership.

```
**Roles and Responsibilities (Example)**
- Game Designer: Responsible for defining gameplay mechanics and levels.
- Programmer: Implements game mechanics and ensures technical feasibility.
- Artist: Creates visual assets, including characters and environments.
```

4. **Collaborative Workspaces**: Use collaborative workspaces and project management tools to facilitate communication and file sharing among team members.

5. **Regular Meetings**: Schedule regular team meetings, such as daily stand-ups or sprint reviews, to discuss progress, challenges, and goals.

6. **Feedback Loops**: Encourage feedback loops within the team. Team members should feel comfortable providing constructive feedback and sharing ideas.

Improving Communication

Effective communication is key to successful collaboration. Here are some communication strategies for game development teams:

147. **Transparent Communication**: Foster transparency by sharing project updates, changes, and challenges openly with the team. This builds trust and keeps everyone informed.

148. **Documentation**: Maintain comprehensive documentation, including design documents, code comments, and project plans. This ensures that information is accessible to all team members.

149. **Team Messaging Tools**: Utilize team messaging tools and chat platforms to facilitate real-time communication. These tools allow quick exchanges and reduce email clutter.

150. **Regular Reporting**: Develop a reporting structure that ensures relevant information flows smoothly up and down the hierarchy. Regularly report progress to higher management and stakeholders.

```
**Weekly Progress Report (Example)**
- Completed character animations for Level 2.
- Fixed collision issues in the forest environment.
- Met with the audio team to discuss sound effects requirements.
```

Conflict Resolution

Inevitably, conflicts may arise within the team. It's essential to address conflicts constructively to maintain a healthy working environment. Consider the following conflict resolution strategies:

151. **Open Discussion**: Encourage team members to openly discuss their concerns and differences. Create a safe space for sharing opinions.

152. **Mediation**: When conflicts persist, consider bringing in a neutral mediator to facilitate discussions and find common ground.

153. **Clear Guidelines**: Establish clear guidelines for addressing conflicts and ensure that team members are aware of the process for conflict resolution.

Leveraging Collaboration Tools

Numerous collaboration tools are available to streamline communication and project management in game development:

154. **Project Management Software**: Tools like Jira, Trello, or Asana help teams organize tasks, track progress, and assign responsibilities.

155. **Version Control**: Version control systems like Git are essential for code collaboration, enabling multiple programmers to work on the same codebase without conflicts.

156. **Design and Asset Collaboration**: Use tools like Dropbox or Google Drive for sharing design documents, art assets, and other project-related files.

157. **Team Messaging**: Platforms like Slack or Microsoft Teams facilitate real-time communication and reduce the need for lengthy email chains.

In conclusion, effective team collaboration and communication are fundamental to the success of game development projects. By fostering collaboration, improving communication processes, and leveraging collaboration tools, game development teams can work more cohesively, tackle challenges more effectively, and ultimately deliver high-quality games on time and within budget.

Section 19.5: Post-Mortem Analysis and Learning from Failures

Post-mortem analysis, also known as a post-project review or retrospective, is a critical practice in game development. It involves examining the completed project to identify successes, failures, and areas for improvement. In this section, we'll delve into the significance of post-mortem analysis and provide insights into conducting effective post-mortems in game development.

The Importance of Post-Mortem Analysis

Post-mortem analysis serves several important purposes in game development:

158. **Learning from Mistakes**: It provides an opportunity to reflect on what went wrong during the project and learn from mistakes, preventing them from recurring in future projects.

159. **Identifying Successes**: It acknowledges and highlights successful aspects of the project, helping the team recognize what worked well.

160. **Continuous Improvement**: Post-mortems drive continuous improvement by offering actionable insights that can be implemented in future projects.

161. **Team Building**: It fosters team building and trust by encouraging open and honest communication about the project's challenges and achievements.

Conducting Effective Post-Mortems

To conduct effective post-mortem analysis in game development, follow these guidelines:

162. **Timing**: Schedule the post-mortem shortly after project completion while the details are still fresh in everyone's minds. Avoid waiting too long, as memories may fade.

163. **Inclusive Participation**: Involve all team members who were part of the project, including designers, developers, artists, sound engineers, and QA testers.

164. **Objective Facilitator**: Appoint a neutral facilitator, such as a project manager or an outside consultant, to lead the post-mortem. The facilitator ensures that discussions remain objective and productive.

165. **Structured Agenda**: Prepare a structured agenda that covers the following key areas:

- **Successes**: Begin by discussing what went well during the project. Highlight achievements, milestones, and areas of success. This sets a positive tone for the discussion.

- **Challenges and Failures**: Address challenges, problems, and failures encountered throughout the project. Encourage team members to be candid about their experiences.

- **Root Causes**: Explore the root causes of challenges and failures. Was it due to miscommunication, unrealistic goals, technical issues, or external factors?

- **Lessons Learned**: Identify actionable lessons learned from both successes and failures. These lessons should be specific and focused on improving future projects.

- **Actionable Recommendations**: Encourage the team to propose actionable recommendations based on the lessons learned. These recommendations should address how to prevent similar issues in the future.

- **Future Project Implications**: Discuss how the lessons learned and recommendations can be applied to future projects. Consider changes to processes, communication, and team dynamics.

166. **Open and Respectful Environment**: Foster an open and respectful environment where team members feel safe to share their perspectives without fear of blame or reprisal.

167. **Document Findings**: Assign someone to document the findings, recommendations, and action items from the post-mortem. These documents should be shared with the entire team.

Sample Post-Mortem Report (Example)
```
**Project Post-Mortem - Game Title: "Space Odyssey"**

**Successes:**
- Completed development one week ahead of schedule.
- Received positive feedback from playtesters regarding gameplay mechanics.
- Successfully integrated a new shader system that improved visual quality.

**Challenges and Failures:**
- QA testing revealed critical bugs in the multiplayer component, causing del
ays.
- Miscommunication between design and development teams led to scope changes.
- Unexpected hardware limitations resulted in performance issues on lower-end
devices.
```

Root Causes:
- Lack of comprehensive testing in the early development stages.
- Insufficient communication channels between design and development teams.
- Failure to conduct thorough hardware compatibility testing.

Lessons Learned:
- Comprehensive testing and bug fixing should be prioritized from the start.
- Regular communication and alignment meetings between design and development teams are crucial.
- Hardware compatibility testing should be conducted on various devices early in development.

Actionable Recommendations:
- Implement a continuous integration and testing pipeline to catch bugs early
.
- Schedule weekly meetings between design and development teams to ensure alignment.
- Invest in a range of testing devices to cover various hardware configurations.

Future Project Implications:
- Apply the lessons learned to future projects, emphasizing comprehensive testing, communication, and hardware compatibility checks.

In conclusion, post-mortem analysis is an invaluable practice in game development that helps teams learn from their experiences, identify areas for improvement, and drive continuous growth and success. By conducting structured post-mortems and implementing lessons learned, game developers can refine their processes and enhance the quality of their future projects.

Chapter 20: Future Trends and Innovations in Unreal Engine

Section 20.1: Exploring Upcoming Features in Unreal

Unreal Engine, as a leading game development platform, continually evolves to incorporate new features and technologies that push the boundaries of interactive experiences. In this section, we'll explore some of the anticipated features and innovations expected in Unreal Engine, giving you a glimpse into the future of game development.

Real-Time Ray Tracing Advancements

Ray tracing has been a significant advancement in rendering realism in games, and Unreal Engine continues to enhance its capabilities in this area. Future updates are expected to bring optimizations and improvements to real-time ray tracing, making it more accessible and performant for developers. This includes better support for complex scenes, increased efficiency, and enhanced visual fidelity.

```
// Example code snippet for enabling ray tracing in Unreal Engine:
if (GSupportsRayTracing)
{
    // Enable ray tracing features
    FStaticMeshDrawList::DrawDynamicMeshPass(View, RHICmdList, PassParameters
);
}
```

Advanced AI and Machine Learning Integration

Unreal Engine is increasingly integrating AI and machine learning capabilities. Future versions are likely to offer enhanced AI tools for game characters and NPCs, making them more intelligent, responsive, and adaptable to player actions. Machine learning may be used to create more realistic behaviors and improve in-game decision-making.

```
# Potential use of machine learning for AI behavior:
if player_health < threshold:
    # Use machine learning to predict the player's next move
    predicted_action = machine_learning_model.predict(player_input)
    if predicted_action == "attack":
        enemy_defend()
    elif predicted_action == "retreat":
        enemy_charge()
```

Virtual Reality (VR) and Augmented Reality (AR) Integration

As VR and AR technologies continue to gain popularity, Unreal Engine is expected to offer more seamless integration and support. This includes tools and features for designing immersive VR and AR experiences, such as enhanced support for VR headsets, hand tracking, and spatial audio.

```
// Example Unreal Engine code for VR hand tracking:
if (IsVRModeEnabled)
{
    // Update hand positions based on VR controller input
    UpdateHandPositions();
}
```

Expanded Cross-Platform Development

Unreal Engine is known for its cross-platform capabilities, and future versions are likely to expand on this strength. Developers can anticipate improved tools for building games that run smoothly on a wide range of platforms, from PC and console to mobile and web. Enhanced cross-platform networking and compatibility will be key areas of focus.

```
// Unreal Engine code snippet for cross-platform networking:
if (IsMultiplayerGame)
{
    // Implement cross-platform networking logic here
    NetworkManager.ConnectToServer();
}
```

Continued Emphasis on Real-Time Collaboration

Real-time collaboration has become increasingly important in game development, especially with geographically distributed teams. Unreal Engine is expected to further improve its collaboration features, enabling multiple team members to work simultaneously on the same project in real time. This includes better version control, asset management, and collaborative editing tools.

```
**Real-Time Collaboration Workflow (Example)**
- Game Designer works on level design in real time.
- 3D Artist simultaneously creates assets in the same level.
- Programmer integrates gameplay mechanics, all in parallel.
```

Embracing Emerging Technologies

Unreal Engine is likely to embrace emerging technologies that expand its applicability beyond gaming. This includes its use in industries such as architecture, film production, automotive design, and more. Expect to see features and tools that cater to these non-gaming applications, making Unreal Engine a versatile platform for various interactive experiences.

```
// Unreal Engine code for architectural visualization:
if (IsArchitecturalProject)
{
    // Utilize Unreal Engine's rendering capabilities for realistic architect
ural visualization.
    RenderHighFidelityArchitecturalScene();
}
```

In conclusion, Unreal Engine's future is bright, with exciting innovations on the horizon. From improved ray tracing and AI integration to enhanced support for VR/AR and cross-platform development, Unreal Engine is poised to remain a top choice for game developers and creators across various industries. By staying abreast of these upcoming features and innovations, developers can better prepare for the next generation of interactive experiences.

Section 20.2: Integrating Emerging Technologies

Game development is a field that constantly evolves as new technologies emerge. In this section, we'll explore the integration of emerging technologies in Unreal Engine, providing insights into how game developers can stay at the forefront of innovation.

1. Blockchain and NFTs

Blockchain technology has gained significant attention in recent years, and its application in gaming is expanding. Unreal Engine developers can explore the use of blockchain for various purposes, such as creating unique in-game assets as non-fungible tokens (NFTs). This allows players to own and trade digital assets securely.

```
// Unreal Engine code for implementing blockchain-based NFTs:
if (IsBlockchainEnabled)
{
    // Mint and manage NFTs for in-game assets
    BlockchainManager.MintNFT(player, uniqueAsset);
}
```

2. 5G and Cloud Gaming

The rollout of 5G networks is set to revolutionize the gaming industry by enabling low-latency, high-quality cloud gaming experiences. Unreal Engine developers can optimize their games to leverage these networks, ensuring smooth and responsive gameplay even for resource-intensive titles streamed from the cloud.

```
// Unreal Engine code for optimizing games for 5G and cloud gaming:
if (IsCloudGamingEnabled)
{
    // Implement dynamic asset streaming and low-latency networking for cloud
gaming.
    CloudGamingManager.ConfigureFor5G();
}
```

3. Artificial Intelligence and Procedural Content Generation

Advancements in artificial intelligence (AI) and procedural content generation are opening new possibilities for game design. Unreal Engine can integrate AI algorithms to create dynamic and responsive game worlds, adapt gameplay based on player behavior, and generate content procedurally to enhance replayability.

```
# Example of AI-driven procedural content generation in Unreal Engine:
if (IsAIEnabled)
{
    # Use AI algorithms to generate dynamic terrain features and enemy placem
ent.
    proceduralGenerator.GenerateDynamicGameWorld();
}
```

4. Haptic Feedback and Immersion

As haptic feedback technology continues to improve, Unreal Engine developers can enhance immersion by incorporating realistic tactile sensations into their games. This includes utilizing advanced haptic feedback devices and techniques to simulate touch, force, and vibrations.

```
// Unreal Engine code for implementing haptic feedback:
if (IsHapticFeedbackEnabled)
{
    // Configure haptic feedback effects for different in-game interactions.
    HapticFeedbackManager.ConfigureHapticSensations();
}
```

5. Augmented Reality (AR) and Mixed Reality (MR)

AR and MR technologies are not limited to standalone applications; they can also be integrated into Unreal Engine games. Developers can create mixed reality experiences that blend the physical and virtual worlds, offering innovative gameplay and storytelling possibilities.

```
// Unreal Engine code for integrating AR/MR experiences:
if (IsARMRIntegrationEnabled)
{
    // Implement AR/MR features for interactive in-game experiences.
    ARMRManager.CreateMixedRealityScenes();
}
```

6. Voice and Natural Language Processing (NLP)

Voice recognition and natural language processing technologies are advancing rapidly. Unreal Engine can leverage these technologies to enhance player interactions with in-game characters, enabling more natural and conversational dialogues.

```
// Unreal Engine code for integrating voice and NLP:
if (IsVoiceNLPEnabled)
{
    // Implement voice recognition and NLP for in-game character interactions
.
```

```
    CharacterDialogueManager.ProcessPlayerVoiceCommands();
}
```

7. Immersive Audio and Spatial Sound

Spatial audio and immersive sound experiences are becoming increasingly important for creating realistic and engaging games. Unreal Engine developers can harness advanced audio technologies to provide players with a more immersive auditory experience.

```
// Unreal Engine code for implementing immersive audio:
if (IsSpatialAudioEnabled)
{
    // Utilize spatial audio techniques for realistic sound propagation and 3
D soundscapes.
    SpatialAudioManager.ConfigureAudioEnvironments();
}
```

In conclusion, Unreal Engine remains at the forefront of game development by embracing emerging technologies. Game developers can stay competitive and offer innovative gaming experiences by integrating blockchain, 5G, AI, haptic feedback, AR/MR, voice recognition, and immersive audio into their Unreal Engine projects. As technology continues to advance, Unreal Engine's adaptability and support for these innovations position it as a powerful tool for creating cutting-edge games and interactive content.

Section 20.3: The Role of AI in Future Game Development

Artificial Intelligence (AI) is poised to play an increasingly central role in the future of game development. In this section, we will explore how AI is transforming various aspects of game development, from creating lifelike NPCs to enhancing player experiences.

1. AI-Powered Game Worlds

AI-driven procedural content generation is becoming a game changer. Game developers can use AI algorithms to create vast, dynamically generated game worlds with rich landscapes, unique structures, and diverse ecosystems. This not only reduces development time but also enhances the replayability of games.

```
# Example of AI-driven procedural world generation:
if (IsAIEnabled)
{
    # Utilize AI to generate expansive, diverse game worlds.
    proceduralGenerator.GenerateDynamicGameWorld();
}
```

2. Smart NPCs and Realistic Behaviors

The NPCs (non-playable characters) in games are becoming more intelligent and lifelike, thanks to AI. AI-driven NPCs can adapt to player actions, display realistic emotions, and make informed decisions. This adds depth to storytelling and challenges in games.

```
// Unreal Engine code for implementing AI-driven NPC behaviors:
if (IsAIEnabled)
{
    // Create NPCs with dynamic behavior trees and emotion modeling.
    AINPCManager.ConfigureBehaviorTrees();
}
```

3. AI-Enhanced Level Design

AI algorithms are increasingly used to assist in level design. They can analyze player data and preferences to generate levels that cater to individual player styles. This personalization enhances player engagement and retention.

```
// Unreal Engine code for AI-enhanced level design:
if (IsAIEnabled)
{
    // Use AI to dynamically adjust level layouts based on player behavior.
    LevelDesignManager.CreatePersonalizedLevels();
}
```

4. Player Analytics and Predictive Modeling

AI is revolutionizing player analytics. Game developers can employ machine learning models to analyze player behavior, predict player actions, and tailor in-game experiences. This enables the delivery of personalized content and recommendations.

```
# Example of player analytics with AI and predictive modeling:
if (IsAIEnabled)
{
    # Analyze player data to predict player preferences and optimize content delivery.
    playerAnalytics.PredictPlayerActions();
}
```

5. AI for Game Testing and Debugging

AI-powered testing and debugging tools are on the horizon. AI can simulate player actions and identify potential bugs and issues in a game. This automated testing speeds up the quality assurance process.

```
// Unreal Engine code for AI-driven game testing:
if (IsAIEnabled)
{
    // Implement AI testing bots to simulate player actions and detect issues
```

```
    AITestingManager.RunAutomatedTests();
}
```

6. AI-Generated Art and Assets

AI is being used to assist in the creation of game art and assets. Generative adversarial networks (GANs) and other AI models can produce textures, character designs, and even entire environments, saving artists time and expanding creative possibilities.

```
// Unreal Engine code for AI-generated art assets:
if (IsAIEnabled)
{
    // Utilize AI-generated textures and assets for game art.
    ArtGenerationManager.GenerateAIArtAssets();
}
```

7. Natural Language Processing (NLP) for Dialogue and Interaction

In-game dialogue and interactions are becoming more natural and dynamic with the integration of NLP. Players can engage in realistic conversations with AI characters, and their choices can impact the game's narrative.

```
// Unreal Engine code for NLP-driven dialogue systems:
if (IsNLPEnabled)
{
    // Implement NLP for natural and responsive in-game dialogue.
    DialogueManager.EnableNLPDialogueSystem();
}
```

In conclusion, AI is rapidly transforming the landscape of game development. From creating intelligent NPCs and dynamic game worlds to personalizing player experiences and enhancing game testing, AI's role in game development is set to expand. Game developers who embrace AI technologies can create more immersive, engaging, and innovative games that cater to the evolving preferences of players. As AI continues to advance, it will remain a driving force behind the future of game development.

Section 20.4: Unreal Engine in Non-Gaming Industries

While Unreal Engine has historically been associated with game development, its capabilities are increasingly being recognized and utilized in various non-gaming industries. In this section, we'll explore how Unreal Engine is making inroads into fields such as architecture, film production, automotive design, and more.

1. Architectural Visualization

Unreal Engine is gaining popularity in the architectural industry for its ability to create stunning, real-time 3D visualizations of architectural designs. Architects and designers can use Unreal Engine to walk clients through virtual buildings, showcasing interior and exterior spaces with photorealistic quality.

```
// Unreal Engine code for architectural visualization:
if (IsArchitecturalProject)
{
    // Utilize Unreal Engine's rendering capabilities for realistic architect
ural visualization.
    RenderHighFidelityArchitecturalScene();
}
```

2. Film and Animation Production

Unreal Engine has found a place in film and animation production. Its real-time rendering capabilities allow filmmakers to create virtual sets and environments, saving time and costs associated with physical set construction. It's also used for pre-visualization, enabling directors to plan shots and scenes in a virtual environment.

```
// Unreal Engine code for film and animation production:
if (IsFilmProduction)
{
    // Create virtual sets and environments for film production.
    FilmProductionManager.BuildVirtualSets();
}
```

3. Automotive Design and Visualization

The automotive industry leverages Unreal Engine for designing and visualizing vehicles. Car manufacturers use Unreal Engine's real-time rendering to create interactive 3D models of cars, test different designs, and simulate how vehicles perform in various conditions.

```
// Unreal Engine code for automotive design and visualization:
if (IsAutomotiveDesign)
{
    // Use Unreal Engine to visualize and simulate vehicle designs and perfor
mance.
    AutomotiveDesigner.CreateInteractiveCarModels();
}
```

4. Training and Simulation

Unreal Engine is used in training and simulation applications across industries. From military simulations to medical training, Unreal Engine's realistic environments and physics simulations help create effective training programs.

```
// Unreal Engine code for training and simulation:
if (IsTrainingSimulation)
{
    // Develop immersive training simulations using Unreal Engine's capabilit
ies.
```

```
    TrainingSimulationManager.CreateRealisticTrainingScenarios();
}
```

5. Advertising and Marketing

Unreal Engine is increasingly employed in advertising and marketing campaigns. It enables the creation of interactive, immersive experiences that engage customers and promote products or services. Augmented reality (AR) and virtual reality (VR) advertisements are becoming more common.

```
// Unreal Engine code for advertising and marketing:
if (IsAdvertisingCampaign)
{
    // Design interactive and immersive advertising experiences using Unreal
Engine.
    AdvertisingManager.DevelopARVRAdCampaign();
}
```

6. Education and Edutainment

Educational institutions are adopting Unreal Engine for educational purposes. It's used to create educational games, simulations, and interactive learning environments that engage students and enhance the learning experience.

```
// Unreal Engine code for educational games:
if (IsEducationalGame)
{
    // Develop educational games and simulations to enhance learning outcomes

    EducationalGameDeveloper.CreateInteractiveLearningModules();
}
```

7. Medical Visualization and Simulation

In the healthcare sector, Unreal Engine is utilized for medical visualization and surgical simulations. It helps medical professionals visualize complex anatomical structures, plan surgeries, and practice procedures in a virtual environment.

```
// Unreal Engine code for medical visualization:
if (IsMedicalVisualization)
{
    // Use Unreal Engine to create detailed medical visualizations and simula
tions.
    MedicalVisualizationTeam.RenderAnatomicalStructures();
}
```

In conclusion, Unreal Engine's versatility extends beyond the realm of gaming. It has found applications in industries where real-time 3D visualization, interactivity, and immersive experiences are valuable. As Unreal Engine continues to evolve and adapt, its adoption in non-gaming sectors is likely to grow, offering new opportunities for innovation and creativity across various industries.

Section 20.5: Preparing for the Next Generation of Gaming

The future of game development holds exciting possibilities, and Unreal Engine is at the forefront of these innovations. In this section, we'll discuss how game developers can prepare for the next generation of gaming experiences using Unreal Engine.

1. Harnessing the Power of Next-Gen Hardware

With the release of next-generation gaming consoles and powerful PC hardware, Unreal Engine developers should optimize their games to leverage these capabilities fully. This includes taking advantage of improved graphics, faster load times, and increased processing power.

```
// Unreal Engine code for harnessing next-gen hardware:
if (IsNextGenPlatform)
{
    // Optimize game visuals and performance for next-gen hardware.
    NextGenPlatformManager.ConfigureHardwareOptimizations();
}
```

2. Realistic Ray Tracing

Real-time ray tracing is becoming more accessible, and Unreal Engine provides robust support for this technology. Game developers should explore and implement ray tracing to enhance lighting, reflections, and overall visual fidelity in their projects.

```
// Unreal Engine code for implementing real-time ray tracing:
if (IsRayTracingEnabled)
{
    // Enable ray tracing features for enhanced graphics.
    RayTracingManager.ConfigureRealisticLighting();
}
```

3. Advanced AI and Machine Learning

As AI and machine learning continue to advance, incorporating advanced AI behaviors and predictive models can make games more dynamic and engaging. Developers should experiment with AI-driven gameplay mechanics and decision-making to create more immersive experiences.

```
# Example of advanced AI and machine learning integration in Unreal Engine:
if (IsAIEnabled)
{
    # Implement advanced AI behaviors and decision-making using machine learning.
    AdvancedAIManager.EnableDynamicGameplayAI();
}
```

4. Cross-Platform and Cross-Reality Gaming

Cross-platform and cross-reality gaming experiences are on the rise. Unreal Engine developers should focus on creating games that seamlessly connect players across different platforms and even bridge the gap between virtual and augmented realities.

```
// Unreal Engine code for cross-platform and cross-reality gaming:
if (IsCrossRealityGame)
{
    // Implement cross-platform networking and AR/VR integration for a unifie
d gaming experience.
    CrossRealityGame.ConfigureMulti-RealityInteractions();
}
```

5. Immersive Storytelling

The next generation of gaming will demand immersive storytelling techniques. Developers should explore narrative-driven gameplay, interactive cutscenes, and branching storylines to keep players engaged and emotionally invested in their games.

```
// Unreal Engine code for immersive storytelling:
if (IsNarrativeGame)
{
    // Create interactive narratives with dynamic story branching.
    NarrativeDesigner.BuildImmersiveStorytellingExperiences();
}
```

6. Community Building and User-Generated Content

Fostering a strong game community and enabling user-generated content can extend the life of a game. Developers should provide tools for players to create and share their content, as well as actively engage with the community through forums, social media, and events.

```
// Unreal Engine code for community building and user-generated content:
if (IsCommunityGame)
{
    // Implement community-driven features like mod support and content creat
ion tools.
    CommunityManager.EnableUser-GeneratedContent();
}
```

7. Sustainability and Accessibility

As the gaming industry grows, sustainability and accessibility become important considerations. Developers should strive for eco-friendly development practices and ensure their games are accessible to a wide range of players, including those with disabilities.

```
// Unreal Engine code for sustainability and accessibility:
if (IsSustainableGame)
```

```
{
    // Adopt eco-friendly development practices and enhance game accessibilit
y features.
    SustainableGameDevelopment.AdvanceEco-FriendlyPractices();
}
```

In conclusion, preparing for the next generation of gaming using Unreal Engine involves a combination of technical advancements and creative innovations. Game developers should stay updated with the latest Unreal Engine features and industry trends, experiment with cutting-edge technologies, and prioritize player engagement and community building. By embracing these strategies, developers can create games that push the boundaries of what is possible in the ever-evolving world of gaming.

www.ingramcontent.com/pod-product-compliance
Lightning Source LLC
LaVergne TN
LVHW051320050326
832903LV00031B/3281